Table Of Contents

What Are WOWBugs, Anyway? • WOWBugs As A Classroom Insect • WOWBugs And The National Science Education Standards (NSES) • WOWBugs And Science Process Skills • Evaluating Attitudes: An Overview • Attitudes Toward Wasps • Evaluating Attitudes: A Draw-A-Wasp Activity • Student Activity Pages

Hoppin' Bug Connect-A-Dot • Speedy WOWBugs: How Fast? How Far? • The Great WOWBug Roundup • Courtship Communication: An Overview • Courtship Communication • Student Activity Pages

Form And Function: Insect Anatomy • Scale And Accuracy: Just How Big Are WOWBugs — Really? • Size And Athletic Ability: The Insect Olympics • Student Activity Pages

A Life Cycle Mystery: An Overview • A Life Cycle Mystery • Time Lines, Cylinders, And The Cycle Of Life • Effects Of Diet On Development: An Overview • Effects Of Diet On Development • Mission: Entomological • Student Activity Pages

WOWBugs™:
New Life For Life Science

Robert W. Matthews
Thomas R. Koballa, Jr.
Lynda R. Flage
Eric J. Pyle

illustrations by Paul H. Matthews

RIVERVIEW
PRESS LLC

Matthews, Robert W., Koballa, Thomas R., Jr., Flage, Lynda R., and Pyle, Eric J.
    WOWBugs™: New Life For Life Science.

Includes index.

ISBN No.1-888499-06-0

1. Biology—Study and teaching. 2. Insects– behavior.   I. Matthews, Robert W.

Cover design and layout: Paul H. Matthews
Illustrations: Paul H. Matthews

Additional copies may be obtained from the publisher:

Riverview Press LLC
Post Office Box 5955
Athens, GA 30604-5955
USA

Printed and bound in the United States of America.

WOWBug and WOWBugs are trademarks of the University of
Georgia Research Foundation, Inc.

This project was supported in part by the National Science
Foundation under Grant Number ESI-9353040. Opinions
expressed are those of the authors and do not necessarily
reflect the views of the National Science Foundation.

Preface

Books of life science activities are not unusual — but this one is. First, it introduces a new experimental animal — the WOWBug, *Melittobia digitata* — that is commonly found in nature but has never before been used in the pre-college classroom.

Second, the animal is not only new, but also absolutely bizarre. For capturing student interest, it's hard to top an insect that has wings but hops and plays possum, takes only 3 weeks to complete its life cycle, produces up to 700 offspring (95% of them female), and includes blind males who kill their brothers and mate with their sisters!

At the same time, these strange creatures have been found to be admirably suitable for teaching a wide variety of fundamental biological concepts and life science skills. This volume, for example, includes 20 activities and experiments that cover topics from basic orientation to ecological interactions, from physical science relationships and muscle power to effects of diet on development.

Female

Each of these activities has been explicitly designed to mesh with 1996 NSES Content Standards developed by the National Research Council of the National Academy of Sciences. Each helps students learn several different process skills.

Some of these investigations take only a small part of a regular class period; many take one to two periods; a few are long-range studies that require several weeks to complete. Some are quite open-ended, and might serve as a springboard to individual science fair projects. Some adapt particularly well to use in teaching across the curriculum. Most are real experiments in the academic sense of employing methods scientists use and producing new information of scientific value.

For three years, nearly 100 middle-grade classroom teachers and several university researchers have worked side by side to develop and test these materials. The synergy has been incredible. Any errors are, of course, our own. But we're extremely grateful for the cooperative efforts involved in developing these activities and (if you'll excuse the pun) working the bugs out!

The result is a book of brand-new activities that are not only scientifically accurate; they also work, and they're fun! May you and your students enjoy using WOWBugs as much as we do!

The authors
September 1996

Acknowledgements

We thank the National Science Foundation, which funded this project under Grant ESI-9353040. We also extend our grateful appreciation to our editor Janice R. Matthews and our illustrator Paul H. Matthews, whose untiring efforts vastly improved this book.

Introduction

In many ways, insects are far more suitable than vertebrates for classroom use. They are more approachable, easier to handle, and far less expensive. Experimentation with them usually requires no special permits and incurs no public criticism. Replication of observations is easier. Many are relatively easy to maintain, take little space, and are readily available in large numbers. As three-quarters of the animal world, they deserve a larger role in science education.

Male

In 1993, the Georgia WOWBugs™ Project was established to bring new life into life science classrooms by way of a "new" organism: *Melittobia digitata*, a harmless insect about the size of a fruit fly, found world wide but never before used in the pre-college classroom.

One of the Project's major goals has been to involve teachers in developing materials that use these insects, the WOWBugs*, to teach biological concepts and principles. Another has been to provide explicit guidance to teachers as they incorporate new dimensions into their teaching practice.

This book is one outcome in support of that first goal. As teachers and university researchers have worked together to develop it, four objectives have guided the process. The first of these is balanced diversity. Activities have been chosen to cover a variety of topics usually presented in a well-balanced life sciences course. Both traditional and non-traditional exercises have been included. There is diversification

*WOWBug and WOWBugs are registered trademarks of the University of Georgia Research Foundation, Inc.

between observational and experimental studies. Most take one to two standard class periods to complete, but some take less and a few stretch over several weeks. Most activities can stand alone, but they appear in a sequence that allows one to build on another, if desired.

Second, though WOWBugs are the experimental subjects, the focus has been on fundamental ideas of contemporary life science study — both the "big concepts" that stretch beyond the boundaries of a single organism or a single discipline and current thinking about the pedagogy by which they should be delivered. The activities focus on concepts developed by students through dynamic, inquiry-centered investigations, rather than on terminology embedded in a rhetoric of conclusions.

The third objective is adaptability. The activities presented here may be easily incorporated into a variety of biology courses for enrichment or as substitutes for activities that use more expensive and/or less readily available organisms. Nearly all of these activities can be used equally sucessfully with students of widely different ages and abilities. No entomological background is needed to understand them. Quantitative procedures are suggested and encouraged where appropriate, but only a rudimentary knowledge of mathematics is assumed. Because many courses include independent study, additional projects and ideas are suggested that show particular promise as the basis for individual research projects, and reinforce or extend basic concepts.

The final and most over-arching objective for the book has been to present these materials in the way that is most interesting, enjoyable, and above all, useful for teachers and students. Each activity includes both an extensively annotated teacher's guide and pages suitable for duplication for student use. Detailed preparation information, descriptions of handling methods, hints, cautions, additional background, and, where helpful, sample results are included. To further increase the book's utility, additional chapters provide background about WOWBugs and their mud dauber hosts, as well as classroom tips, transparency masters, and other teaching aids.

Workshops and seminars are now being conducted at various locations across the United States. We invite you to join us. The WOWBug adventure is just beginning!

Chapter One. WOWBugs And The Life Science Curriculum

By grades 5-8, students can begin to recognize ways that explanation and evidence are related. They need opportunities to develop and refine this recognition, and should be given as many occasions as possible to engage in full and in partial inquiries. In high school and beyond, these opportunities should continue and, whenever possible, accelerate. The WOWBugs activities in this book present many engaging opportunities for both levels of inquiry.

What Are WOWBugs, Anyway?

WOWBugs (*Melittobia digitata*) are harmless, non-stinging parasitic wasps about the size of a fruit fly which have been developed as new organisms for use in classroom life science curricula. Scientifically, they are a species of non-social wasp in the family Eulophidae, order Hymenoptera. They are found all around the world, often inadvertently transported there by human commerce.

There are a number of different *Melittobia* species — 14 have been described in the scientific literature. However, only *M. digitata* is the WOWBug; the biology of the others differs in various respects, and using them in these activities could have uncertain results.

In nature, WOWBugs are "parasitoids." They lay their eggs on the outside of the larvae or pupae of other insects. Their natural hosts include a great number of different insect species, especially mud dauber wasps. In the classroom or laboratory, WOWBugs can reproduce successfully upon blow fly puparia (which are commercially available through biological supply companies). Currently researchers are working to develop an encapsulated artificial diet medium which will be even easier to use.

WOWBugs As A Classroom Insect

Thirty years of working with *Melittobia* in a variety of situations, including the college classroom, have shown that these insects have a number of biological attributes that uniquely suit them to use as a living classroom subject.

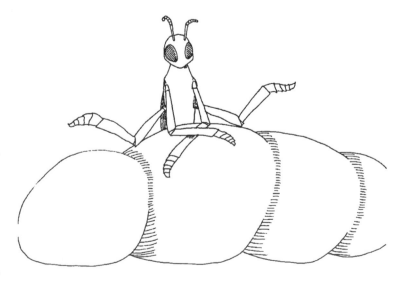

Here are twenty attributes. As you work with WOWBugs, you will probably count even more.

1. WOWBugs are abundant.

A single mud dauber cocoon can give rise to between 300 and 900 individuals, enough for several classes to do several activities.

2. WOWBugs are simple to maintain.

Continuous rearing requires nothing more than placing a few newly emerged adults on a new host once a month, a process that takes only a few minutes.

3. WOWBugs are inexpensive.

Or free, depending on how you get them. Cultures are available commercially (Carolina Biological Supply) and the insects can be easily found in nature, in nests of mud dauber wasps.

4. WOWBugs take very little classroom space.

Even if each student is given their own culture, this amounts only to a row of small containers tucked away in a corner.

5. WOWBugs require no special environmental manipulations.

They thrive at typical room temperature and humidity ranges, inside cotton-stoppered vials or small plastic chambers which require little space in the classroom or laboratory. Temperature fluctuations, such as those which occur in school buildings during holiday breaks, are of no consequence for WOWBugs.

6. WOWBugs are easily reared.

Various inexpensive suitable hosts (e.g., blow fly puparia) are available to teachers from biological supply houses. Chemically defined artificial diets are on the horizon.

7. WOWBugs pose no environmental risks.

WOWBugs are cosmopolitan in distribution, and have been so spread about the world by commerce that their actual geographic origin is unknown. Because they already occur so widely, there is no risk of introducing an unwanted alien insect, should individuals escape from cultures or experiments. In the classroom, escaped individuals seem to just disappear.

Neither sex is dependent on photoperiod or emergence rhythms for behavior expression.

8. WOWBugs are reliable performers.

Males are blind and flightless. Although females have wings, they seldom fly. Pupae and adults can be easily moved about on the bristles of an inexpensive watercolor paint brush or the nap of a pipe cleaner.

9. WOWBugs are easy to handle.

Because they develop on the external surface of the host, even eggs can be easily viewed, counted, or even transferred to a different host. Each subsequent life cycle stage is similarly distinct and visible.

10. WOWBugs are easily observed during all life stages.

They have no odor or other objectionable features. Although they possess a tiny stinger, they are incapable of stinging people.

11. WOWBugs are harmless.

At normal room temperatures, the total life cycle takes only about 18 to 21 days.

12. WOWBugs have a rapid life cycle.

Even as pupae, WOWBugs can be separated by sex, because of the absence of eyes in males. Adults exhibit extreme sexual dimorphism. Males have greatly reduced wings, lack functional eyes, and have striking antler-like antennae. Female have normal eyes, antennae, and wings.

13. WOWBug sexes are extremely distinct.

Unmated females given a host first produce a few sons parthenogenetically, then mate with these offspring to produce a normal mixed-sex clutch on the same host. In the absence of a host, females are capable of delaying oviposition for considerable periods (over 200 days under laboratory conditions).

14. Female WOWBug reproductive behavior is extremely flexible.

Males produce a sex pheromone odor which attracts unmated females.

15. WOWBugs have an unusual chemical communication system.

16. WOWBugs have a broad host range.

They have been reared successfully from over 20 different insect species representing at least 4 different orders, ranging from cockroaches to flies to honeybees. This host breadth makes it potentially easy to switch them from one host to another, and even to an artificial diet.

17. WOWBug courtship is elaborate and reliably observable.

Males avidly and continuously court females, and unmated females become receptive almost immediately upon placement with a male. Males engage in a highly ritualized display involving antennal contact and synchronized leg lifting movements.

18. Male WOWBug competition is extreme.

WOWBug males attack one another ferociously, often mutilating and even killing one another if the loser cannot escape. There is even some evidence for male cannibalism.

19. WOWBug sex ratios and high inbreeding suggest interesting genetic questions.

Females comprise about 95% of the progeny in every generation, and sisters normally mate with their brothers.

20. WOWBugs don't need to be fed as adults.

What could be easier?

WOWBugs and the National Science Education Standards (NSES)

Early in 1996, science educators welcomed the publication of an immense new science education effort: The National Science Education Standards. The intent of this comprehensive effort, in its compilers' words, was "science standards for all students... both excellence and equity."

Hundreds of people cooperated to develop the NSES, from teachers and parents to scientists, engineers, and government officials. Thousands reviewed various drafts. Major corporations, foundations, and organizations joined in a massive effort to combine the results of research, earlier reform efforts, and personal insights to produce a broad consensus about the elements of science education needed to permit all students to achieve their scientific potential.

The Standards are grouped into six sets, organized around six basic questions about science education.
1. What should science teachers know and do?
2. What professional development experiences should science teachers be provided with?
3. What criteria are appropriate to judge the quality of assessment practices in science education?
4. What should students know, understand, and be able to do in the natural sciences?
5. What conditions are necessary for quality school science programs?
6. What criteria are appropriate to judge the performance of the overall science education system?

The overall goals of NSES, which "define a scientifically literate society" are to educate students who are able to:

• experience the richness and excitement of knowing about and understanding the natural world;

• use appropriate scientific processes and principles in making personal decisions;

• engage intelligently in public discourse and debate about matters of scientific and technological concern; and

• increase their economic productivity through the use of the knowledge, understanding, and skills of the scientifically literate person in their careers.

The fourth set, Science Content Standards, has been of particular interest and guidance to the Georgia WOWBugs Project. We believe that in the years ahead, the NSES effort will influence and guide U.S. science education in a positive direction, and will touch the lives of all of those who are concerned about America's educational efforts.

Each of the activities in this manual was guided by specific Science Content Standards. The chart on the following page cross-references the activities and the standards we feel they address. However, we recognize that the degree to which these standards are explicitly expressed sometimes is influenced by individual teaching and learning styles.

One of the strengths of this new classroom organism is that **WOWBugs can be used with students of many different ages and abilities.** In this manual, we focus on grades 5-12. The initial development effort funded by the National Science Foundation targeted students in grades 5 through 9, but we quickly found that the activities we present here could be used with success in high school, and even in college undergraduate and graduate-level classes. Some creative teachers also have adapted these materials successfully for children as young as second grade.

Content is what students should learn. Curriculum is the way content is presented, organized, and emphasized. **WOWBugs can — and should — be used in many different ways in many different curricula.** The Content Standards recognize, respect, and explicitly reinforce the need for many different curricula with many different emphases and perspectives to meet the goal of educating all our nation's children. So do we.

WOWBugs And Science Process Skills

Skills used daily by scientists should be introduced and reinforced in science curricular materials at every grade level. WOWBug activities in this book do so.

In this chapter, we've provided a chart with science process skills cross-referenced to each activity to help teachers identify at a glance those process skills involved in each. Alternatively, a quick check of the chart will enable one to identify those activities that feature a particular desired skill.

National Science Education Standards Related to WOWBug Activities

Content Standards	Systems, Order, & Organization	Evidence, Models, & Explanation	Constancy, Change, & Measurement	Evolution & Equilibrium	Form & Function	Abilities Necessary To Do Scientific Inquiry	Understanding About Scientific Inquiry	Structure & Function In Living Systems	Reproduction & Heredity	Regulation & Behavior	Populations & Ecosystems	Diversity & Adaptations Of Organisms	Science & Technology In Society	Science As A Human Endeavor (5-8)	Nature Of Science	History Of Science	Biological Evolution	Interdependence Of Organisms	Matter, Energy, & Organization In Living Systems	Behavior Of Organisms	Population Growth	Science As A Human Endeavor (9-12)	Nature Of Scientific Knowledge
Darwinian Selection		X		X		X	X					X		X			X					X	X
Mud Dauber Nest Ecosystem	X	X	X		X	X	X				X		X	X				X	X			X	X
Momma's Boys	X	X	X	X	X	X	X		X			X	X	X						X		X	X
Population Sex Ratios	X	X	X	X		X	X		X		X		X	X							X	X	X
Hot Stuff & Cold Feet		X	X			X	X	X				X	X	X								X	X
Rockin' WOWBugs		X	X			X	X	X				X	X	X								X	X
Tastes Good		X	X			X	X	X				X	X	X								X	X
Odor Responses		X	X			X	X	X				X	X	X								X	X
Light At End Of Tunnel		X	X			X	X	X				X	X	X								X	X
Mission: Entomological		X						X				X		X								X	
Diet & Development				X		X	X					X		X			X		X			X	
Time Lines	X	X	X									X											
Life Cycle Mystery	X		X			X	X		X			X		X					X				
Size & Athletic Ability	X		X	X		X	X	X	X		X			X									
Scale & Accuracy			X		X	X	X	X			X		X	X								X	
Form & Function		X		X				X			X	X											
Courtship Communication	X		X	X		X	X	X		X	X			X									
WOWBug Roundup		X				X	X	X	X	X	X												
Speedy WOWBugs	X		X			X	X	X	X	X	X												
Hoppin' Bug Connect-a-dot		X		X		X		X		X	X			X									
Draw-A-Wasp	X			X		X		X					X									X	

Science Process Skills Related to WOWBug Activities

Activity	Observation	Classification	Communication	Measurement	Prediction	Inference	Identifying Variables	Constructing A Table Of Data	Describing Relationships Between Variables	Acquiring & Processing Your Own Data	Analyzing Investigations	Constructing A Hypothesis	Defining Variables Operationally	Designing An Investigation	Experimenting
Basic Skills															
Darwinian Selection	X		X	X	X	X		X			X	X			
Mud Dauber Nest Ecosystem	X	X	X	X	X	X			X	X	X	X			
Momma's Boys	X		X	X	X	X	X		X	X	X	X			
Population Sex Ratios	X		X	X	X	X				X	X	X	X		
Hot Stuff & Cold Feet	X		X	X	X	X	X	X	X	X	X	X	X		
Rockin' WOWBugs	X	X	X	X	X	X	X	X	X	X	X	X	X	X	
Tastes Good	X		X	X	X	X	X	X	X	X	X	X	X	X	
Odor Responses	X		X	X	X	X	X	X	X	X	X	X	X	X	
Light At End Of Tunnel	X		X	X	X	X	X	X	X	X	X	X	X	X	
Mission: Entomological			X				X		X		X	X		X	
Diet & Development	X		X	X	X	X	X	X	X	X	X	X		X	
Time Lines			X	X	X	X	X		X	X	X				
Life Cycle Mystery	X		X	X	X	X			X	X	X		X		
Size & Athletic Ability	X		X	X	X	X	X	X		X	X				
Scale & Accuracy	X		X	X	X		X			X		X			
Form & Function	X		X		X	X	X						X	X	
Courtship Communication	X		X	X	X	X	X	X	X		X	X	X	X	X
WOWBug Roundup			X	X	X	X	X		X		X	X	X	X	X
Speedy WOWBugs	X		X	X	X	X	X	X	X	X	X	X	X	X	X
Integrated Skills															
Hoppin' Bug Connect-a-dot	X		X	X	X	X	X		X	X	X	X	X	X	X
Draw-A-Wasp			X												

Process Skills*

*Based on Funk, H.J. et al. 1985. Learning Science Process Skills. 2nd ed., Dubuque: Kendall/Hunt.

Evaluating Student Attitudes: An Overview

Whenever a new situation is presented to a group of learners, certain preconceived notions are brought to mind, especially when the learner has had some personal or anecdotal experience with a similar situation.

The process of information-gathering in the form of visual-spatial images begins years before children make sense of the spoken word. Children's knowledge of animals, particularly information about their size, shape, color and patterns of movement, is stored as visual-spatial images, not words, in separate subsystems of the brain (Peterson, 1996).

Attitudes Toward Wasps

Wasps are commonly thought of as swarming insect pests that can cause pain and sometimes death by stinging. This is true of some of the large social wasps like hornets and yellow jackets, which aggressively defend their nests. The fear of an allergic reaction to a social wasp sting is understandable since no completely reliable test exists for predicting who will have an exaggerated immune response. For this reason, the general attitude toward wasps ranges from extreme aversion to one of hysterical dislike (Olkowski & Olkowski, 1976).

Further contributing to wasps' reputation as pest insects is a history of human ignorance about their role in nature. Most people are unaware that most wasps are predators or parasites on spiders and insects (including other members of their own order).

In addition, most people's awareness of wasps is limited to social forms. However, the vast majority — about 90% — of all wasps are nonsocial, not aggressive and do not defend their nests against intruders. The WOWBug, *Mellitobia digitata*, is a species of nonsocial wasp. WOWBugs go virtually unnoticed in nature because they do not live in colonies and because they are so small their stingers are unable to pierce human skin.

In the experience of teachers affiliated with the Georgia WOWBugs Project, most students' understanding of wasps has been broadened by working with the WOWBug materials. They have come to view insects in general less as organisms to be feared and hated and more as organisms valued for their contributions to the natural world.

As an evaluation method, consider having students assess their own knowledge about and feelings toward wasps by comparative drawings (see the activity on the next page). If the activity is done before and after a unit on WOWBugs, students can use the drawings as evidence of their own cognitive and affective growth.

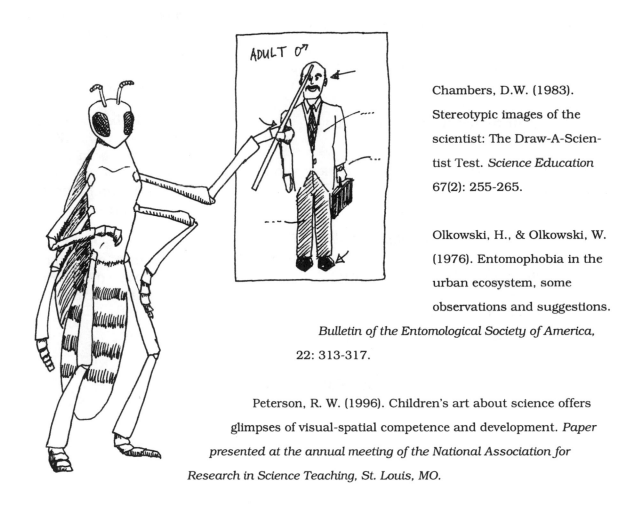

Chambers, D.W. (1983). Stereotypic images of the scientist: The Draw-A-Scientist Test. *Science Education* 67(2): 255-265.

Olkowski, H., & Olkowski, W. (1976). Entomophobia in the urban ecosystem, some observations and suggestions. *Bulletin of the Entomological Society of America,* 22: 313-317.

Peterson, R. W. (1996). Children's art about science offers glimpses of visual-spatial competence and development. *Paper presented at the annual meeting of the National Association for Research in Science Teaching, St. Louis, MO.*

Evaluating Attitudes: A Draw-a-Wasp Activity

Most of us have had at least some experience with wasps, or know of a friend or family member who has. What do you know about wasps and how they live?

Materials (per student):

• a piece of unlined paper

• two or three felt tip markers of different colors

Use only dark colored markers if drawings will be photocopied.

1. Gather your materials and return to your seat.

2. Draw a picture that tells what you know about wasps and how they live.

Repeat these instructions orally, and also write on the chalkboard or a projected transparency to ensure that no students are confused about what to do.

3. As you draw your wasp picture, feel free to label anything you want to identify in your drawing.

4. Make sure your name and today's date are on the drawing.

This will enable you to match pre- and post-unit drawings.

Optional: If your teacher tells you to, write a brief description of your drawing on the back of the paper.

The descriptions may prove helpful in trying to understand the drawing or to compare the visual-spatial presentation of ideas with the verbal presentation.

Key Concepts: Attitudinal change; Insect morphology; Diversity of organisms.

Prerequisites: None but the learners' own life experiences. This activity can serve as an important springboard to a discussion of the human factor in the history of science.

Time: To be done twice (once before the WOWBug unit, and again after it has been completed). 30 minutes per administration, plus discussion.

Objectives: Observe changes in one's own knowledge about, and attitude towards, wasps.

5. Repeat this activity after you have studied WOWBugs.

Discussion:

1. Compare your drawings from the beginning and end of the activity. What differences do you notice?

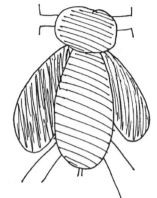

Here are some suggestions for things to look for:

• combinations of proper and improper anatomy (e.g., legs drawn in the wrong place, human faces).

• associations with social and aggressive bees and wasps (e.g., swarming, nests, attacks on humans).

• expressions of human fear, flight or pain (e.g., sting marks on human body, comments such as "Help, Wasp" or "Ouch!").

• gender identification clues. Male and female wasps may be distinguished based on either appearance or behavior.

• changes in wasp anatomy drawn.

• wasps shown as insect parasites or predators, rather than as attackers of humans.

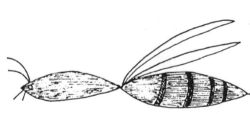

• wasps shown as insects that undergo complete metamorphosis (i.e., evidence of egg, larva, pupa, adult).

*Typical 5th Graders'
"Before" Drawings*

• variability in wasp size, from microscopic to a length of several centimeters.

• evidence of changes in feelings toward wasps. Wasps may take on a friendly appearance. Fewer pictures may show signs of fear, flight or pain.

2. How did your ideas about wasps change as a result of working with WOWBugs?

Help students see that at every point in history, people's preconceptions have influenced the way they see the world around them. This includes scientists. Encourage students to read more about a famous example such as Clever Hans, the mathematically gifted horse. Encourage discussion about the ways in which all of us are a product of our experience.

Concept Application And Elaboration:

1. Draw another type of dangerous animal.

Encourage students to choose other animal groups where only a few species are actually harmful to humans, such as spiders, snakes, sharks, etc. Encourage investigations of the degree of danger such groups actually present.

2. Display the drawings in your school's central hallway or public shopping mall.

3. How did you learn to feel this way about wasps? Interview parents, other relatives, and friends about their memories of your early encounters with wasps, stories told about wasps, or family or cultural practices related to wasp encounters. Share your results with the class in an oral or written report.

4. Write a report on one of these books:

Evans, H. E., & Eberhard, M. J. (1970). *The wasps.* Ann Arbor: University of Michigan Press.

Spradbery, J. P. (1973). *Wasps: an account of the biology and natural history of solitary and social wasps.* Seattle: University of Washington Press.

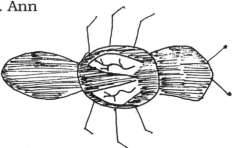

Typical 5th Graders' "After" Drawings

***Key to Secret Code on p. 24**: A, 26; B, 11; C, 24; D, 23; E, 22; F, 21; G, 20; H, 19; I, 25; J, 12; K, 18; L, 17; M, 16; N, 15; O, 14; P, 13; Q, 10; R, 9; S, 8; T, 7; U, 6; V, 5; W, 4; X, 3; Y, 2; Z, 1.*
"Female WOWBugs can live for up to two hundred days."

Evaluating Attitudes: A Draw-a-Wasp Activity

Objectives: Observe changes in one's own knowledge about, and attitude towards, wasps.

Materials (per student):

• *a piece of unlined paper*

• *two or three felt tip markers of different colors*

Most of us have had a least some experience with wasps, or know of a friend or family member who has. What do you know about wasps and how they live?

1. Gather your materials and return to your seat.

2. Draw a picture that tells what you know about wasps and how they live.

3. As you draw your wasp picture, feel free to label anything you want to identify in your drawing.

4. Make sure your name and today's date are on the drawing.

Optional: If your teacher tells you to, write a brief description of your drawing on the back of the paper.

5. Repeat this activity after you have studied WOWBugs.

Discussion:

1. Compare your drawings from the beginning and end of the activity. What differences do you notice?

2. How did your ideas about wasps change as a result of working with WOWBugs?

Just For Fun: A WOWBug Secret Code Game

The answers to these clues are in a secret code. Each number takes the place of a letter of the alphabet. As you do the WOWBug activities, answer the clues below. Then solve the code. Use it to decode the secret message and learn a new fact about WOWBugs.

1. The Organ Pipe Mud Dauber's scientific name is 7-9-2-13-14-3-2-17-14-15.

2. The WOWBug's scientific name is 16-22-17-25-7-7-14-11-25-26.

3. The Y-tube used to test WOWBug sensory choices is called a 24-19-14-25-24-22

7-6-15-15-22-17.

4. Male and female animals that look very different are said to be 23-25-16-14-9-13-19-25-24.

5. An animal's oriented response to gravity is called 20-22-14-7-26-3-25-8.

6. A network of food chains, all linked together, is a 21-14-14-23   4-22-11.

7. Anything changeable is a 5-26-9-25-26-11-17-22.

Secret Message: 21-22-16-26-17-22   4-14-4-11-6-20-8   24-26-15
17-25-5-22   21-14-9   6-13   7-14   7-4-14   19-6-15-23-9-22-23
23-26-2-8.

Answer key for secret code is on p. 22

Chapter Two. Observing Animal Behavior

Behavior can be defined as what animals do. More precisely, it is the ways in which an organism adjusts to and interacts with its environment. Some behaviors – locomotion, grooming, and feeding, for example – are essentially individual matters. These maintenance activities keep an insect in good shape, but usually have little influence on others of its kind. Many actions, however, are communicatory; they are clearly "other oriented" and concerned with conveying information and influencing the moods and activities of others.

This chapter includes a look at orientation and locomotion, two fundamental maintenance activities, and male-female attraction, the most basic of all communicatory activities.

Hoppin' Bug Connect-A-Dot

The ability to move around in the environment is essential to the survival of nearly all insects. Escape from predators, food gathering, mate location, adjustment to environmental variables such as temperature and humidity — these and other important behaviors all depend upon an insect's ability to change its position. To understand ways in which insects solve their very specific spatial problems, let's consider their **locomotion**, how they move within their environment.

Melittobia are small insects, but they are found around the world. How does a WOWBug move about?

Materials (per pair):

- several live female WOWBugs
- temporary containment chambers

(stoppered vials, test tubes, baby food jars, etc.)

- pipe cleaner or small watercolor brush
- sheet of unlined white paper
- pencil
- metric ruler

Key Concepts: Insect locomotion.

Prerequisites: None. This is an entertaining introduction to WOWBug behavior which can be adapted for students of almost any age.

Time: One class period or less.

Getting Ready: Make sure that living adult female WOWBugs are available.

Objectives: Observe WOWBugs' unusual form of insect locomotion; Consider possible advantages of various locomotion methods; Calculate distance covered.

1. Working in pairs or teams, gather your supplies. Then let the teacher know you are ready for your WOWBugs.

When a student group is ready, gently tap WOWBugs out of the culture vial into their temporary container (which can be anything from a small vial to a petri dish or a baby food jar). By dispensing the insects yourself, you can maintain better control over the number that are released. Each group will need 3-5 insects, because some will perform more reliably than others and a few may be accidentally maimed or killed. One stock culture should provide enough for several classes.

2. Transfer one WOWBug from the container onto the blank white sheet of paper, using the pipe cleaner or brush bristles to lift it carefully.

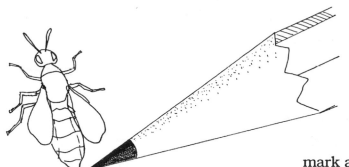

Inexperienced students may wish to practice their transfer technique by first using their brush or pipe cleaner to pick up and move grains of kosher salt.

3. Gently prod its abdomen with a pencil tip. At the same time, mark a small pencil dot on the paper to show where you touched the WOWBug. Label that dot 1.

4. How did the WOWBug respond to your pencil's touch? If it moved, make another mark to show where it stopped. Label that dot 2. If it became motionless, do not prematurely decide that it's dead. Watch for a few moments and see what happens. What might be an advantage of this behavior?

Most of the insects will hop. Only very rarely will one fly away. A few may "play possum." After lying deathly still for a few moments, they will slowly crawl away. This is probably a way to fool predators, just as real opossums feign death to escape attack. Many predators will not touch motionless prey.

5. Continue this process until you have marked at least 10 dots. If you can't finish that many with one WOWBug, switch to a new one. When finished, return the WOWBug to its container.

6. Use the ruler to draw a straight line between each number and the next higher one. Measure the length of the lines between dots 1 and 2, 2 and 3, etc. Record these distances in millimeters (mm) on the chart below.

Charts are provided on the student pages.

7. To find the average jump length, add all jump distances, then divide this total by the number of jumps.

Average jump distance: *usually on the order of 8-10 mm*

8. Record the average WOWBug jump distance for each group of students in your class. Find the average for all the WOWBugs measured by your class. The average is also called the **mean**.

9. When scientists speak of the **range**, they mean the difference between the smallest and largest values in a series of data. The jump distances for all the WOWBugs measured by the class ranged from ____ to ____.

Jump distance varies considerably, a range between 1 and 20 mm being common. If students report distances greater than 25 mm, help them consider the possibility that the wasps were actually making short flights.

Discussion:

1. In what three ways do WOWBugs move about? Which method of locomotion do they appear to use most? Least? What seems to influence the locomotion method they choose?

WOWBugs walk, hop, and fly. Left undisturbed, they most often walk. When disturbed, they almost always hop. Flying is seldom observed.

2. Why would a WOWBug hop rather than crawl when disturbed? How else can it respond to being disturbed?

Hopping adds an element of surprise and also makes it difficult for a predator to determine the direction of the insect's escape. Playing possum, which also can be a surprise, is another option.

3. Female WOWBugs have perfectly normal-looking wings. Why do they usually hop rather than flying away?

Encourage students to brainstorm on this point, and compile a blackboard or transparency list of their responses.

Students often suggest that the wings only look normal but don't really work for some reason. However, female WOWBugs are perfectly capable of flight, and occasionally a student may see one fly (usually toward light).

Scientists have postulated that the reason they seldom fly is because they are so light-weight and delicate that if they were to rise into the air, any wind currents might blow them away from their host's habitat. Their mud dauber hosts usually nest near the place where they were born, and tend to aggregate their nests in suitable sites under bridges, decks, etc. Therefore, in most cases new adult WOWBugs wouldn't have to travel very far to find new hosts.

4. Name at least three other animals that hop.

Kangaroos, crickets, fleas, grasshoppers, frogs, and rabbits are the most commonly mentioned.

5. What sort of adaptations for hopping do these animals have? What sort of adaptations do WOWBugs have?

All of the animals mentioned above have modified legs. WOWBugs, however, have no obvious modifications for hopping. This suggests that their hopping behavior has developed more recently than these other examples. Biologists point out that beneficial behavioral adaptations generally develop more quickly in a population than morphological ones do.

Concept Application And Elaboration:

1. Research and report on how insects such as grass-hoppers, larvae in Mexican jumping beans, springtails, fleas, or click beetles jump.

2. Look up the definition of the word "saltation." How does it apply to WOWBugs?

New Terms:

locomotion

3. Make a poster that shows insects moving in at least five different ways.

mean

range

Hopping, leaping, crawling, flying, gliding, swimming, burrowing, and climbing are common possibilities. More unusual methods include jet propulsion (some dragonfly larvae), riding on other organisms (some parasites), and by release of stored energy (fleas, click beetles).

4. For an entertaining challenge, play "WOWBugs Back Words." Divide the class into teams of 4 or 5. Each team will need a pencil and paper. Call out a word which has four or more letters (such as one of the examples below). Each team writes the word vertically down the left side of the paper. On the right side, the word is written vertically but backwards.

Example: N   o   T
E xercise S
S cienc   E
T oke   N

Between the two columns, each team tries to fit in any number of letters needed to make a word. The first team to complete their chart scores a point. At the end of 5 minutes, if no team has completed the chart, award a point to the team with the greatest number of words. Then, for any word that a team can relate to WOWBugs, give them an extra point.

Be generous in scoring. Strange, convoluted explanations of relationships are part of the fun!

Short words such as BRUSH, ADULT, or MATE work well. Words with repeated letters (pupae, cocoon, etc.) are quite difficult. This can be a tough game!

Speedy WOWBugs: How Fast? How Far?

Key Concepts: Insect locomotion behaviors; Relative speed.

Prerequisites: None. An entertaining introduction to WOWBug behavior which can be adapted for students of almost any age.

Time: One class period.

Getting Ready: Make sure that living adult WOWBugs are available. One culture will provide more than enough for several classes.

If time is short and you want to provide data charts rather than having students make their own, copy page 55 in the student pages. If you want to provide a ready-made racing arena, copy the one on the next page.

Objectives: Observe WOWBugs' unusual form of insect locomotion; Consider possible advantages of various locomotion methods; Calculate distance covered.

Insects move about in a variety of ways, including walking, flying, and hopping. Flying is usually considered the fastest, but scurrying about on six legs can also be wonderfully efficient. Cockroaches, for example, have been clocked at speeds of nearly three miles per hour — a remarkably high speed in relation to their body size. However, there's an old saying that "slow and steady wins the race," and even slow insects can cover more distance than one might expect.

The ability to move about by hopping or jumping is another means of locomotion that has repeatedly and independently arisen in animals of all sizes. It appears to have many advantages. How does it compare with walking as a way to get about?

Materials (per pair or team):

- living adult female WOWBugs
- a sheet of unlined white paper
- pencil
- metric ruler
- drawing compass
- pipe cleaner or small watercolor brush
- stopwatch, or a wrist watch with a second hand
- two temporary WOWBug storage containers
- a laboratory notebook or pad of paper

Part A. Crawling WOWBug Races

1. Working in pairs or teams, gather your supplies. With the metric rule and the compass, draw a circle with a radius of 75 millimeters (3 inches) on the sheet of paper. Mark the center of the circle with a penciled dot, and draw a circle with a 10 mm radius around the dot to

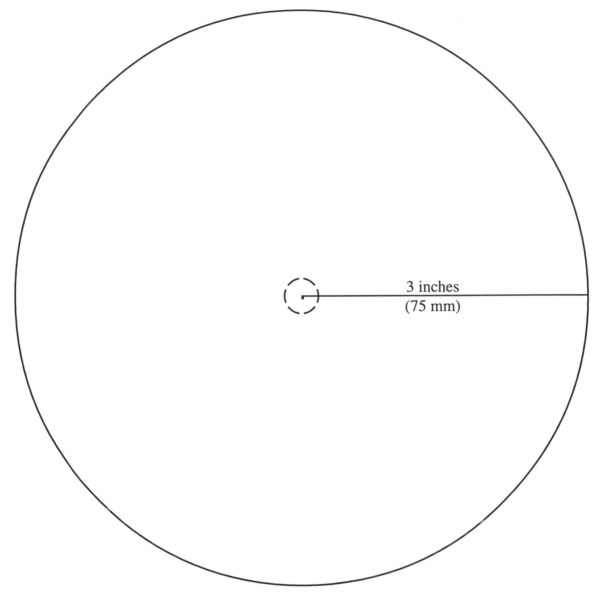

3 inches
(75 mm)

serve as the starting arena. Then let the teacher know you are ready for your WOWBugs.

If class time is really short, you can photocopy and distribute copies of this arena instead.

By dispensing the insects yourself, you can maintain better control over the number released. Tap 3-5 WOWBugs out of the culture vial into one of the two temporary storage containers.

2. As one of you picks up the WOWBug with the pipe cleaner or brush and gently places it in the center starting arena, another should begin timing it.

3. Record how long it takes the WOWBug to reach the outer pencil circle (the "finish line"). Put the information into a data chart. Then use the pipe cleaner or brush bristle to gently pick up the insect and place it in the other storage container.

Students can easily make their own charts, and it's a worthwhile practice. However, if time is short or you want to show an example, use the master in the student pages.

4. Repeat four more times with other WOWBugs from the starting container. Disregard any trial in which the WOWBug simply wanders aimlessly about rather than traveling in a relatively straight line.

WOWBugs usually cover the distance in 10 to 25 seconds.

5. Average the times for your own races, and record this information on your data chart. Add your data together with those of other teams and determine an average for all of the WOWBug races in your class.

Part B. Calculating WOWBug Ground Speed

6. With the pipe cleaner or the brush bristles, gently pick up a WOWBug and place it in the center of the sheet of paper.

7. Have one team member start timing with the watch while another uses the tip of the pencil to gently prod the insect's abdomen until it hops. When the WOWBug lands, immediately prod it again. Count how many times the insect can be made to hop in exactly 30 seconds. Record this number. Then return this WOWBug to its temporary container. Remember, sometimes the insects will "play dead."

Number of jumps in 30 seconds:

Number of jumps in 1 minute (double the previous answer):

8. If you have previously done the "Hoppin' Bug Connect-a-Dot" activity, use your data from that activity, and go to step 12. If you haven't, turn over your sheet of paper and continue.

9. Pick up another WOWBug and place it in the center of the paper. Prod it as before, but instead of timing it, slide the pencil to draw a line from where you touched the WOWBug to where it landed after its hop. If the insect approaches the paper's edge, you should move it back toward the center before you continue.

10. Repeat this until you have at least 10 good marks on the sheet to show hopping distances. Measure these distances in millimeters (mm), and record these in a data chart.

See the second chart in the student masters for an example.

11. Add all of the distances together, then divide by the number of jumps. This gives you the average jump distance.

Average jump distance is usually on the order of 8-10 mm, but varies considerably, with a range between 1-20 mm. If students report distances greater than 25 mm help them consider the possibility that the wasps were actually making short flights.

12. What was your WOWBug's hopping speed in millimeters per minute? Use this formula to figure it out.

Hopping speed per minute = (number of jumps per minute) x (average jump length in millimeters).

Number of jumps per minute is from #7, the doubled answer; average jump length is from #11. Average hopping speed is usually on the order of 275 to 400 mm per minute.

13. What was your WOWBug's walking speed in millimeters per minute? Use this formula to figure it out.

Walking speed per minute = (4500)/ (average time to

reach the finish line).

Average time is from #5. This formula results from converting the ratio of the 75-mm distance to the finish line/average time required to travel the 75 mm to an equivalent distance (x) for 60 seconds (1 minute). The formula is x = (75 x 60)/Ave. time or 4500/Ave. time. Walking speed usually is about 250 mm per minute.

14. Record your team's average on the class master list. Working together, calculate average WOWBug walking speed in meters per hour and feet per hour for all the WOWBugs measured by your class.

You may need to review the meaning of the term "average" with younger students, and walk them through the conversions necessary to switch from meters to feet per hour. It's worth the effort. (1 meter=3.28 feet.)

With more advanced classes, you might expand these calculations to include standard deviation and standard error of the mean.

Discussion:

1. What was the average time for a WOWBug to cover a 75-mm distance without prodding? What was the range in times? What was the average unprodded WOWBug speed in millimeters per minute?

WOWBugs usually cover the distance in 10-25 seconds, at a speed of about 250 mm per minute.

2. What would the average time be for a WOWBug to cover that same 75-mm distance if it had hopped steadily along in a straight line? Is it likely that it would do so?

To calculate this, divide the observed speed by 60 (to convert it to speed per second), then divide this number into the distance (which is 75 mm). Depending on the student's speed calculations, this should be on the order of 10-18 seconds. WOWBugs generally don't hop in a straight line.

3. Many **variables** (things that can change) can affect the distance an insect can cover. What are some? How do they affect each other?

At first, students will probably name environmental variables such as wind. Ask how they calculated distance. Lead them to consider the most fundamental variables: the distance each hop covers, and the rate of hopping (hops per minute or second). Each multiplies the effects of the other. Increases in either can compensate for a decrease in the other in a way that keeps the final distance the same.

4. Which was a faster way to cover distance, crawling or hopping? Which takes more energy? Which would work better as a way to escape predators? Which would work better to find a food source an insect could see?

Hopping generally is somewhat faster, takes more energy and is much more variable in direction. It would be better for escaping predators. Crawling or walking is slower, but takes less energy and is straighter, so it would be better for finding the source of a stimulus.

5. Suppose two mud-dauber nests are located under bridges half a mile (800 meters) apart. If WOWBugs can walk 12 hours a day at a speed of 250 mm per minute, how long would those from one nest take to reach the other? Show your calculations.

For younger students, you may wish to omit this question or work on it as a whole-class activity. However, it's quite straight-forward if set up like this:

800 meters x 1000 mm/meter x 1 min/250 mm x 1 hr/60 min = 53.3 hours.

6. Is covering this distance biologically realistic?

If the WOWBugs travel for 12 hours a day, they'll reach the other nest on the fifth day. Because WOWBugs can easily live for one to two weeks, this is clearly possible, assuming they walk in a straight line..

7. Did anyone in your class see a WOWBug fly? How did flying seem to compare in speed to walking and hopping?

They fly occasionally, and it is many times faster than ground transportation.

8. Describe an experiment a scientist could design to test flying speed. What would you do to measure the movement of the insects?

Brainstorm about experimental design. One possibility would be to use a very high speed camera which shoots a known number of frames per second. Then analyze the film. You may wish to show students the beautiful photography in Borne on the Wind: The Extraordinary World of Insects in Flight, *by Stephen Dalton (1975, E. P. Dutton, New York), who has actually done such work.*

Concept Application And Elaboration:

1. Migration or "adaptive traveling" is one of the most spectacular forms of insect travel, and monarch butterflies are undoubtedly the best publicized North American example. Some excellent film footage is available. An older film worth finding to show is "Strategy for Survival: Behavioral Ecology of the Monarch Butterfly." (30 min., Harper and Row Media, New York. 1977.)

2. Could the dispersal of female WOWBugs be called a migration? Working together, research migration in the scientific literature, and hold a mock debate on the subject in your classroom.

3. Just for fun, play the "I Saw A WOWBug" Rhyming Game. It can be done either as a whole class or in teams or groups.

Each group will need a pencil and paper, and a person

designated as the recorder. The teacher begins by recit-
ing a line of verse intended to form an original jingle. For
example, one might say, "I saw a WOWBug on a nest..."
The next player on the team or in the group adds another original line which rhymes with the previous one,
such as "She hopped to show she liked me best..." (Silly
rhymes are fine!) Each player adds a line until no one
can invent any more.

*In teams, the activity can be either competitive (who can develop
the longest poem around a single rhyme?) or cooperative (start
each team with a different first line, ask for the same number of
lines, and link rhymes into a single long poem for classroom
display).*

Some sample first lines:

I saw a WOWBug hopping by...

I saw a WOWBug playing dead...

I saw a WOWBug find a host...

I saw a WOWBug near a light...

The Great WOWBug Roundup

Key Concepts: Animal behavior; Phototaxis; Orientation; Light reactions; Dispersal.

Prerequisites: None. An excellent introduction for students of any age who have never seen WOWBugs before. Can be used as a stand-alone activity or in tandem with any other WOWBug activity.

Time: About 15 minutes, including discussion.

Getting Ready: No advance preparation needed.

Objective: Determine an effective technique for gathering and collecting Melittobia digitata; Discover positive phototaxic behavior and recognize its importance as a variable that must be controlled in many biological experiments.

A major part of an insect's behavior is turning towards, or away from, factors like food, mate, prey, host, etc. Scientists look at this **orientation** in two very different ways. Some study how they move, others study why they move. Let's try to use the "why" to our advantage to solve a simple but important task — the job of trying to recapture WOWBugs after taking them out to study. What is the most effective way to "round up" WOWBugs when they are outside of their container?

Materials (per pair or team):
• a culture of living adult WOWBugs
• small watercolor brushes
• pipe cleaners
• construction or photocopy paper in white and other light colors
• various sizes and colors of glass or plastic containers (such as pill bottles) with lids, stoppers, or tightly packed cotton plugs
• light sources such as flashlights, pen lights, or table lamps

1. Working in pairs or teams, gather your laboratory supplies.

2. Let the teacher know you are ready for your WOWBugs. (If you already have your WOWBugs, skip this step.)

To dispense them, gently tap WOWBugs out of the culture vial onto the white paper. By dispensing the insects yourself, you can maintain better control over the number that are released. Give each team about 10 insects. (The exact number does not matter, but more than this many can be difficult to keep on the paper.)

3. Figure out a way to get all the WOWBugs back into captivity. You may use any of the materials you have in any way that makes sense, as long as you don't injure or kill the WOWBugs. You may want to try out several techniques to find the one that seems the most effective.

Be enthusiastic about whatever creative ideas students come up with. Among the ones we've seen tried with varying degrees of success:

• *herding WOWBugs along with a brush*
• *picking individuals up with the pipe cleaner and tapping them into the vial*
• *inverting the container over individuals and letting them crawl in by themselves*
• *making a paper funnel of the white sheet and pouring the insects into the vial*
• *setting a light behind a clear container and letting WOWBugs crawl toward it*

Have the class list and describe the methods they tried, and discussing the advantages, disadvantages, and relative efficiency of each. Then discuss the questions on the activity sheet.

Discussion:

1. What sorts of WOWBug movement did you observe?

List should include walking, hopping, and perhaps short flights and playing "dead."

2. Did the WOWBugs consistently move toward or away from anything?

In various ways, nearly everyone should have been able to observe the insects moving upward and toward light.

3. Which behaviors did your most efficient "round up" technique take advantage of?

Answers will vary, but should be centered around use of movement toward light and away from gravity.

Encourage further discussion of this behavior. What happened when the light direction changed? What would happen if they were to pick up the paper and turn it upside down? Ask whether students are sure that the insects are actually moving toward light, and not just away from gravity. How could they test this idea? (Move the light to a position below the insects and see what happens.)

How can they be sure the insects are not just moving toward the heat generated by the light source? What could they do to eliminate this possibility? (Shine the light through a glass of water. The water would absorb the heat, but not the light.)

4. Look up the terms **phototaxis** and **geotaxis**. What does "taxis" mean?

The movement of an animal in response to some external stimulus, from the Greek word for "arrangement."

5. Movement toward something is called **positive**, and away is called **negative**. How would you describe WOWBug orientation using the words in questions 4 and 5?

WOWBugs show positive phototaxis (they move toward light) and negative geotaxis (they move away from gravity).

6. A scientist tried to test whether WOWBugs prefer the smell of vinegar or water. He placed cotton balls soaked with the two liquids on a table, then placed WOWBugs on a paper midway between them. After 5 minutes, he counted the number that crawled off the paper toward each cotton ball. What was wrong with his experimental design?

Answers will vary, but should include that he failed to control for the possible influence of light.

7. Male WOWBugs are blind. Would you predict that they would react in the same way? How could you set up an experiment to test your hypothesis?

Most will predict that the blind males will not be influenced by light. However, you may wish to point out to students that studies of orientation are seldom as simple as they first appear to be. For example, scientists have never even determined whether the WOWBug's light reaction is through its compound eyes, its tiny simple eyes (ocelli), or perhaps another body region entirely. Although males do not have compound eyes, they do have a pigmented spot on each side of the head where an eye would be. No one yet knows if these spots retain any working neural connections. They also have ocelli that look fairly normal, and might detect light.

Experimental design ideas will vary, but should include a control group not exposed to directional light, and a way to measure whether the movement observed is just chance wandering. You may wish to give interested students the opportunity to actually conduct these experiments. This is truly new research. We'd be interested in your results.

New Terms:

orientation

phototaxis

geotaxis

Concept Application And Elaboration:

1. Honeybees orient to gravity while communicating with other bees in the hive. How do they do it? See if you can find out.

The answer, with pictures, can be found in Matthews and Matthews (1978), p. 85–86.

2. Would other insects react to light in the same way that WOWBugs do? Conduct some trials with other species such as ants or beetles. Report your results to the class.

3. Write a limerick about WOWBug locomotion.

Here's a rip-off of an old classic, just to get your creative juices flowing:

There was a WOWBug of Devizes,
Whose wings were of two different sizes.
The one that was small
Was of no use at all,
But the other one won several prizes.

Courtship Communication: An Overview

When we speak of communication with each other, we usually mean talking. But doesn't body language also communicate? What about perfume? Or romantic music? Communication can, in fact, take many forms, so it's probably best defined broadly —sharing information coded in the form of signals. More precisely, communication is the production of a signal, measurable in the language of physics or chemistry, that alters the response patterns of another individual. (For the true word-lover among us, the study of all animal communication is called **zoosemiotics**.)

For most types of animals, finding a mate is an important priority. For animals which are relatively short-lived, as most insects are, time is of the essence. Mate location and identification must occur quickly, in order to leave sufficient time to reproduce. In the insect world, communication that helps an individual quickly recognize potential mates is particularly important. **Courtship signals** are the cues used.

Courtship signals can be sent and received in many ways. Firefly flashing, for example, is a visual mate location signal. Crickets, on the other hand, chirp out an auditory cue. But by far the vast majority of insect courtship signals are chemical in nature.

Chemical signals that communicate information between different individuals of the same species are called **pheromones**. These highly distinctive odors (or distinctive mixtures of odors) allow an insect to recognize another of the same species and to identify it as the opposite sex.

Courtship Communication

Within the cocoon of their host, WOWBugs live in the dark, amidst hundreds of others of their kind. How do WOWBugs find and recognize others of the opposite sex?

These experiments are a bit more complex than the preceding ones, and require more advance preparation. However, the time spent is well worth it, for this is an excellent avenue for learning several essential abilities necessary to do scientific inquiry.

To answer such a question is a challenging task. Since insects can't talk to us, we must design experiments that let us clearly recognize when communication about these matters takes place. Such experiments usually involve a **bioassay** — a test in which an organism is offered a choice of stimuli that may have significance in its biology, and its reaction to the various stimuli is measured.

You may wish to discuss with students the fact that the choice of which stimuli to use in a bioassay is critical. By its behavior in a bioassay, the insect tells the scientists which of the choices offered is more important and relevant to it. But if all of the choices are biological nonsense, it is possible to get results that look plausible, but are nonsense as well. As the computer saying goes, "garbage in, garbage out."

Key Concepts: Insect sexual attraction; Chemical communication.

Prerequisites: Basic familiarity with WOWBugs, including ability to recognize males and females and some practice handling and moving the insects. An understanding of the concept of controlling variables.

Time: One class period for the activity itself; parts of one or two other periods for discussions.

Getting Ready: Two to three days in advance, isolate at least 10 dark (late stage) female pupae for each team or group (see Chapter 7). Prepare bioassay chambers (see Chapter 8).

Objectives: Use a simple bioassay to demonstrate that unmated female WOWBugs recognize and distinguish between males and other females; Discover chemically-mediated attraction of female WOWBugs to males; Recognize and control variables; Recognize the importance of asking biologically meaningful research questions.

To be successful, it is imperative to use unmated females. If there is time and students are able to reliably recognize and sort female pupae, you may wish to enlist their aid in preparations.

Materials (per team):

• live unmated female and male *Melittobia digitata* in separate containment chambers
• two double-ended cotton swabs
• small watercolor brush
• millimeter ruler
• scissors
• one sheet of unlined white paper
• one small sheet of tissue paper
• one bioassay chamber
• one cotton ball
• stop watch or wrist watch with ability to time seconds

Part A. Designing A Bioassay

1. The most effective research builds on what a researcher already knows. How do male and female WOWBugs find each other? Which sex is more likely to be the attraction? Which the attracted? The clues are in what you and your classmates already know about the WOWBug life cycle. Share your ideas.

2. Courtship cues can involve any of an insect's senses — vision, hearing, smell, taste, or touch. Which would seem most reasonable for WOWBugs? Which most unlikely? Again, think about what you already know.

In nature, a newly adult WOWBug is in the dark, literally. The females emerge from their pupae while still within the cocoon of their host and mate, then immediately begin to try to escape to the world outside. The males are blind, and stay behind. This suggests that vision is not a major clue. It also suggests that if there is an attraction, it probably occurs only before mating.

Several hundred WOWBugs emerge from a single host, and female WOWBugs outnumber males by approximately 20:1. Taste and touch require close contact, and would be of limited use in this situation.

This leaves hearing and smell. Because the females are more active, have "normal" appearing antennae, and outnumber the males so greatly, it is reasonable to hypothesize that they are the ones attracted by the cues, and thus that the males are the attractions.

3. Working together, state your prediction in the form of a general hypothesis.

Examples include "Unmated female Melittobia are attracted to males by an odor which the males produce" or "Unmated female WOWBugs go to males because the males make a sound which females find attractive."

4. Examine the bioassay chamber. Insects to be tested will be placed in the dark bottom section, from which they are free to move up into the clear straw tubes. Test stimuli will be placed behind a tissue paper "screen" in each of the tubes.

See the illustration of the bioassay chamber on the first page of this exercise. Construction directions are included in Chapter 8.

5. To be testable, a hypothesis must include something that can be measured. The choice of experimental apparatus often determines what that will be. With these bioassay chambers, it's easy to count the number of insects entering each clear tube over a given amount of time, such as 3 minutes. Re-state your hypothesis in a more specific, measurable form.

An example might be "In 3 minutes, more unmated female WOWBugs will enter a straw where there is a male than a straw without a male."

6. What types of cues could best be tested in this particular type of bioassay chamber? What types of cues would be better tested in a chamber that was differently designed?

This type of chamber works best for bioassays of odors or auditory cues. The test stimuli are visually hidden, but odors or sounds can readily diffuse through the tissue. Tests of visual or tactile (touch) cues would need a different type of design.

Unmated Female WOWBug Entries In 3 Minutes (Empty Tubes)	
Tube #:	# Of Entries:
1	
2	
3	
4	
Total:	

Part A. What You See Is What You Get?

It's a favorite saying, but is it true? Conducting an experiment is often relatively easy, scientists say. Having confidence in the results is harder. One of the marks of good research is the care which is taken to be sure that the results are really due to the experimental variables being examined. This is the reason a well-designed experiment always has one or more control groups.

7. Prepare the bioassay chamber. Use the scissors and ruler to cut several small (about 1 cm x 1 cm) squares from the tissue paper. Lay a single square of tissue over the end of the brush handle, and gently press it around the end. Then use the brush handle to gently push the tissue into the straw about 2 cm. Take care not to tear the tissue.

8. Repeat this for each of the tubes. Then cut the stems of two double-ended cotton swabs in half. Push one into each straw. (Your bioassay chamber should now look like the one in the illustration.)

9. Suppose nothing were placed in any of the tubes. What would you predict about the choices the test organisms would make? What would a different result suggest? How should a careful researcher respond?

An approximately equal number of organisms would enter each of the tubes, indicating that choices were made randomly in the absence of any other cues. A consistently non-random result would indicate that some non-controlled variable was acting. The investigators' task should be to identify and remove (or at least account for) this extra variable.

10. Let's test our prediction. Open the lid of the bioassay chamber. Open the vial of unmated female WOWBugs, invert it over the chamber, and flick your finger sharply against the side of the vial so that the insects all fall to the bottom of the test chamber at once. Quickly replace

the lid on the chamber, and place it, lid-side-down, on the sheet of white paper. Mark the direction in which the #1 straw is facing.

11. Immediately begin timing. For the next 3 minutes, watch carefully. Count each time an insect enters a straw, even if it leaves before the end of the time period. Record your tally on the chart provided.

12. Open the bioassay chamber, invert it on the sheet of paper, and tap the side to remove the WOWBugs. Invert the vial over individual insects until they crawl up inside the vial. Stopper the vial with the cotton plug. Count to be sure you have recaptured all 10 WOWBugs. (You'll use them again in the next experiment.)

13. Add your team's tally to the class master chart. How did your results compare with those of other teams?

When the first team has finished, have them make a master chart for all class results. When all have completed this trial, discuss the results. Chance variation in results from one team to another will be evident, but the class average should not be significantly different from random. More advanced students might be shown how to perform a chi-square test on the class data set. (See Chapter 8.)

14. How did the female WOWBugs react? Why?

They went to different straws, more or less randomly or stayed within the dark bioassay chamber. There was nothing to attract them in any particular direction.

Alternative: Strong room light from one direction could result in a directional response (but such a response is much more pronounced with mated than with unmated females). Consider setting up this situation intentionally, in order to give students an opportunity to discover and deal with this variable. Help students discover the necessity for a second set of trials with the light source

Class Master Chart
Unmated Female WOWBug Entries In 3 Minutes (Empty Tubes)

Tube #:	# Of Entries:
1	
2	
3	
4	
Total:	

Unmated Female WOWBug Entries In 3 Minutes (Male In Tube 1)	
Tube #:	# Of Entries:
1	
2	
3	
4	
Total:	

removed, or adjusted for uniform illumination on all four tubes, to confirm that this variable has been controlled.

15. Did the same number of insects enter each tube? Why or why not?

Probably not, since with only 10 insects an equal distribution is unlikely. Moreover, in practice WOWBugs tend to enter each of the straws, explore briefly, then reenter the main chamber without staying for long in any one tube.

Part C. Testing WOWBug Courtship Attraction

How does the presence of a male WOWBug affect the way unmated females react? What cue or cues are responsible? It's time to find out.

16. Remove the cotton swab from straw #1. Use the paintbrush bristles or pipe cleaner to put a male WOWBug gently into the straw tube. Stick the cotton swab back in behind him to make sure he doesn't escape.

17. As before, place 10 unmated females in the dark bioassay chamber, then place the chamber lid-side-down on the paper. Be sure the #1 tube is facing the same way it faced before.

18. Immediately begin timing for 3 minutes. As before, count the number of WOWBugs entering each tube. Record your tally on the chart. As before, at the end of the experiment, replace the female WOWBugs back into their original vial.

19. With a male WOWBug in tube # 1, how did the results compare to those in the first experiment? What does this indicate?

Most of the females should have entered the tube with the male, and the majority will have stayed there. This indicates that the male is somehow attracting them.

20. Do you think the cue is a sound or an odor? Remove the male, and repeat the experiment without changing the swab or the tissue. Record your data on the chart.

21. What does the tally show? Which hypothesis does it support?

Even with the male gone, the swab and tissue continue to attract females. This suggests an odor-based communication system. The male has left behind an attractive pheromone.

Unmated Female WOWBug Entries In 3 Minutes (Male Gone From Tube 1)	
Tube #:	# Of Entries:
1	
2	
3	
4	
Total:	

22. What do you think the results would be if you repeated this experiment with females that had already been allowed to mate?

They would not be interested in seeking out the male wasp. If time allows, you can let your students try this experiment with 10 females taken from the stock culture.

23. What do you think would be the result if the WOWBug in tube # 1 were another female instead of a male?

Again, the other females should not be particularly attracted to another female. You can let your students run this experiment, too. However, be sure to use a new straw tube, tissue, and cotton swab so there are no residual pheromones.

A few students may generalize this line of thinking and want to put a male WOWBug into straw # 1 and a set of 10 males in the bioassay chamber. They will guess, wrongly, that like with two females there would be no attraction. This experiment is to be avoided, however, because the 10 test males will seek each other out to fight for dominance, often killing or injuring one another in the chamber. (Males move more slowly, but the victors will eventually crawl into the male-occupied tube.) See "Darwinian Selection" in Chapter 6.

New Terms:

bioassay

courtship signal

pheromones

zoosemiotics

Concept Application And Elaboration:

1. What other insects use odors to bring the sexes together? What other senses are often used by insects to attract mates? Research the answer, and write a short report.

2. Working together, prepare a skit that has to do with WOWBug courtship attraction. Use at least 4 props. Present the skit to your class.

3. We used bioassay chambers made from a dark canister. Based on what you know about WOWBug behavior, how would our results have differed if the canister had been clear? Make such a bioassay chamber and test your predictions.

Hoppin' Bug Connect-A-Dot

The ability to move around in the environment is essential to the survival of nearly all insects. Escape from predators, food gathering, mate location, adjustment to environmental variables such as temperature and humidity — these and other important behaviors all depend upon an insect's ability to change its position. To understand ways in which insects solve their very specific spatial problems, let's consider their **locomotion**, how they move within their environment.

Melittobia are small insects, but they are found around the world. How does a WOWBug move about?

Objectives: Observe WOWBugs' unusual form of insect locomotion; Consider possible advantages of various locomotion methods; Calculate distance covered.

Procedure:

1. Working in pairs or teams, gather your supplies. Then let the teacher know you are ready for your WOWBugs.

2. Transfer one WOWBug from the container onto the blank white sheet of paper, using the pipe cleaner or brush bristles to lift it carefully.

3. Gently prod its abdomen with a pencil. At the same time, mark a small pencil dot on the paper to show where you put the WOWBug down. Label that dot 1.

Materials (per pair):

• *several live female WOWBugs*
• *temporary containment chambers*
• *pipe cleaner or small water-color brush*
• *sheet of unlined white paper*
• *pencil*
• *metric ruler*

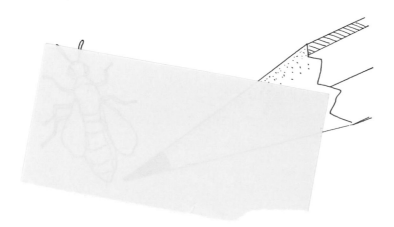

4. How did the WOWBug respond to your pencil's touch? If it moved, make another mark to show where it stopped. Label that dot 2. If it became motionless, do not prematurely decide that it's dead. Watch for a few minutes and see what happens. What might be an advantage of this behavior?

_____

_____

_____

5. Continue this process until you have marked at least 10 dots. If you can't finish that many with one WOWBug, switch to a new one. When finished, return the WOWBug to its container.

6. Use the ruler to draw a straight line between each number and the next higher one. Measure the length of the lines between dots 1 and 2, 2 and 3, etc. Record these distances in millimeters (mm) on the chart below.

WOWBug Jumping Distance in Millimeters	
Jump	Distance
1	
2	
3	
4	
5	
6	
7	
8	
9	
10	
Total distance:	
Average jump:	

7. To find the average jump length, add all jump distances, then divide this total by the number of jumps.

Average jump distance: _____

8. Record the average WOWBug jump distance for each group of students in your class. Find the average for all the WOWBugs measured by your class. The average is also called the **mean**.

9. When scientists speak of the **range**, they mean the difference between the smallest and largest values in a series of data. The jump distances for all the WOWBugs measured by the class ranged from _____ to _____.

Discussion:

1. In what three ways do WOWBugs move about? Which method of locomotion do they appear to use most? Least? What seems to influence the locomotion method they choose?

_____

_____

2. Why would a WOWBug hop rather than crawl when disturbed? How else can it respond to being disturbed?

_____

_____

3. Female WOWBugs have perfectly normal-looking wings. Why do they usually hop rather than flying away?

_____

_____

4. Name at least three other animals that hop.

_____

_____

5. What sort of adaptations for hopping do these animals have? What sort of adaptations do WOWBugs have?

_____

_____

_____

Data Charts For Use With "Speedy WOWBugs: How Fast? How Far?"

Data Chart. Crawling WOWBugs

Trial Number	Seconds to Finish
1.	
2.	
3.	
4.	
5.	

Total time in seconds:

Average time:

Data Chart. WOWBug Ground Speed

Jump Number	Distance (mm)
1.	
2.	
3.	
4.	
5.	
6.	
7.	
8.	
9.	
10.	

Total distance:

Average jump length:

Range:

Speedy WOWBugs: How Fast? How Far?

Objectives: Observe WOWBugs' unusual form of insect locomotion; Consider possible advantages of various locomotion methods; Calculate distance covered.

Materials (per pair or team):

- *living adult female WOWBugs (Melittobia digitata)*
- *a sheet of unlined white paper*
- *pencil*
- *metric ruler*
- *drawing compass*
- *pipe cleaner or small water-color brush*
- *stopwatch, or a wrist watch with a second hand*
- *two temporary WOWBug storage containers*
- *a laboratory notebook or pad of paper*

Insects move about in a variety of ways, including walking, flying, and hopping. Flying is usually considered the fastest, but scurrying about on six legs can also be wonderfully efficient. Cockroaches, for example, have been clocked at speeds of nearly three miles per hour — a remarkably high speed in relation to their body size. However, there's an old saying that "slow and steady wins the race," and even slow insects can cover more distance than one might expect.

The ability to move about by hopping or jumping is another means of locomotion that has repeatedly and independently arisen in animals of all sizes. It appears to have many advantages. How does it compare with walking as a way to get about?

Part A. Crawling WOWBug Races

1. Working in pairs or teams, gather your supplies. With the metric rule and the compass, draw a circle with a radius of 75 millimeters (3 inches) on the sheet of paper. Mark the center of the circle with a penciled dot, and draw a circle with a 10 mm radius around the dot to serve as the starting arena. Then let the teacher know you are ready for your WOWBugs.

2. As one of you picks up the WOWBug with the pipe cleaner or brush and gently places it in the center starting arena, another should begin timing it.

3. Record how long it takes the WOWBug to reach the outer pencil circle (the "finish line"). Put the information into a data chart. Then use the pipe cleaner or brush bristle to gently pick up the insect and place it in the other storage container.

4. Repeat four more times with other WOWBugs from the starting container. Disregard any trial in which the

WOWBug simply wanders aimlessly about rather than traveling in a relatively straight line.

5. Average the times for your own races, and record this information on your data chart. Add your data together with those of other teams and determine an average for all of the WOWBug races in your class.

Part B. Calculating WOWBug Ground Speed

6. With the pipe cleaner or the brush bristles, gently pick up a WOWBug and place it in the center of the sheet of paper.

7. Have one team member start timing with the watch while another uses the tip of the pencil to gently prod the insect's abdomen until it hops. When the WOWBug lands, immediately prod it again. Count how many times the insect can be made to hop in exactly 30 seconds. Record this number. Then return this WOWBug to its temporary container. Remember, sometimes the insects will "play dead."

Number of jumps in 30 seconds: _____

Number of jumps in 1 minute (double the previous answer): _____

8. If you have previously done the "Hoppin' Bug Connect-a-Dot" activity, use your data from that activity, and go to step 12. If you haven't, turn over your sheet of paper and continue.

9. Pick up another WOWBug and place it in the center of the paper. Prod it as before, but instead of timing it, slide the pencil to draw a line from where you touched the WOWBug to where it landed after its hop. If the insect approaches the paper's edge, you should move it back toward the center before you continue.

10. Repeat this until you have at least 10 good marks on the sheet to show hopping distances. Measure these distances in millimeters (mm), and record these in a data chart.

11. Add all of the distances together, then divide by the number of jumps. This gives you the average jump distance.

Average jump distance: _____ millimeters

12. What was your WOWBug's hopping speed in millimeters per minute? Use this formula to figure it out:

Hopping speed per min. = (number of jumps per min.) x (average jump length in mm)

Our WOWBug's hopping speed: _____

13. What was your WOWBug's walking speed in millimeters per minute? Use this formula to figure it out.

Walking speed per minute = (4500)/ (average time to reach the finish line).

Our WOWBug's walking speed: _____

14. Record your team's average on the class master list. Working together, calculate average WOWBug walking speed in meters per hour and feet per hour for all the WOWBugs measured by your class.

Discussion:

1. What was the average time for a WOWBug to cover a 75-mm distance without prodding? What was the range in times? What was the average unprodded WOWBug speed in millimeters per minute?

_____

2. What would the average time be for a WOWBug to cover that same 75-mm distance if it had hopped steadily along in a straight line? Is it likely that it would do so?

_____

3. Many **variables** (things that can change) can affect the distance an insect can cover. What are some? How do they affect each other?

_____

_____

_____

_____

4. Which was a faster way to cover distance, crawling or hopping? Which takes more energy? Which would work better as a way to escape predators? Which would work better to find a food source an insect could see?

_____

_____

_____

5. Suppose two mud-dauber nests are located under bridges half a mile (800 meters) apart. If WOWBugs can walk 12 hours a day at a speed of 250 mm per minute, how long would those from one nest take to reach the other? Show your calculations.

6. Is covering this distance biologically realistic? Why or why not?

_____

_____

_____

7. Did anyone in your class see a WOWBug fly? How did flying seem to compare in speed to walking and hopping?

_____

_____

8. Describe an experiment a scientist could design to test flying speed. What would you do to measure the movement of the insects?

_____

_____

_____

The Great WOWBug Roundup

A major part of an insect's behavior is turning towards, or away from, factors like food, mate, prey, host, etc. Scientists look at this **orientation** in two very different ways. Some study how they move, others study why they move. Let's try to use the "why" to our advantage to solve a simple but important task — the job of trying to recapture WOWBugs after taking them out to study. What is the most effective way to "round up" WOWBugs when they are outside of their container?

Objective: Determine an effective technique for gathering and collecting Melittobia digitata; *Discover positive phototaxic behavior and recognize its importance as a variable that must be controlled in many biological experiments.*

Materials (per pair or team):

• *a culture of living adult WOWBugs*
• *small watercolor brushes*
• *pipe cleaners*
• *construction paper in white and other light colors*
• *various sizes and colors of glass or plastic containers (such as pill bottles) with lids, stoppers, or tightly packed cotton plugs*
• *light sources such as flashlights, pen lights, or table lamps*

Procedure:

1. Working in pairs or teams, gather your laboratory supplies.

2. Let the teacher know you are ready for your WOWBugs. (If you already have your WOWBugs, skip this step.)

3. Figure out a way to get all the WOWBugs back into captivity. You may use any of the materials you have in any way that makes sense, as long as you don't injure or kill the WOWBugs. You may want to try out several techniques to find the one that seems the most effective.

Discussion:

1. What sorts of WOWBug movement did you observe?

_____

2. Did the WOWBugs consistently move toward or away from anything?

_____

3. Which behaviors did your most efficient "round up" technique take advantage of?

_____

4. Look up the terms **phototaxis** and **geotaxis**. What does "taxis" mean?

_____

5. Movement toward something is called **positive**, and away is called **negative**. How would you describe WOWBug orientation using the words in questions 4 and 5?

_____

6. Male WOWBugs are blind. Would you predict that they would react in the same way? How could you set up an experiment to test your hypothesis?

_____

_____

_____

_____

7. A scientist tried to test whether WOWBugs prefer the smell of vinegar or water. He placed cotton balls soaked with the two liquids on a table, then placed WOWBugs on a paper midway between them. After 5 minutes, he counted the number that crawled off the paper toward each cotton ball. What was wrong with his experimental design?

_____

_____

_____

Courtship Communication

Within the cocoon of their host, WOWBugs live in the dark, amidst hundreds of others of their kind. How do WOWBugs find and recognize others of the opposite sex?

To answer such a question is a challenging task. Since insects can't talk to us, we must design experiments that let us clearly recognize when communication about these matters takes place. Such experiments usually involve a **bioassay** — a test in which an organism is offered a choice of stimuli that may have significance in its biology, and its reaction to the various stimuli is measured.

Objectives: Use a simple bioassay to demonstrate that unmated female WOWBugs recognize and distinguish between males and other females; Discover chemically-mediated attraction of female WOWBugs to males; Recognize and control variables; Recognize the importance of asking biologically meaningful research questions.

Part A. Designing A Bioassay.

1. The most effective research builds on what a researcher already knows. Which sex is more likely to be the attraction? Which the attracted? The clues are in what you and your classmates already know about the WOWBug life cycle. Share your ideas.

_____

_____

Materials (per team):

• *live unmated female and male* Melittobia digitata *in separate containment chambers*
• *two double-ended cotton swabs*
• *small watercolor brush*
• *millimeter ruler*
• *scissors*
• *one sheet of unlined white paper*
• *one small sheet of tissue paper*
• *one bioassay chamber*
• *one cotton ball*
• *stop watch or wrist watch with ability to time seconds*

2. Courtship cues might involve any or all of an insect's senses — vision, hearing, smell, taste, or touch. Which would seem most reasonable for WOWBugs? Which most unlikely? Again, think about what you already know.

_____

_____

_____

3. Working together, state your prediction in the form of a general hypothesis.

_____

_____

4. Examine the bioassay chamber. Insects to be tested will be placed in the dark bottom section, from which they are free to move up into the clear straw tubes. Test stimuli will be placed behind a tissue paper "screen" in each of the tubes.

5. To be testable, a hypothesis must include something that can be measured. The choice of experimental apparatus often determines what that will be. With these bioassay chambers, it's easy to count the number of insects entering each clear tube over a given amount of time, such as 3 minutes. Re-state your hypothesis in a more specific, measurable form.

_____

_____

6. What types of cues could best be tested in this particular type of bioassay chamber? What types of cues would be better tested in a chamber that was differently designed?

_____

_____

_____

Part B. What You See Is What You Get?

It's a favorite saying, but is it true? Conducting an experiment is often relatively easy, scientists say. Having confidence in the results is harder. One of the marks of good research is the care which is taken to be sure that the results are really due to the experimental variables being examined. This is the reason a well-designed experiment always has one or more control groups.

7. Prepare the bioassay chamber. Use the scissors and ruler to cut several small (about 1 cm x 1 cm) squares from the tissue paper. Lay a single square of tissue over the end of the brush handle, and gently press it around the end. Then use the brush handle to gently push the tissue into the straw about 2 cm. Take care not to tear the tissue.

8. Repeat this for each of the tubes. Then cut the stems of two double-ended cotton swabs in half. Push one into each straw. (Your bioassay chamber should now look like the one in the illustration.)

9. Suppose nothing were placed in any of the tubes. What would you predict about the choices the test organisms would make? What would a different result suggest? How should a careful researcher respond?

_____

_____

_____

10. Let's test our prediction. Open the lid of the bioassay chamber. Open the vial of unmated female WOWBugs, invert it over the chamber, and flick your finger sharply against the side of the vial so that the insects all fall to the bottom of the test chamber at once. Quickly replace the lid on the chamber, and place it, lid-side-down, on the sheet of white paper. Mark the direction in which the #1 straw is facing.

11. Immediately begin timing. For the next 3 minutes, watch carefully. Count each time an insect enters a straw, even if it leaves before the end of the time period. Record your tally on the chart provided.

12. Open the bioassay chamber, invert it on the sheet of paper, and tap the side to remove the WOWBugs. Invert the vial over individual insects until they crawl up inside the vial. Stopper the vial with the cotton plug. Count to be sure you have recaptured all 10 WOWBugs. (You'll use them again in the next experiment.)

Unmated Female WOWBug Entries In 3 Minutes (Empty Tubes)	
Tube #:	# Of Entries:
1	
2	
3	
4	
Total:	

13. Add your team's tally to the class master chart. How did your results compare with those of other teams?

_____

_____

14. How did the female WOWBugs react? Why?

_____

_____

15. Did the same number of insects enter each tube? Why or why not?

_____

_____

_____

Part C. Testing WOWBug Courtship Attraction

How does the presence of a male WOWBug affect the way unmated females react? What cue or cues are responsible? It's time to find out.

16. Remove the cotton swab from straw #1. Use the paintbrush bristles or pipe cleaner to put a male WOWBug gently into the straw tube. Stick the cotton swab back in behind him to make sure he doesn't escape.

17. As before, place 10 unmated females in the dark bioassay chamber, then place the chamber lid-side-down on the paper. Be sure the #1 tube is facing the same way it faced before.

18. Immediately begin timing for 3 minutes. As before, count the number of WOWBugs entering each tube. Record your tally on the chart. As before, at the end of the experiment, replace the female WOWBugs back into their original vial.

19. With a male WOWBug in tube # 1, how did the results compare to those in the first experiment? What does

Unmated Female WOWBug Entries In 3 Minutes (Male In Tube 1)	
Tube #:	# Of Entries:
1	
2	
3	
4	
Total:	

this indicate?

_____

_____

_____

_____

_____

20. Do you think the cue is a sound or an odor? Remove the male, and repeat the experiment without changing the swab or the tissue. Record your data on the chart.

21. What does the tally show? Which hypothesis does it support?

_____

_____

_____

22. What do you think the results would be if you repeated this experiment with females that had already been allowed to mate?

_____

_____

_____

23. What do you think would be the result if the WOWBug in tube # 1 were another female instead of a male?

_____

_____

_____

Unmated Female WOWBug Entries In 3 Minutes (Male Gone From Tube #1)	
Tube #:	# Of Entries:
1	
2	
3	
4	
Total:	

Chapter Three.
Structure And Function
In Living Systems

When we say that certain plants and animals are related to each other, how do we know? Why is the butterfly related to the moth more closely than it is to the mosquito? The answer lies in the fact that butterflies and moths both have two pairs of scale-covered wings, while the mosquito has one pair of clear wings.

All scientific classification is based on similarity in form. How plants or animals are constructed tells a great deal about how they can and will act, and determines in many ways how they can function. Clearly form and function are closely intertwined.

The three activities in this chapter explore patterns in the ways living organisms are constructed, and some ways these structural patterns affect how they live, behave, and interact with each other and with their environment.

Form And Function: Insect Anatomy

In the seas, fresh waters, and on land, they out-number all other animal groups. Only humans can rival them... but we can't live with them, and we can't live without them. They eat our food and buildings, attack our pets and livestock, and spread diseases. At the same time, our very existence depends on them, for they are the vital backbone of most ecosystems all over the planet.

They are the arthropods, by far the most successful animals ever to have evolved on earth, and especially the insects, by far the most successful arthropods.

Why are arthropods so successful? To understand, a person needs to begin by looking at how they are put together. WOWBugs are a good place to start. How are *Melittobia digitata* similar to other insects? How are they different? How do male and female WOWBugs differ from each other?

This activity can be conducted with either live or dead speci-mens, or both, as long as each group of students has male and female specimens to observe. Remember that living males must be separated from one another.

In most insects, the differences between the sexes are rather subtle, to human eyes at least. However, Melittobia females are black and have normal wings, compound eyes, and anten-nae that can easily be seen with a dissecting microscope. Males have reduced wings incapable of flight, lack functional eyes, and have strikingly modified antennae used in courtship. In addition, the male body is the color of honey or amber.

Materials (per pair):

• live or dead female and male WOWBugs in separate containment chambers
• two plastic well slides

Key Concepts: The insect body plan; Sexual dimorphism.

Prerequisites: Basic micro-scope skills.

Time: One class period or less.

Getting Ready: Place male and female WOWBugs in separate chambers. Prepare transparency of male and female WOWBugs. Assemble pictures of various insects.

Objectives: Describe major structures and functions of external parts of WOWBugs; Describe how male Melittobia digitata differ from females; Infer major structure and functions of basic insect external body parts.

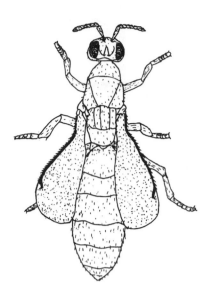

Female Melittobia digitata

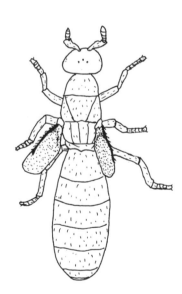

Male Melittobia digitata

• pipe cleaner or small watercolor paint brush

• Magiscope® or dissecting microscope

• pencil

• unlined paper

Part A. Female WOWBug Anatomy

1. Using the pipe cleaner or brush bristles, carefully move the female *Melittobia* from the containment vessel to a clean plastic well slide and snap the lid over it.

Students often ask if the WOWBug will be able to breathe. Reassure them that enough air circulates around the lip of the lid and the slide bottom to keep the wasp alive for several days.

2. Place the well slide on the stage of the microscope and adjust the focus of the microscope at the lowest magnification until the bug is clearly visible. As the WOWBug crawls around, move the well slide around to keep it in view.

3. Observe the external features of the WOWBug through the dissecting microscope. What color is its outside covering, or **cuticle**?

4. Carefully move the slide on the microscope stage to observe its head, **thorax**, abdomen, legs, wings, antennae, and compound eyes.

5. Sketch the major external features of the female wasp. Begin at the **anterior** (head) end of the body and slowly work to the **posterior** (tail) end. Include enough detail to make the features clear. Label the structures identified in steps 3 and 4.

6. Are you looking at the insect's back or its belly? Scientists call the back the **dorsum.** Looking at it gives you a **dorsal** view. Scientists call the belly the **sternum.** Looking at it gives you a **ventral** view. Label your drawing to indicate your view.

7. Observe the last segment of the abdomen. Female insects typically have an egg-laying tube, called an **ovipositor**. In *Melittobia digitata* females the ovipositor is pulled into the abdomen and is hard to see, but you may detect a small projection on the tip of the abdomen.

8. Carefully and gently return the female bug to the containment vessel.

Part B. Male WOWBug Anatomy

9. Repeat steps 1 to 8 for the male WOWBug. Carefully draw and label any differences you see.

Discussion:

1. What external features did you see on the male that you also saw on the female?

Like the female, the male has a head, thorax, and abdomen. The male also has 6 legs.

2. How is the male different from the female?

The male differs from the female in that he has reduced wings, no ovipositor, and no compound eyes. His antennae are clubbed, and his body is lighter in color.

3. While *Melittobia digitata* are harmless to humans, females do sting and paralyze the larvae of insects that serve as the hosts for their eggs. What body part of the female WOWBug has been modified into a stinger?

The ovipositor has been modified for stinging.

4. Compare your sketches of *Melittobia digitata* with pictures and sketches of other insects, including the grasshopper and honeybee. Which part of the insect do the legs come out of? Which part do the wings come out of? Based on your observations, describe a typical insect in terms of body segments, legs, eyes, and antennae.

A typical insect has a head, thorax, and abdomen; 6 legs;

compound eyes; and a pair of antennae. Legs and wings always attach to the thorax, antennae always come off the head, etc. (The fleshy appendages at the end of a caterpillar's body are not true legs, but fleshy outpockets pumped along by changes in body fluid.)

5. Some scientists describe the insect body as being like three boxes fastened together. In many ways this is true. Only the insect's nerve cord, gut, and heart run the length of the body, traveling through all segments. The other parts are confined to one section. What are some possible advantages of this arrangement?

One advantage is that injury to a single body section has less overall effect. A preying mantis without a head can still walk and strike, for example. In fact, because he saw examples like this, Carolus Linnaeus (the first scientist to systematically classify the animal kingdom) said that one of the criteria that applied to insects was that they lacked a brain! This is, of course, untrue.

6. When males and females of the same species are of two distinct forms, it is called **sexual dimorphism**. How many other animals can you name that have sexual dimorphism? What are some possible advantages of it?

Encourage brainstorming an extensive list. Make two columns, one to describe the male, the other the female. Just to start, consider many birds such as mallard ducks with brightly colored males and camouflaged females, deer with antlers and does without, and male lions with manes and females without.

7. Do an insect's legs fasten to its body near the top or bottom of the "box" that forms its thorax? Look at pictures of an insect such as a grasshopper. Scientists have suggested that the legs are arranged like this because they increase the insect's **stability**. What does the word mean? How could you design an experiment to test this hypothesis? (Hint: would constructing models help?) What variables might you need to control? How could you define stability in a way you could measure? (This is called an **operational definition**.)

Legs generally fasten near the top of most insects' bodies, as viewed from the side. This suspends the body below the legs in a hammock-like arrangement. Encourage students to brainstorm about ways they could design models and test whether they could be blown over by an air stream. You'll get many inventive ideas! They would need to control body (model) size and weight, air current strength, and "leg" length, as a minimum. Relative stability could be operationally defined by how many minutes or seconds the model resisted being blown over, or by weight (how light the model could be and still stand for a given number of seconds), to give two examples.

New Terms:

anterior

cuticle

dorsal

dorsum

operational definition

ovipositor

posterior

sexual dimorphism

stability

sternum

thorax

ventral

Concept Application And Elaboration:

1. Invent a new species of insect. Write a "scientific paper" describing what it looks like, its behavior, and any other interesting facts you have "discovered" about it. Be sure to include illustrations of both sexes.

2. Write an operational definition for friendliness, cooperation, or wakefulness.

This is harder than it sounds!

3. Make a poster that shows the external anatomy of a typical member of each of the four largest insect orders: Lepidoptera, Coleoptera, Hymenoptera, and Diptera. Indicate the function of any unusual structures not shared by all of these orders.

Scale and Accuracy: Just How Big Are WOWBugs — Really?

Key Concepts: Relative size; Measurement and accuracy; Use of ratios; Insect morphology; Estimation.

Prerequisites: Basic microscope skills.

Time: 1–2 class periods.

Getting Ready: This is an excellent use for dead WOWBugs. Glue them down, either on a professionally prepared slide or one you make yourself (Chapter 8). Make a transparency (Chapter 8) of an electronmicrograph of male and female WOWBugs.

Objectives: Learn how to measure microscopic objects; Compare the sizes of WOWBugs and other insects; Examine measurement scale and accuracy; Learn how to use ratios to find an unknown quantity; Realize that all measurements are estimations.

Big insects get most of the attention in our human-centered world. We notice butterflies, bumblebees, fireflies, and cockroaches. However, most insects on earth today are not large. In fact, three-quarters of all living insects are less than 1/4 inch (6.4 mm) long.

How big are WOWBugs? It's easy to measure something when you can place the ruler beside it, line the object up with a point on the ruler, and figure out how many units it stretches along. But what do you do to measure something so small it takes a microscope to look at it? You could, of course, use a microscope with its own fancy little measurement scale attachment. These do exist. But what if you don't have one? What can you do then? And how accurate can you be?

Materials (per pair):

- Magiscope® or dissecting microscope
- Slides of male and female WOWBugs
- Transparent ruler with millimeter markings
- Lab sheet or notebook
- Meter stick

One meter stick per class is enough if doing part B as a whole-class activity.

Since students will be placing the smaller ruler next to the object for viewing with the microscope, use a ruler which is transparent. These can be found in discount stores, or ordered from school or science supply catalogs. However, an easy, inexpensive alternative is to make a quantity of them yourself. Photocopy one ruler several times, paste the copies together, and print the result on transparency film. Then just cut the sheet apart to have enough transparent rulers for every team in the class.

Part A. Estimating WOWBug Size

Things can be measured in various ways, and with
varying degrees of accuracy. In this activity, we'll be
measuring WOWBugs with and without a ruler and a
microscope. All measurements are somewhat inexact,
and all our measurements of *Melittobia* will be estimates.
However, by working carefully, they will be fairly accurate estimates — much more accurate than we could
ever get by measuring them directly without a microscope.

1. Working in pairs, gather your materials. You and your
partner will each measure one male and one female
WOWBug by various methods. Then everyone will pool
their results.

2. Lay the ruler directly on the slide and measure female
and male WOWBug body lengths as well as you can.
Record your measurements.

3. Would a microscope help? Even without a ruler, it's
possible to estimate the size of something by comparing
it with something else whose size you already know.
Under a microscope, the thing you can know most easily
is the size of the **field of view** — the area you can see
when you look into it.

4. To measure your microscope's field of view,
adjust the microscope for the **viewing power** recommended for the organism. For WOWBugs, this
should be 30 or 40 power. Remember that viewing
power is determined by the magnification of the
eyepiece (what you look into) times the magnification of the **objective lens** (the lens that is just
above the microscope stage).

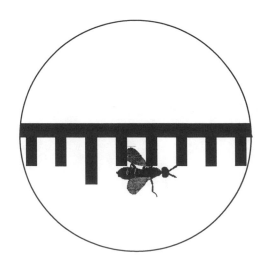

5. Put the metric edge of the ruler across the center
of the field so it looks like the illustration. Focus
the microscope. You should see the millimeter
marks on the ruler in the field of view.

Many rulers have the millimeters marked with lines, but have only the designation "cm" spelled out on that edge of the ruler. Students easily confuse "cm" with "mm" unless you point out the difference.

6. Line up the one-millimeter mark with the left side of your field of view. Count the millimeters along the center of your field of view, to the right. Add any fraction of millimeters (for instance, 1/2 millimeter). How many millimeters is your field of view?

About 7.5 mm in a 30-power Magiscope®. Make sure students align the far edge of the millimeter lines with the edge of the field of view, rather than "centering" it.

7. Remove the ruler and place a WOWBug slide into the field of view. Focus the microscope on the female insect. (She's the one with the longer wings.) Estimate the female's size by seeing how much she fills the field of view. She appears to be about how long? Repeat with the male WOWBug. Does he seem to be any different in length?

She is about one to two mm long. He is about the same or just slightly shorter.

8. A more accurate estimation can be made by putting the ruler under the microscope with the insects. Place the female WOWBug on the microscope stage near the ruler. Slide the ruler to match the far end of a millimeter mark to the tip of the abdomen of the wasp (not the wing tips). Measure from the tip of the abdomen to the top of its head. Don't include the antennae. What is your estimation of the female's **body length** to the nearest tenth of a millimeter? Repeat with the male WOWBug. To the nearest tenth-millimeter, he is about how long?

She is about 1.5 mm. He also appears to be about 1.5 mm or a little less. Make SURE that your students understand that they need to line the insect's abdomen tip up to the FAR end of one of the black ruler lines. If they "center" the insect , it will measure as being longer than it actually is. Be aware that, at low magnification, it may be difficult for students to accurately estimate to the tenth of a millimeter.

9. Taking turns, have each person in your group measure two WOWBugs: one male and one female. Record your data for all measuring methods on the chart and in the front of the room for everyone in the class to share.

WOWBug Body Length By Various Methods: My Results in Millimeters		
Method	Female	Male
With ruler, no magnification		
Based on field of view		
With ruler under microscope		

While the class is working, set up a chart like the one in this exercise, but label it "Average WOWBug Size, Based on Different Methods of Estimating." Leave space for each team to record their results. At the bottom of each column, leave space to calculate the average. Depending upon the age and experience of your students, either walk them through the calculations or have individuals calculate the averages themselves.

Discussion (Part A):

1. Based on your class measurements with microscope and ruler, what is the average length for female WOWBugs? What range of lengths did your class observe?

Students usually find an average of about 1.35 mm, and a range of 1.2 to 1.7 mm. If a specimen is somewhat curled then it will measure even shorter.

2. What is the average length for male WOWBugs? What range of lengths did your class observe?

Students usually find an average of about 1.25 mm for males, ranging between 1.1 and 1.6 mm (sometimes shorter if a specimen is curled). Males are only slightly shorter, but may be noticeably broader.

3. Why didn't you include wings and antennae in your measurements of body length?

Both can be moved about, and their position could influence the measurement.

4. Why might different individuals from the same species be different sizes?

This could be the result of environmental factors such as nutrition or stress, or just natural genetic variation. Also position or orientation can affect measurements.

5. Do female WOWBugs differ greatly from males in their size? How might any size variation of the different sexes in a species contribute to the survival of that species?

The sexes don't differ much, but slightly larger females might be able to lay more eggs, and might have more energy and/or nutritional reserves to survive better in their trip out into the world to find new hosts.

6. The smallest adult insects in the world are less than 0.2 mm long. How many times larger are WOWBugs than these tiniest of wasps? Where do you think the tiniest parasitic wasps might lay their eggs?

WOWBugs are actually over seven times as large (1.5 mm/0.2 mm = 7.5). The tiniest parasitic wasps are called fairy flies (Family Mymaridae). These parasites lay their eggs inside the eggs of other insects such as butterflies and moths. (Some tiny parasitic wasps are in fact smaller than some of the largest protists.)

Part B. Increasing Measurement Accuracy

As soon as everyone has finished Part A, work as a class for the rest of this activity.

1. How can we increase the **accuracy** of our WOWBug measurements? Share your ideas with classmates.

Discuss with the students what accuracy really means: exact correctness, precision, or freedom from error.

2. Because WOWBugs are small, with millimeters it's difficult to be accurate, and it's even more difficult to tell whether one individual differs in size from another. It would be nice to use a more precise, smaller unit of measurement. A tiny unit often used for measuring small objects is the **micron**. You may have heard another name for micron — **micrometer**. The symbol for micron is the Greek letter μ, pronounced "myoo." The symbol for micrometer is μm. Either designation is correct.

Why do two names, micron and micrometer, exist side by side? Those of us that use the English system of measurement have more than one way to express a quantity. For example, we might say "two cups" or "one pint." In the metric system, various ways of stating the same quantity also have developed.

About twenty years ago, a concerted effort arose to standardize metric terms, and correct some confusion and inconsistencies in the traditional metric system. The result was what is called the SI System.

The SI (Systeme International d'Unites) is an international system based on eight fundamental units of measurement. Other units are derived from these base units. Prefixes join base units to express multiples, and are based on powers of ten. For example, meter is the basic unit of length and "micro" is the prefix to indicate the factor 10^6 so what used to be called a micron became a micrometer. But to add to the confusion, the term "micrometer" is also used as the name of various measuring instruments.

The SI System sounds very logical, but it does require changing some habits and terminology. Such terms as liter and hour would disappear, for example. Thus, change has been relatively slow in coming. Most scientists now use the SI system but also permit some widely used units outside the SI system.

SI Fundamental Units of Measurement

Property	Base unit	Symbol
Length	meter	m
Mass	kilogram	kg
Time	second	s
Concentration	molar	M
Amount	mole	mol
Thermodynamic temperature	kelvin	K
Electric current	ampere	A
Luminous intensity	candela	cd

Purists also now avoid prefixes such as hecto-, deca-, deci-, and centi- because they are not standard SI prefixes.

If you or your students would like to pursue additional information concerning use of SI units, it's worth searching out this reference:

Young, D.S. 1987. Implementation of SI units for clinical laboratory data: Style specifications and conversion tables. Annals of Internal Medicine *106: 114-129.*

No regular ruler measures in microns or micrometers. They are too small. Each millimeter equals one thousand of them. Another way to say this is that one micron is 1/1000th of a millimeter, or one millionth of a meter. To understand the size of a micron, do this simple conversion. Convert your microscope's field of view in millimeters to microns by multiplying by 1,000. How many microns is your field of view?

About 7500 μ, for a Magiscope®.

3. Return to your WOWBug measurements from Part A. Convert the millimeters to microns by multiplying by 1,000. What are your WOWBug body lengths in microns? I estimate that the female is _____ μ. I estimate that the male is _____ μ. Are these measurements more accurate than the ones you made in millimeters?

These measurements are no more accurate. Only the units have changed. This concept may require some additional time and thought to bring the point home to students.

4. Is there a way to use a regular ruler and still measure WOWBugs in microns? Yes, but it involves being able to look more closely. That is, you need to magnify the WOWBugs more. Scientists have done this with an **electron microscope**, an instrument that focuses rays of electrons rather than light rays. It is much more powerful than any microscope that uses glass lenses to focus light like yours does.

Your teacher will show you a picture of WOWBugs taken with an electron microscope. (Such a picture is called an **electronmicrograph**.) Using just this picture and what you already know, could you estimate their size? Can you just measure the picture directly? Why or why not?

Project a transparency of the electronmicrograph provided in Chapter 8. Elicit discussion of ways the class could determine WOWBug size more accurately using just a ruler or meter stick.

No, you can't measure it directly. The picture could be made any size you wanted. This can be demonstrated by alternately moving the projector closer or farther from the screen. Have a student measure length directly on the screen with a meter stick. Students will quickly realize that the result is way too big for a WOWBug!

5. Scientists often include a **scale bar** in their photographs. This lets the reader determine the actual size of the object. If there is no scale bar, you still can figure it out. To do so, you would need to compare the object to something whose exact size you know.

Here's a hint. Consider the following problem: You and your father plan to cut down a large tree in your yard, but you don't know how tall it is and are worried that it might fall onto your house, which is 50 feet away. The tree is too tall to climb and measure, but it makes a nice shadow on the ground, and you can measure that. You notice that your dad has a shadow, too, and it's easy to measure. Your 6-foot-tall dad has a shadow exactly 4 feet long. The tree's shadow measures 32 feet long. Can you use this information to measure the tree? How? (Show

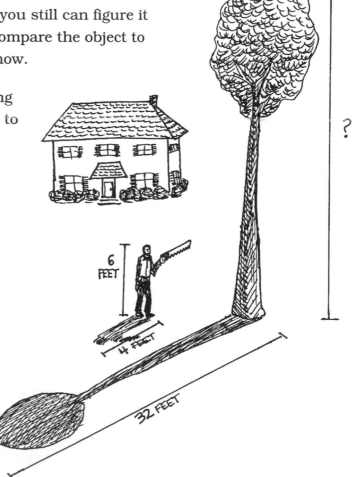

your calculations.)

Help students see that they can set up an equation that compares the ratios:

$$\frac{Dad's\ height}{Dad's\ shadow} = \frac{Tree's\ height}{Tree's\ shadow}$$

Substituting your measurements and cross-multiplying gives 6/4 = ?/32. Solving for the unknown gives an answer of 48 feet.

We've used the English system of measurement in this example because that is what most of us in the United States would use for such a problem. Furthermore, students can see the reasoning more easily when they aren't also grappling with conversions. See the Concept Application And Elaboration section of this activity for suggestions concerning metric follow-ups to this example.

Will the tree hit the house?

The tree will miss the house.

6. Let's return to metric units. Suppose scientists have carefully measured the wings of female WOWBugs many times and found the wings to be exactly 1000 µm long. How can we use the same sort of reasoning we did with the tree to find out the length of the WOWBug in the electronmicrograph?

We can find the length of the wing and body in the electronmicrograph, then set up a proportion like we did for the tree. The unknown in this example will be body length.

7. Use a meter stick to measure the length of the female's wing and body on the projected electronmicrograph again.

If necessary, remind students that each individual mark on a meter stick represents 1 mm.

WOWBug wing length (mm) <u>320</u>

WOWBug body length (mm) <u>415</u>

8. Using this information, set up an equation using ratios. Use it to calculate the true body length of a WOWBug.

measured wing length (mm)   = *known exact wing length (μm)*
measured body length (mm)   *? exact body length (μm)*

Substituting your measurements and cross-multiplying gives
320/415 = 1000/?

The female WOWBug body length equals *1297 μm.*

Stress to the students that despite how exact they look, even these measurements of Melittobia *are estimates. How precisely the measurer works makes a big difference in how accurate the estimates are, but nothing can change the fact that they are never exact. No matter how highly you magnify the WOWBug and how small the measurement scale is, there will always be some error. This is a difficult concept for some students, but an intriguing thought for most. If several groups measure the same projected image and make their calculations independently, then share them with the class, this point will be more obvious. They are unlikely to all get the same result.*

Discussion (Part B):

1. The largest insects living today are some stick insects, which are over 30 cm (12 inches) long, and some beetles which weigh as much as 100 grams (3.5 ounces). Yet we know that about 300 million years ago, much larger insects existed. Ancient dragonflies, for example, had wingspreads over two feet. What hypotheses might explain why today's insects aren't any larger than they are?

Many answers are possible.

2. What information would be helpful in answering this question? What things are different about the world today? (In other words, what variables might you need to consider?)

Many answers are possible. Here are some you might like to guide students' thinking toward.

1. It would help to know what other animals were around. Scientists often point out that niches for larger species are now occupied by more successful vertebrates such as birds. These competitors were absent 300 million years ago.

2. It would help to know how long early insects lived. One of the main disadvantages of having a skeleton on the outside of one's body, as insects do, is that it limits growth. The only time an insect can grow is during the short period after it molts, or sheds its outer covering, or exoskeleton. Before the new outer covering hardens, it is flexible and can be stretched.

If a very large arthropod were to try to grow an enormous amount during a single molt, it might collapse under its own weight before a newly secreted exoskeleton hardened. So external hard cuticles work best for relatively small and/or slowly growing creatures. Present-day insects seem to have taken an evolutionary direction that favors smallness and producing more generations rapidly, rather than producing fewer, longer-living, much larger individuals.

3. It might help to know what advantages there might be in small size. Perhaps being small was just so much more advantageous that it simply won out over large size. In fact, small size has some compelling advantages. The number of individuals can be greater. The reproductive rate (and hence the rate of evolutionary adaptation) can be higher. And the number of available niches is enormously greater. The smaller the insect, the more incredibly variable its ecological world becomes.

4. It might help to know if the atmosphere was different then. For example, there might have been less air pressure or more oxygen, factors that might make it easier for a large insect to breathe. Since insects can't breathe in and out of lungs (because of their exoskeleton), they have to breathe through a system of tubes. The limits of this system might be one of the things that keep them relatively small today.

Concept Application And Elaboration:

1. In most of the rest of the world, the father and son in our tree-cutting example would use a metric scale rather

than measuring in feet as we did. Suppose the tree's shadow were 12 meters long. Would the tree hit the house?

1 ft = 0.305 m
1 m = 3.28 ft

1.83 m/1.22 m = tree ht./12 m.
tree ht. = 21.96 m/1.22 m = 18 m.
18 m x 3.28 ft/m = 59.04 ft.

This tree would hit the house.

2. A British scientist has discovered a rare new beetle in the Amazon jungle. He sends a fax to his colleagues in London, showing a photograph of it covering exactly half the length of his notebook. Even though he has neglected to include a scale bar, his astute colleagues immediately are able to determine its size. The notebook shown in the fax is 15.25 cm. Their own similar notebooks are 30.5 cm long. How big is the beetle? Is it larger than the current American record of 5.5 inches?

The beetle is half of 15.25, or 7.625 cm in the fax.
actual beetle length/7.625 cm = 30.5 cm/15.25 cm.
actual beetle length = 15.25 cm.
15.25 cm x 1 inch/2.54 cm = 6.0 in.
The beetle is a new record!

3. What is the largest insect known, in terms of body weight? Make a poster that shows its actual size in comparison to a hummingbird.

The tropical Goliath Beetle can grow to 20 cm (8 inches) and weigh 100 grams (3.5 ounces). Hummingbirds can weigh as little as 2 grams (0.07 ounces).

New Terms:

accuracy

body length

electron microscope

electronmicrograph

eyepiece

field of view

micron (= micrometer)

objective lens

scale bar

viewing power

Size And Athletic Ability:
The Insect Olympics

Key Concepts: Insect locomotion; Surface:mass relationships.

Prerequisites: None. In addition to serving as a hands-on investigation of one type of insect locomotion, this is an excellent "discrepant event" activity to introduce a discussion of the biological implications of body size.

Time: One class period.

Getting Ready: Have living adult female WOWBugs available. Have one or more uninflated balloons, but keep them hidden until the class discussion. Set up a jumping range marked in centimeters on the classroom floor.

Objectives: Observe and compare modes of insect locomotion; Understand the changing relationships of surface and mass in relation to an object's size.

Insects move about in a variety of ways, and in the process, they often perform activities that seem extremely impressive when judged by human standards. "Believe It Or Not" columnists are particularly fond of stories about what great powers insects have. They tell of a blood-sucking bug that drinks 10 to 12 times its weight, corresponding to a human drinking 200 gallons weighing a ton. Or they mention the flea, able to leap 10 inches, a feat equivalent to a human jump covering 780 feet. How might WOWBugs fare in an Insect Olympics? Let's look at their jumping ability, and compare it to our own.

Materials (per pair or team):

• adult female WOWBugs

One culture will provide more than enough for several classes.

• sheet of unlined white paper (8 1/2 x 11 inches)
• pencil
• short metric ruler that measures millimeters
• meter stick
• pipe cleaner or small watercolor paint brush
• laboratory notebooks or writing pad

Part A. The WOWBug Long Jump

If you have already done the "Hoppin' Bug Connect-A-Dot" activity, turn to the data you collected in your laboratory notebook, and move on to part B. If you have not done that activity, then follow the steps below.

1. Working in pairs or teams, gather your supplies. Then let the teacher know you are ready for your WOWBugs.

By dispensing the insects yourself, you can maintain better control over the number that are released. Each group will need 3-5 insects, because some will perform more reliably than others and a few may be accidentally maimed or killed by inexperienced handlers.

2. With the pipe cleaner or the brush bristles, gently pick up a WOWBug and place it in the center of the sheet of paper.

3. With the tip of the pencil, gently prod the insect's abdomen. At the same time, mark a small pencil dot on the paper to show where you put the WOWBug down. Label that dot 1.

4. How did the WOWBug respond to your pencil's touch? If it moved, make another mark to show where it stopped. Label that dot 2. If it became motionless, do not prematurely declare it dead. Watch for a few moments and see what happens. What might be an advantage of this behavior?

Most of the insects will hop. Only very rarely will one fly away. A few will briefly "play possum." Presumably this is another way to fool predators, just as real opossums feign death to escape attack. Many predators will not touch motionless prey.

5. Repeat this process until you have marked at least 5 dots, and as many as 10 if you can. If you are unable to complete this many with one WOWBug, switch to a new one and continue.

6. Use the short ruler to draw a straight line between each number and the next higher one. Measure the distances between dots 1 and 2, 2 and 3, etc. Record these distances in millimeters (mm) on the data chart.

Part B. Putting Insect Athletics in Perspective

7. Could you win a jumping competition against a WOWBug? Just for fun, convert the WOWBug's athletic abilities into personal terms. It wouldn't be fair not to consider size. So let's put the competition in terms of

WOWBug Long Jump	
	Distance Between Dots (mm)
1 to 2	
2 to 3	
3 to 4	
4 to 5	
5 to 6	
6 to 7	
7 to 8	
8 to 9	
9 to 10	
TOTAL	
AVERAGE	
RANGE	

relative body length. For you, that would be your height. Stand against a wall while another student measures your body height to the nearest centimeter with the meter stick. Convert this to a decimal expression in meters. My height = _____ m.

For example, a height of 165 centimeters tall would be 1.65 meters.

8. Set up a ratio like this:

insect length (mm)/longest jump (mm)= my height (m)/my jump (m)

Assume an average female WOWBug is 1.5 mm long. To find the distance you'd have to jump to win, cross multiply the longest WOWBug jump distance (in mm) times your own height. Divide by the insect length.

A person my size would have to jump _____ meters to out-hop a WOWBug.

9. How far can you actually jump? Your teacher has set up a jumping range in the classroom. Jump three times without a running start. (After all, the WOWBugs didn't get one!) Average the numbers.

I can actually jump _____ meters.

Discussion:

1. How long is an average WOWBug jump? What was the longest jump you saw? What was the longest jump made by any insect in your class?

Jumps average about 8 mm long. Jumps reported to be greater than 18-20 mm were probably short flights instead.

2. Could you win the Insect Olympics if you had to compete on equal terms by body size? Why or why not?

With younger students, the "gee whiz" factor will be the main take-home message. However, with advanced students it may be appropriate to continue the discussion through questions 3 to

5, and include the mathematical relationships that lie behind these seeming anomalies.

3. Small animals can seem very powerful for their size. What lies behind insects' seemingly amazing power? Do insects have tremendous muscular strength? Or a different sort of muscles from those we possess? Not really. Scientific studies show that insect muscles are quite similar in almost all respects to our own. If this is so, then something else must be changing as size changes. Actually, two things change. What could they be?

Help students see that as an object changes size, two variables are actually changing: surface area and volume. For a visual demonstration, have one or more students blow up a balloon to various sizes.

4. A strange thing happens to these two variables as an object changes size. See if you can figure out what it is by looking at these two mathematical formulas.

volume of a sphere = $4/3\ \pi\ r^3$

surface of a sphere = $4\ \pi\ r^2$

Which has more relative surface area – a small organism or a large one? Why?

Because volume is changing by a cubed amount, and surface is only changing by a squared amount, as the size or mass of any object gets larger, the relative amount of its surface decreases. Looking at it in the other direction, as the size or mass gets smaller, the relative amount of its surface increases. Work with students until they become comfortable with this idea.

5. In fact, many of the strange powers and extraordinary abilities that insects appear to have come from the effects of these relationships. Something critical happens to muscle power as muscle size increases. The power of a muscle is proportional to the area of its cross section. The mass it has to move is proportional to volume. For an organism as small as an insect, this relationship has

a marked effect on muscle power. Can you explain what it is?

As the body becomes smaller the muscles become relatively more powerful.(In addition, smaller size changes things like wind resistance and center of gravity.)

Can we really speak of insect powers in terms of human size? Why or why not?

We're amazed by the jump of a flea or a WOWBug, but (however much fun it may be) it's simply not correct — either biologically or mathematically — to extrapolate the jump directly into human equivalents. A flea or WOWBug the size of a man would have relatively much more mass per unit cross-sectional area of muscle than a normal-sized flea or WOWBug. Thus if it were human-sized it would no longer seem to have extraordinary abilities.

Concept Application And Elaboration:

1. Refer back to the flea in the introduction to this activity. How high are its jumps on a metric scale? If a WOWBug can hop 8 mm, to the nearest whole number, how many times farther than a WOWBug can a flea jump?

10 inches x 2.54 cm/in. = 25.4 cm. or 254 mm.
254 mm/8 mm = 31.75, or about 32 times as far.

2. Make a poster that shows the jumping distance of a kangaroo, a frog, a grasshopper, and a WOWBug. Report them in absolute distance, and in comparison with some measure of their body size such as length or weight.

Form And Function: Insect Anatomy

In the seas, fresh waters, and on land, they out-number all other animal groups. Only humans can rival them... but we can't live with them, and we can't live without them. They eat our food and buildings, attack our pets and livestock, and spread diseases. At the same time, our very existence depends on them, for they are the vital backbone of most ecosystems all over the planet.

They are the arthropods, by far the most successful animals ever to have evolved on earth, and especially the insects, by far the most successful arthropods.

Why are arthropods so successful? To understand, a person needs to begin by looking at how they are put together. WOWBugs are a good place to start. How are *Melittobia digitata* similar to other insects? How are they different? How do male and female WOWBugs differ from each other?

Part A. Female WOWBug Anatomy

1. Using the pipe cleaner or brush bristles, carefully move the female *Melittobia* from the containment vessel to a clean plastic well slide and snap the lid over it.

2. Place the well slide on the stage of the microscope and adjust the focus of the microscope at the lowest magnification until the bug is clearly visible. As the WOWBug crawls around, move the well slide around to keep it in view.

3. Observe the external features of the WOWBug through the dissecting microscope. What color is its outside covering, or **cuticle**? _____

4. Carefully move the slide on the microscope stage to observe its head, **thorax**, abdomen, legs, wings, anten-

Objectives: Describe major structures and functions of external parts of WOWBugs; Describe how male Melittobia digitata *differ from females; Infer major structure and functions of basic insect external body parts.*

Materials (per pair):

- *live or dead female and male WOWBugs in separate containment chambers*
- *two plastic well slides*
- *pipe cleaner or small water-color paint brush*
- *Magiscope® or dissecting microscope*
- *pencil*
- *unlined paper*

Female *Melittobia digitata*

Male *Melittobia digitata*

nae, and compound eyes.

5. Sketch the major external features of the female wasp. Begin at the **anterior** (head) end of the body and slowly work to the **posterior** (tail) end. Include enough detail to make the features clear. Label the structures identified in steps 3 and 4.

6. Are you looking at the insect's back or its belly? Scientists call the back the **dorsum.** Looking at it gives you a **dorsal** view. Scientists call the belly the **sternum.** Looking at it gives you a **ventral** view. Label your drawing to indicate your view.

7. Observe the last segment of the abdomen. Female insects typically have an egg-laying tube, called an **ovipositor.** In *Melittobia digitata* females the ovipositor is pulled into the abdomen and is hard to see, but you may detect a small projection on the tip of the abdomen.

8. Carefully and gently return the female bug to the containment vessel.

Part B. Male WOWBug Anatomy

9. Repeat steps 1 to 8 for the male WOWBug. Carefully draw and label any differences you see.

Discussion:

1. What external features did you see on the male that you also saw on the female?

_____

_____

2. How is the male different from the female?

_____

_____

3. While *Melittobia digitata* are harmless to humans, females do sting and paralyze the larvae of insects that serve as the hosts for their eggs. What body part of the female WOWBug has been modified into a stinger? _____

4. Compare your sketches of *Melittobia digitata* with pictures and sketches of other insects, including the grasshopper and honeybee. Which part of the insect do the legs come out of? Which part do the wings come out of? Based on your observations, describe a typical insect in terms of body segments, legs, eyes, and antennae.

_____

_____

_____

5. Some scientists describe the insect body as being like three boxes fastened together. In many ways this is true. Only the insect's nerve cord, gut, and heart run the length of the body, traveling through all segments. The other parts are confined to one section. What are some possible advantages of this arrangement?

_____

_____

6. When males and females of the same species are of two distinct forms, it is called

sexual dimorphism. How many other animals can you name that have sexual dimorphism? What are some possible advantages of it?

_____

_____

_____

_____

7. Do an insect's legs fasten to its body near the top or bottom of the "box" that forms its thorax? Look at pictures of an insect such as a grasshopper. Scientists have suggested that the legs are arranged like this because they increase the insect's **stability**. What does the word mean? _____

_____

How could you design an experiment to test this hypothesis? (Hint: would constructing models help?) What variables might you need to control? How could you define stability in a way you could measure? (This is called an **operational definition**.)

_____

_____

_____

_____

_____

_____

_____

_____

_____

Scale and Accuracy: Just How Big Are WOWBugs — Really?

Objectives: Learn how to measure microscopic objects; Compare the sizes of WOWBugs and other insects; Examine measurement scale and accuracy; Learn how to use ratios to find an unknown quantity; Realize that all measurements are estimations.

Materials (per pair):

- *Magiscope® or dissecting microscope*
- *Slides of male and female WOWBugs*
- *Transparent ruler with millimeter markings*
- *Lab sheet or notebook*
- *Meter stick*

Big insects get most of the attention in our human-centered world. We notice butterflies, bumblebees, fireflies, and cockroaches. However, most insects on earth today are not large. In fact, three-quarters of all living insects are less than 1/4 inch (6.4 mm) long.

How big are WOWBugs? It's easy to measure something when you can place the ruler beside it, line the object up with a point on the ruler, and figure out how many units it stretches along. But what do you do to measure something so small it takes a microscope to look at it? You could, of course, use a microscope with its own fancy little measurement scale attachment. These do exist. But what if you don't have one? What can you do then? And how accurate can you be?

Part A. Estimating WOWBug Size

Things can be measured in various ways, and with varying degrees of accuracy. In this activity, we'll be measuring WOWBugs with and without a ruler and a microscope. It's important to see that all measurements are somewhat inexact, and all our measurements of *Melittobia* will be estimates. However, by working carefully, they will be fairly accurate estimates — much more accurate than we could ever get by measuring them directly without a microscope.

1. Working in pairs, gather your materials. You and your partner will each measure one male and one female WOWBug by various methods. Then everyone will pool their results.

2. Lay the ruler directly on the slide and measure female and male WOWBug body lengths as well as you can. Record your measurements on the data chart.

3. Would a microscope help? Even without a ruler, it's possible to estimate the size of something by comparing it with something else whose size you already know. Under a microscope, the thing you can know most easily is the size of the **field of view** — the area you can see when you look into it.

4. To measure your microscope's field of view, adjust the microscope for the **viewing power** recommended for the organism. For WOWBugs, this should be 30 or 40 power. Remember that viewing power is determined by the magnification of the **eyepiece** (what you look into) times the magnification of the **objective lens** (the lens that is just above the microscope stage).

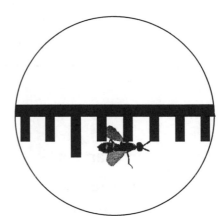

5. Put the metric edge of the ruler across the center of the field so it looks like the illustration. Focus the microscope. You should see the millimeter marks on the ruler in the field of view.

6. Line up the one-millimeter mark with the left side of your field of view. Count the millimeters along the center of your field of view, to the right. Add any fraction of millimeters (for instance, 1/2 millimeter). How many millimeters is your field of view? _____

7. Remove the ruler and place a WOWBug slide into the field of view. Focus the microscope on the female insect. (She's the one with the longer wings.) Estimate the female's size by seeing how much she fills the field of view. She appears to be about how long? _____ Repeat with the male WOWBug. Does he seem to be any different in length? _____

8. A more accurate estimation can be made by putting the ruler under the microscope with the insects. Place the female WOWBug on the microscope stage near the ruler. Slide the ruler to match the far end of a millimeter mark to the tip of the abdomen of the wasp (not the wing tips). Measure from the tip of the abdomen to the top of its head. Don't include the antennae. What is your estimation of the female's **body length** to the nearest tenth of a millimeter? _____

Repeat with the male WOWBug. To the nearest tenth-millimeter, he is about how long? _____

9. Taking turns, have each person in your group measure two WOWBugs: one male and one female. Record your data for all measuring methods on the chart and in the

WOWBug Body Length By Various Methods: My Results in Millimeters		
Method	Female	Male
With ruler, no magnification		
Based on field of view		
With ruler under microscope		

front of the room for everyone in the class to share.

Discussion (Part A):

1. Based on your class measurements with microscope and ruler, what is the average length for female WOWBugs? What range of lengths did your class observe?

_____

 2. What is the average length for male WOWBugs? What range of lengths did your class observe? _____

3. Why didn't you include wings and antennae in your measurements of body length?

_____

4. Why might different individuals from the same species be different sizes?

_____

_____

5. Do female WOWBugs differ greatly from males in their size? How might any size variation of the different sexes in a species contribute to the survival of that species?

_____

_____

6. The smallest adult insects in the world are less than 0.2 mm long. How many times

larger are WOWBugs than these tiniest of wasps? Where do you think the tiniest parasitic wasps might lay their eggs?

_____

_____

Part B. Increasing Measurement Accuracy

As soon as everyone has finished Part A, work as a class for the rest of this activity.

1. How can we increase the **accuracy** of our WOWBug measurements? Share your ideas with classmates.

2. Because WOWBugs are small, with millimeters it's difficult to be accurate, and it's even more difficult to tell whether one individual differs in size from another. It would be nice to use a more precise, smaller unit of measurement. A tiny unit often used for measuring small objects is the **micron**. You may have heard another name for micron — **micrometer**. The symbol for micron is the Greek letter μ, pronounced "myoo." The symbol for micrometer is μm. Either designation is correct.

No regular ruler measures in microns or micrometers. They are too small. Each millimeter equals one thousand of them. Another way to say this is that one micron is 1/1000th of a millimeter, or one millionth of a meter. To understand the size of a micron, do this simple conversion. Convert your microscope's field of view in millimeters to microns by multiplying by 1,000. How many microns is your field of view? _____

3. Return to your WOWBug measurements from Part A. Convert the millimeters to microns by multiplying by 1,000. What are your WOWBug body lengths in microns? I estimate that the female is _____ μ. I estimate that the male is _____ μ.

Are these measurements more accurate than the ones you made in millimeters? _____

4. Is there a way to use a regular ruler and still measure WOWBugs in microns? Yes, but it involves being able to look more closely. That is, you need to magnify the WOWBugs more. Scientists have done this with an **electron microscope**, an instrument that focuses rays of electrons rather than light rays. It is much more powerful than any microscope that uses glass lenses to focus light like yours does.

Your teacher will show you a picture of WOWBugs taken with an electron microscope. (Such a picture is called an **electronmicrograph**.) Using just this picture and what you already know, could you estimate their size? Can you just measure the picture directly? Why or why not? _____

_____

5. Scientists often include a **scale bar** in their photographs. This lets the reader determine the actual size of the object. If there is no scale bar, you still can figure it out. To do so, you would need to compare the object to something whose exact size you know.

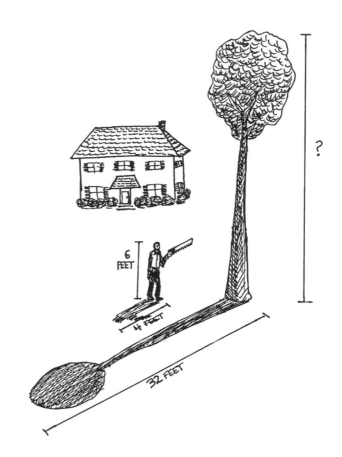

Here's a hint. Consider the following problem: You and your father plan to cut down a large tree in your yard, but you don't know how tall it is and are worried that it might fall onto your house, which is 50 feet away. The tree is too tall to climb and measure, but it makes a nice shadow on the ground, and you can measure that. You notice that your dad has a shadow, too, and it's easy to measure. Your 6-foot-tall dad has a shadow exactly 4 feet long. The tree's shadow measures 32 feet long. Can you use this information to measure the tree? How? (Show your calculations.)

Will the tree hit the house? _____

6. Let's return to metric units. Suppose scientists have carefully measured the wings of female WOWBugs many times and found the wings to be exactly 1000 μm long. How can we use the same sort of reasoning we did with the tree to find out the length of the WOWBug in the electronmicrograph?

_____

_____

_____

7. Use a meter stick to measure the length of the female's wing and body on the projected electronmicrograph again.

WOWBug wing length (mm): _____   WOWBug body length (mm) _____

8. Using this information, set up an equation using ratios. Use it to calculate the true body length of a WOWBug. The female WOWBug body length equals _____

Discussion (Part B):

1. The largest insects living today are some stick insects, which are over 30 cm (12 inches) long, and some beetles which weigh as much as 100 grams (3.5 ounces). Yet we know that about 300 million years ago, much larger insects existed. Ancient dragonflies, for example, had wingspreads over two feet. What hypotheses might explain why today's insects aren't any larger than they are?

_____

_____

_____

_____

2. What information would be helpful in answering this question? What things are different about the world today? (In other words, what variables might you need to consider?)

_____

_____

_____

_____

Size And Athletic Ability: The Insect Olympics

Objectives: Observe and compare modes of insect locomotion; Understand the changing relationships of surface and mass in relation to an object's size.

Materials (per pair or team):

• *adult female WOWBugs*
• *sheet of unlined white paper (8 1/2 x 11 inches)*
• *pencil*
• *short metric ruler that measures millimeters*
• *meter stick*
• *pipecleaner or small watercolor paint brush*
• *laboratory notebooks or writing pad*

Insects move about in a variety of ways, and in the process, they often perform activities that seem extremely impressive when judged by human standards. "Believe It Or Not" columnists are particularly fond of stories about what great powers insects have. They tell of a blood-sucking bug that drinks 10 to 12 times its weight, corresponding to a human drinking 200 gallons weighing a ton. Or they mention the flea, able to leap 10 inches, a feat equivalent to a human jump covering 780 feet. How might WOWBugs fare in an Insect Olympics? Let's look at their jumping ability, and compare it to our own.

Part A. The WOWBug Long Jump

If you have already done the "Hoppin' Bug Connect-A-Dot" activity, turn to the data you collected in your laboratory notebook, and move on to part B. If you have not done that activity, then follow the steps below.

1. Working in pairs or teams, gather your supplies. Then let the teacher know you are ready for your WOWBugs.

2. With the pipecleaner or the brush bristles, gently pick up a WOWBug and place it in the center of the sheet of paper.

3. With the tip of the pencil, gently prod the insect's abdomen. At the same time, mark a small pencil dot on the paper to show where you put the WOWBug down. Label that dot 1.

4. How did the WOWBug respond to your pencil's touch? If it moved, make another mark to show where it stopped. Label that dot 2. If it became motionless, do not prematurely declare it dead. Watch for a few moments and see what happens. What might be an advantage of

this behavior?_____

5. Repeat this process until you have marked at least 5 dots, and as many as 10 if you can. If you are unable to complete this many with one WOWBug, switch to a new one and continue.

6. Use the short ruler to draw a straight line between each number and the next higher one. Measure the distances between dots 1 and 2, 2 and 3, etc. Record these distances in millimeters (mm) on the data chart.

Part B. Putting Insect Athletics in Perspective

7. Could you win a jumping competition against a WOWBug? Just for fun, convert the WOWBug's athletic abilities into personal terms. It wouldn't be fair not to consider size. So let's put the competition in terms of relative body length. For you, that would be your height. Stand against a wall while another student measures your body height to the nearest centimeter with the meter stick. Convert this to a decimal expression in meters.

WOWBug Long Jump	
	Distance Between Dots (mm)
1 to 2	
2 to 3	
3 to 4	
4 to 5	
5 to 6	
6 to 7	
7 to 8	
8 to 9	
9 to 10	
TOTAL	
AVERAGE	
RANGE	

My height = _____ m.

8. Set up a ratio like this: insect length (mm)/longest jump (mm)= my height (m)/my jump (m)

Assume an average female WOWBug is 1.5 mm long. To find the distance you'd have to jump to win, cross multiply the longest WOWBug jump distance (in mm) times your own height. Divide by the insect length.

A person my size would have to jump _____ meters to out-hop a WOWBug.

9. How far can you actually jump? Your teacher has set up a jumping range in the classroom. Jump three times without a running start. (After all, the WOWBugs didn't get one!)

Jump # 1: _____ Jump # 2: _____ Jump # 3: _____

Average the numbers. I can actually jump an average of _____ meters.

Discussion:

1. How long is an average WOWBug jump? What was the longest jump you saw? What was the longest jump made by any insect in your class?

_____

2. Could you win the Insect Olympics if you had to compete on equal terms by body size? Why or why not?_____

3. Small animals can seem very powerful for their size. What lies behind insects' seemingly amazing power? Do insects have tremendous muscular strength? Or a different sort of muscles from those we possess? Not really. Scientific studies show that insect muscles are quite similar in almost all respects to our own. If this is so, then something else must be changing as size changes. Actually, two things change. What could they be? _____ and _____.

4. A strange thing happens to these two variables as an object changes size. See if you can figure out what it is by looking at these two mathematical formulas.

$$\text{volume of a sphere} = 4/3 \; \pi \; r^3 \qquad\qquad \text{surface of a sphere} = 4 \; \pi \; r^2$$

Which has more relative surface area — a small organism or a large one? Why?

_____

_____

5. In fact, many of the strange powers and extraordinary abilities that insects appear to have come from the effects of these relationships. Something critical happens to muscle power as muscle size increases. The power of a muscle is proportional to the area of its cross section. The mass it has to move is proportional to volume.

For an organism as small as an insect, this relationship has a marked effect on muscle power, Can you explain what it is?

_____

_____

Can we really speak of insect powers in terms of human size? Why or why not?

_____

_____

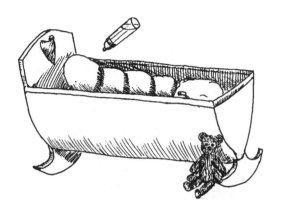

Chapter Four. Change And Constancy: Growth And Development

It was quite an event when some folks discovered that big green tomato hornworms could fly 35 miles an hour — as adult sphinx moths! Others were thrilled to find that the reason why monarch butterflies are safe from birds is because their bodies are chock-full of heart poisons and other toxic chemicals they get from the milkweed plants they eat as caterpillars.

The growth and development of insects can be relatively straightforward or incredibly bizarre, but almost never uninteresting. Of the four activities in this chapter, two are long-term inquiry studies. The other two are brief: an introductory one to pique student interest, and an interesting wrap-up activity.

A Life Cycle Mystery: An Overview

This inquiry approach to the WOWBug life cycle has been very successful. For younger students, we've provided a fair amount of guidance in the student activity sheet. For students with more experience, you may want to make the investigation more open-ended. Don't begin by describing the WOWBugs life stages, or providing terms such as larva or pupae! You'll remove an important element of the inquiry!

Some teachers have quite successfully taken the "mystery" concept a step further, omitted the student activity sheet, and used this activity as students' first experience with WOWBugs. Presenting students with the parasitized host larvae (upon which the eggs are almost invisible), they've spun a story of an organism unknown to science, and students' duty as investigators to learn all they can about it. This adds an interesting twist. Students at first assume the larva is the unknown, then soon discover that something else is growing on it!*

Accurate journal note taking is the basis of all scientific research. This inquiry activity gives the students a chance to develop the skills and habits this requires. The activity can be done by individual students or teams, or as an entire-class cooperative learning activity. Alternatively, observation can be a whole-class demonstration. You can put the culture under a video projection system and have students generate a single data sheet for the whole class.

If you choose to alert students to the presence of the eggs, before class begins, locate WOWBugs eggs on the

Key Concepts: Life cycles; Metamorphosis.

Prerequisites: Basic microscope skills. Students also should have a basic understanding of insect life cycles and metamorphosis.

Time: One class period to start the activity, parts of 6 to 9 subsequent periods for students to make observations, and one class period to conclude the activity.

Getting Ready: You need to have a WOWBugs culture on hand. If you don't already have them, be sure to order some in advance.

For every child or team, you will need to start a separate culture 2–3 days before starting the activity (see Chapter 8). With a fine-tipped permanent marker, code each container with a letter or number. Eggs are generally present 2–4 days after fertilized females are put on a host.

Objectives: Describe changes that occur during the life cycle of an insect.

* An article by L. R. Flage and R. W. Matthews describes student affective and cognitive experiences using WOWBugs presented as mystery organisms (Proceedings, Conf. Invertebrates in Captivity, Tucson, 1996. Prchal, S., ed. Sonoran Arthropod Studies Institute).

eggs

larvae

post defecating larvae

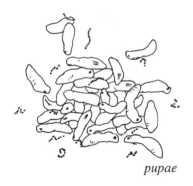

pupae

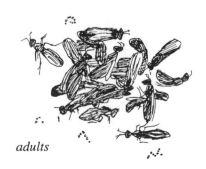

adults

skin of the host larva so that you can point them out to students. If available, use a video projection system to show the eggs to students during the first three days of the activity. (A bioscope can also be used, although it gives off more heat than is desirable.) The eggs are small and nearly transparent. Move the lighting around until you can see them well. Typically eggs are laid in clusters or piles. If you can't locate eggs, you may wish to begin the activity by having students observe WOWBugs larvae. If you do, then tell them that the eggs are very small and take about 3-4 days to hatch into what they are now observing. You should not tell them that these are larvae, since the purpose of this activity is for them to figure this out.

Some insects, such as grasshoppers, undergo a life cycle where nymphs hatch from eggs laid by the adults. The nymphs look similar to the adults, except that they are smaller and do not have wings or reproductive organs. This type of development is called simple or incomplete metamorphosis. Several variations exist, which are given different names by those who study insects.

WOWBugs go through the same kind of metamorphosis that most insects (85% of all the major species) do: complete metamorphosis. Like butterflies and beetles, they develop through a life cycle that has four unique stages: egg, larva, pupa, and adult.

Grub-like larvae hatch from eggs, eat, grow, shed their skins, and defecate.

Once a larva has reached a certain size, it stops moving around. For protection, instead of a cocoon (like caterpillars make), these larvae harden their skin into a tough casing.

Inside this protective shell, the body of the larva breaks down and reorganizes into the body of an adult male or female insect. During this stage, the insect is called a pupa. It looks like a tiny, fat cigar. The pupa does not move around or eat.

Until right before the adult stage, there are no obvious differences between males and females. During the pupa stage, female WOWBugs develop red eyes. By the end of the pupa stage, however, their eyes and body are black.

The final stage is the adult, which courts and mates. The females lay eggs. Most adult insects of different species eat. No one knows for sure, though, that adult WOWBugs do. It appears that adult males may be cannibalistic, eating each other, and that females may feed on juices from their host.

At normal room temperatures (22-30 degrees C; 72-86 degrees F) the entire WOWBug life cycle takes 14-21 days. Eggs hatch in 3-4 days, larvae feed for 7-10 days, and the pupation period requires 4-7 days.

The videotape, "Working With WOWBugs: WOWBug Biology" makes a good capstone for concluding this activity and reviewing the life cycle stages.

A Life Cycle Mystery

One of the most interesting things about WOWBugs is their life cycle. An entire generation develops and grows to adulthood in a very short while. Additionally, they do all this in a container that fits in the palm of your hand, a tiny, self-contained "world" that doesn't require any maintenance.

What is the nature of this life cycle? What do its stages look like? How long do they last? These are things we're going to find out.

Materials (per student or team)

• WOWBugs immatures (eggs or larvae) on host, in numbered container

• dissecting microscope, Magiscope®, or lighted magnifying glass

• composition book (or, at least 12 sheets of lined and 12 sheets of unlined paper, punched and placed in a loose-leaf binder)

• pencil

• millimeter ruler

First Day of Observations

1. If you're not using a composition book for your lab manual, construct a notebook using the lined and unlined paper and loose-leaf binder. Put the paper in the binder so that each two page spread has unlined paper on one side for drawings and lined paper on the other side for notes.

2. Write today's date in the upper right corner of the first lined page of your notebook. Write the date in this location on a new page each time your make observations.

Tell students that the female was put in the vial 2 to 3 days ago. Have them record this date in their notebooks.

3. Get a culture container with a **host** and a female WOWBug. Carefully check to find the identification number of your container. Write this number in your lab notebook, below the date.

4. Keep the container closed to avoid contaminating it. Working slowly and carefully, try to find clusters of eggs on the yellow skin of the host. On the lined page, write a paragraph that describes their appearance. How large are they compared to the host? What color are they? Are they shiny or dull? Do they move? About how many are there?

If students can't find the eggs, tell them to skip these questions. Caution students not to roll the host around in the container. It is best to always keep it in one position. Otherwise, the eggs or host could be injured.

5. Use the ruler to measure the host and to estimate the size of the eggs. Write these numbers down in your notebook.

6. On the unlined paper, draw a sketch of the host and the eggs. Label your sketch. If you are using a microscope to see them, write down the magnification. Using the ruler, draw a **scale bar**, to show how large they actually are.

Stress the need for providing a scale bar or other indicator of the relative magnification to accompany all sketches or drawings. You will need to demonstrate to the class how to do this. For practice with scale bars, see the "Scale and Accuracy" activity in Chapter Three.

7. When you are finished, return the culture to its storage area. Your teacher will tell you where to put it.

Days Three and Beyond
1. Examine your container every other school day for

three weeks. Use a different two-page spread in your laboratory notebook each day. Be sure to write the date and container number in the corner of your notebook page.

2. Ask the same questions you did on the first day. Describe what you see on the lined page and draw what you see on the unlined page. Label all your sketches, and include magnification and a scale bar.

3. At the end of this study, you should have lots of insects. Try to estimate how many are in your vial. Later, your teacher may give you the chance to find out if your guess is accurate.

If you want to include estimation skills, talk to the class about counting the insects in a small area and extrapolating. Another activity in this manual ("Population Sex Ratios," Chapter 6) includes counting the insects. If time permits, have students compare their notes and drawings with those of other students. If short on time, different groups could take notes on different days and share them with the others.

Final Day

Label the final page in your notebook "Results and Discussion." On that page, write the answer to the following questions.

Even if the students did their observations individually, you may wish to let them work together on these questions. Or, you may want to guide the entire class through them as a discussion. Remind your students that you placed the fertilized female in the vial 2–3 days before they began observations.

1. Remember that the female insect was put in the vial a few days before you started your observations. How many days total did it take before the eggs hatched? How did you know when they had hatched?

Responses may vary, but should be within 3-4 days of first observation. The smallest larvae appear to have body segmentation which was not seen in the eggs. Omit this question if the students started their observation with the larval stage.

2. What did the insect that hatched from the egg look like? When and how did it move?

The insect is small and worm-like (no legs or antennae) and initially remains fixed in one position on the host. As they grow, the insects begin to wiggle, but they don't crawl around the vial.

3. What was the yellow-brown, curly material that appeared in the vials (probably between days 7 and 9)? What did it indicate?

These are the larval feces, excreted all at once when the larvae finish feeding. Many larval insects do this. The presence of this material indicates that the larva is fully grown and is ready to begin pupating.

4. When did the insects begin to move off their host? What did they do then? What did the host look like at this point?

*The larvae detach from the host and drop off between days 8 and 10. At this point, the larvae are inactive. If you want to introduce the term, they now technically are called **prepupae**, literally "just before being pupae." The host has been mostly or totally eaten, leaving a dry and shriveled host "mummy."*

5. What was the next change in appearance that you saw? When did it happen? Did all the insects change in the same way?

Near the end of the pupa stage (days 10-14), the female pupae develop red eyes. Look carefully to find the eyeless (blind) males, since there are only about one out of each 20 insects.

6. Your culture started with one fertilized female insect. About how many were there in the vial at the end?

There probably were 400-500 offspring. The number depends on the size of the host.

7. How many different life cycle stages did the WOWBugs go through?

The life cycle includes four stages: egg, larva, pupa, and adult.

8. Is this life cycle more like that of grasshoppers or butterflies? Why?

For this question, you need to make sure your students know about the life cycles of these insects. (See the beginning of this exercise for a summary.)

The life cycle is more like that of butterflies, because it has four stages. Grasshoppers only have three life cycle stages (egg, immature [nymph], and adult).

9. How could the entire WOWBugs life cycle be diagrammed? Use the data collected in your laboratory notebook to draw a diagram that shows the different stages of the life cycle. Be sure to put how many days each stage took.

See the diagram at the beginning of this section. At this point, you may want to share it with the class via a transparency made from the master in Chapter 8.

New Terms:

host

nymph

prepupae

scale bar

Concept Application And Elaboration:

1. Assume that one female WOWBug can produce 500 female offspring from one mating. Assume also that there can be one new generation each month. If each of these 500 offspring successfully survived, mated, and found a host, and each produced 500 more female offspring, what would the total number of WOWBugs be at the end of one calendar year?

You cannot calculate this on the calculator unless it can handle scientific notation or has space for 33 digits! Think of the 500 as 5×10^2. At the end of month 1, there will be 500; at the end of month 2, there will be $500 \times 500 = 500^2$, or 250,000. This continues until the end of month 12, where the number is 500^{12}. This same number could be expressed as 2.4414×10^{32} or as 244,140,000,000,000,000,000,000,000,000,000.

2. If the WOWBug has one of the shortest life cycles in the insect world, the periodical cicada (or so-called "seventeen year locust") certainly has one of the longest. Research the story of its life, and present an illustrated report.

3. Just for fun, have students do the WOWBugs Word Find. The answers are shown below. You'll find the reproducible original on page 248. All the circled words appear in activities in this book.

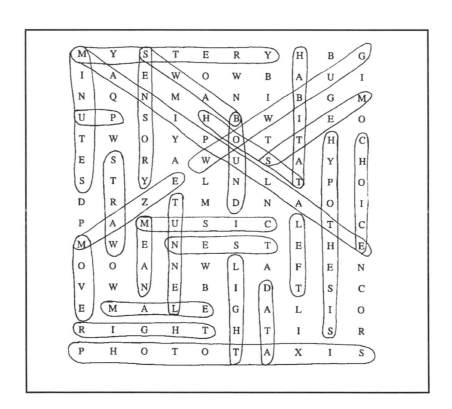

Time-Lines, Cylinders, And The Cycle Of Life

Key Concepts: Visual and tactile reinforcement of life cycles and the continuity of life.

Prerequisites: Students should have data on the life cycle of Melittobia digitata, *ideally obtained from their own laboratory notebooks.*

Time: One to two class periods, depending on student age and abilities.

Getting Ready: You may want to cut the poster board strips in advance to save time. Cutting 14-cm wide strips parallel to the long edge yields 4 strips per sheet. For younger students, cut two 28-cm strips instead, to leave more room for writing and illustration. For older students, you can substitute adding-machine tape to make individual time lines.

Objectives: Develop time-lines to encourage class comparisons, discussions, and evaluations of life history data; Turn time-lines into cylinders to produce visual models that reinforce the concept of the repeating cycle of life.

In biology, we often speak of the **life cycle** of an organism — that is, the genetically programmed sequence of events by which individuals of a species are produced, grow, develop, and themselves reproduce. Life history information can be presented in many different ways. This activity introduces three: tables, time-lines, and time cylinders.

What does the WOWBug life cycle look like, based on our own experimental data?

Materials (per student or team)

• Long poster board strip or length of adding-machine tape
• Pencil
• Colored markers
• Transparent tape
• Meter stick
• Small individual calendars or a few large calendars posted where they can be easily seen
• Student laboratory notebook with data on the WOWBug life cycle

1. Working in pairs or small groups, review the information in your laboratory notebooks. Make a list of events you think were important milestones in the life of your population of *Melittobia digitata.*

Some examples might be when the culture was started, when egg-laying was first noticed, when the first larvae were observed, etc.

2. Make a chart or table that includes each event, its data, and a column to indicate the number of days between events. Use the calendar to determine how to fill

in the last column. How long did the complete WOWBug
life cycle take?

*Ordinarily, the complete life cycle should take 17-21 days,
depending on classroom temperature. Rarely, a longer life cycle
may result if the insects enter diapause, a dormant state
somewhat like hibernation. However, this is an unusual event
under typical classroom conditions.*

3. Measure the length of the poster board strip in centi-
meters. Divide this length by the total days in your
WOWBug life cycle to figure out your time-line scale.
Round your number down to the next half-centimeter.
Use the ruler to draw a line along the length of the
poster board strip, and mark it at the proper intervals.
It's all right to have some extra space at the ends.

*For example, a 71-cm poster board strip
divided by a 20-day life cycle gives 3.55.
Make the scale marks 3.5 cm apart.
You'll have 1 centimeter left at the
end of the line.*

4. Plot, label, and illustrate events on the time
line.

*Have the colored markers
freely available.*

5. To show the repeating
life cycle, roll the time-
line into a cylinder.
Overlap the ends so
that the life cycle time-
line becomes a continu-
ous loop. Fasten the
edges with clear tape.

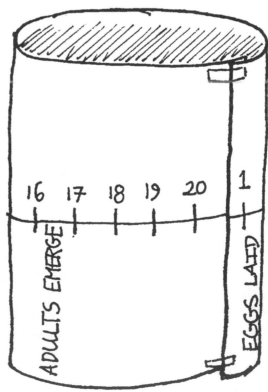

Discussion:

1. Compare your time-line with that of others. Are the life cycle events all on the same days? To the same scale? Why or why not?

They should be within a few days of each other because the WOWBugs were all kept under similar conditions and had similar genetic backgrounds. Slight differences due to different observers are to be expected, however.

2. In nature or under different classroom conditions, how might the time-line you draw be different? What variables might be changed?

Answers will vary, depending on what the students have studied so far. Diapause and slower egg-laying by unmated females are just two of the possibilities.

Concept Application And Elaboration:

1. To visually reinforce the idea of a cycle, invent a way to rotate the cylinder.

Students often think of turntables, such as are used for records, in a microwave, or in a cabinet. Other choices include putting it on a spit or making a rotator with a LEGO™ set.

2. Unlike WOWBugs, some insects such as cicadas, June bugs, and mayflies have very long and/or variable life cycles. When they do appear, it is often in very large numbers. Scientists think this gives them a major advantage over their predators. What could it be?

When the insect hordes appear, it always comes as a "surprise" to their predators. As a result, predator numbers can't increase the way they would if they could count on a reliable number of prey at regular intervals. In addition, the insects' life cycle may actually be much longer than that of the predators. As a result, predators can't learn to expect them based on what they've experienced.

Effects Of Diet On Development: An Overview

This activity involves original research. Students will be discovering facts unknown to published science. It is one of several in this manual that use an inquiry approach with students. Students should work in pairs or teams, pooling their collective abilities, as working scientists themselves are increasingly doing.

Rather than lecturing or dictating, the teacher's role is as a facilitator, leading students to discover background information they need to formulate a question that they can answer using methods scientists use. During the class periods, you can interrupt collaborative team work in order to have whole-group teaching sessions on common questions or problems or to give input that will benefit the whole group.

Refer students to books and articles on parasitic insects, as well as photographs or actual cultures, as appropriate. Chapter 7 includes a helpful bibliography to get you started. The students will decide on the specific materials to use as they design their research question.

This activity presupposes knowledge of the WOWBug life cycle on the mud-dauber host. If the students have not already done the Mystery Life Cycle activity and kept a journal of their observations, they will need some way to see the different stages. This could be a chart with the timing, length and appearance of the stages (see the transparency masters section in Chapter 8). Alternatively, you may wish to have several different cultures at all the different life cycle stages, labeled with the stage and the number of days, or show the class the videotape, "Working With WOWBugs: WOWBug Biology."

Key Concepts: Diet; Life cycles; Factors limiting population growth.

Prerequisites: Basic knowledge of the Melittobia *life cycle; Familiarity with the concepts of hypothesis, variables, and controls.*

Time: At least one class period for background research. Students' experiments could last several weeks, depending on the experiment.

Getting Ready: Have available a WOWBugs culture and a variety of reference and background research materials (see Chapter 7). Also have different diet possibilities, including mud dauber larvae. Other host possibilities are fly pupae, artificial media, or other larvae (see Chapter 8).

Objective: Determine the effects of altered host quantity and quality on parasite growth by examining WOWBug development on various alternative hosts.

Effects Of Diet On Development

Insects are one of the most successful classes of animals. They have survived, adapted, and expanded until there now are more different kinds of insects on our planet than different kinds of any other creature. There are many reasons for this success, but a very important one is the wide range of dietary habits.

Having an exoskeleton is another reason. Still another is insects' small size. The large number of offspring and short length of life cycle which are common to most insects permit rapid adaptation to changing environments.

Many insects are **host specific**, meaning they live on, or off of, one particular species of animal or plant. For the insects that are strictly host specific, absence of the host means death. Not surprisingly, many other insects are able to expand their possibilities when their primary host is not available. An insect or animal that eats a variety of foods is described as being **polyphagous**.

People are polyphagous. We can eat lots of different kinds of food and still survive, even if we don't like the food very much. You might prefer to eat pizza, for example, but you could survive if the only things you had to eat were broccoli, asparagus, and eggplant.

Are WOWBugs host specific or polyphagous? The surprising answer is both! Normally, they live off of one particular species of animal or host, the mud dauber wasp larva. If they find other kinds of larvae, however, they can use them instead. WOWBugs have been successfully reared from over 20 different insect host species, from cockroaches and caterpillars to flies to honeybees.

Dahms (l984) describes this in an article you might want to have on hand for your students' research.

If we humans don't get to eat the food that we like and need, our bodies can suffer from **malnourishment**. This means we don't have enough of a particular vitamin, or nutrient, or something else our body needs from the food. We might be slow to mature. We might not grow very big, and we might be pretty weak or sick.

Does the same thing happen with WOWBugs? When they must use a different host than the mud dauber larvae they prefer, what kinds of effects might it have on their life cycle and development?

Scientists don't know. This is what we will be trying to figure out in this activity.

Materials (per team):
• resource materials on insects and parasites

• diet possibilities

• unmated female WOWBugs

• one male WOWBug

• magnifying lens, stereo microscope, or Magiscope®

• several test tubes or vials

• small watercolor brush or pipe cleaner

• cotton

The diet possibilities will vary, and additional materials may be needed, depending on the experiment the students choose.

Part A. Getting Background Information

Before you design your research project, what does your group need to know? The questions below will help you decide. Some of this information you might already know from earlier studies or observations. You will need to get the rest from the books and articles your teacher has available, and by observing and asking questions.

a. What are **parasites** and **hosts**? Give definitions and examples.

Parasites are animals or plants that live off of other animals or plants, usually hurting the other animal when they do so. Hosts are the animals parasites live off. Some examples are: mistletoe and oak trees; WOWBugs and mud dauber larvae; fleas and dogs.

b. What kind of insect is the WOWBugs' **primary host** (the one they prefer or use most often)? What stage of life are the hosts in? Why is this a good time for WOWBugs to parasitize them?

WOWBugs' primary host is the mud dauber wasp, specifically the larval stage. This is a good stage to parasitize because the larvae do not move around. They cannot get away from the parasite.

c. If WOWBugs were to parasitize a different insect, what kind of problems might develop? Brainstorm with other group members, and see how many ideas you can think of.

Answers will vary. Encourage free-wheeling, non-judgmental discussion. There are many other species that can be used as hosts, but possibly the different host might not be as good nutritionally, or might not provide as safe a shelter.

Part B. Designing An Original Research Study

Now it's time to create your own experiment to test some of the ideas you've been thinking about.

1. First, you need to ask a question that has a **manipulated variable** and a **responding variable**. It also needs to be a question that you can answer by experimentation. This question should have to do with WOWBugs' diet and with their development. It also should include something that can be measured to show a change or difference. (For example, suppose you were studying humans. You might ask, "Do babies fed nothing but pizza gain the same amount of weight as babies that are fed milk?")

A good idea here is for your group to brainstorm a lot of different ideas and questions. Write them down. Circle the one that is the most interesting to you. (Make sure it is one that you can test.)

Make sure that each group of students creates a group of workable questions, and chooses a testable one for this exercise. Review the construction of hypotheses if students seem to be getting off track.

Our Questions Are:

Some ideas to test might include whether a host or diet different than mud dauber larvae makes the WOWBugs take longer to develop; whether they grow to the same size; whether their coloration changes; whether their behavior (aggression, mating, etc.) changes; whether their life expectancy is shorter; etc. A sample question could be "Does use of a different host affect the time to complete the WOWBug life cycle?" Another could be "Does use of a different host affect the ratio of females and males that develop?"

In our most interesting question, the manipulated variable is:

In our most interesting question, the responding variable is:

Answers will vary. Review the concepts of manipulated and responding variables, if necessary.

2. Next, you need a hypothesis. In answer to your circled question, what do you think will happen? How will you measure it? Write a statement that includes the words "if" and "then" and gives your prediction in measurable terms. Be as specific as possible. (For example, your human-babies nutrition question might become the hypothesis, "If human babies are fed nothing but pureed pizza for the first six months of their life, then they will gain less weight than babies that are fed nothing but milk.")

Our Hypothesis Is:

A sample hypothesis might be, "If a blowfly larva instead of a mud dauber larva is used as a host, then the time for Melittobia digitata to complete its life cycle will increase."

3. At the beginning of this activity, some basic supplies were listed. What additional materials would you need to do your specific experiment? Are they obtainable? If not, then you'll need to go back to step 1 and choose another question.

Our Materials:

While you will, of course, want to help students get the materials they need to test a well-reasoned experiment, this step serves as a valuable "reality check" for excessively exuberant hypotheses.

4. What are the exact steps you would need to take to test your hypothesis? Try to be very specific.

Our Procedures:

A sample might be, "In one container, place 5 female WOWBugs on a mud dauber larva and label it. In another container place 5 female WOWBugs with the blowfly host, and label it. The manipulated variable will be the type of host. The responding variable will be the length of time in each development stage, and total time."

5. Remember that it is very important to control all

variables other than the one to be manipulated! Identify all the variables you can. Indicate how you will control each.

A sample might be, "The type of container, temperature, and light are other variables we need to control. We will use the same type of container, and to keep everything under the same temperature and lighting."

6. What sort of **data** (information) will you gather? How will the data be recorded? As numbers of days, sizes, colors, numbers of insects, or something else?

Kind Of Data We Are Collecting:

A sample might be, "The number of days until the first adult female and first adult male appear; possibly also the time until the first larval defecation; the first pupa, etc."

Part C. Carrying Out The Experiment

Talk with your teacher about the experiment you have designed. After your teacher okays your procedure, it is time to actually carry out your experiment.

A review at this point can forestall later problems. It also helps underscore the importance of careful planning.

Gather together the supplies you will need, from the list you wrote. Paying attention to your hypothesis and your variables, go through the steps of the Procedure that you created. In your laboratory notebook or other permanent record, write down all your data and your results as they occur. Then summarize them below:

Depending on what kind of experiment the students design, this could take several weeks of observation. For example, studying the length of the WOWBugs' different stages of life cycle, or their total life span, would take a few weeks.

Summary Of Our Data And Results:

A sample might be, "The mud dauber host produced the first male after 14 days, the first female after 17 days. The blowfly host produced the first male after 13 days, the first female after 17 days."

Now you need to analyze or look at your data and results and decide what they mean. What did you learn as a result of this study?

Our Analysis:

A sample might be, "There was no real difference in life cycle completion time. Possibly the life cycle is completed slightly faster on blowfly pupae, but more trials are needed to confirm this."

How did your results relate to your hypothesis? Did your data support your hypothesis? Or not?

Our Conclusions:

A sample might be, "The hypothesis of increased time to develop on blowflies was not supported."

Remind students that even if their experiment did not support their hypothesis, they are still doing an excellent job as scientists when they test their different ideas in this fashion. In addition, finding no differences in an aspect of development on a different host raises interesting questions. For example, if the alternate host is "just as good", what factors might keep it from being the primary host?

Think about the experiment you designed and what you learned from it. If you wanted to do your experiment again, but better, how would you change it?

One suggestion might be to replicate the experiment five times instead of once, since one test might have been some kind of fluke.

What kind of a follow-up experiment could you do? What other related questions could you test?

These might include some of the brainstormed ideas in answer to question 3.

Concept Application And Elaboration:

1. Write a limerick that draws its inspiration from WOWBug growth and development.

Here's an adaptation of a very old one, to use as an example:

Host-specific young WOWBug Eugene
Soon grew so abnormally lean,
And flat, and compressed,
That his back touched his chest,
And sideways he couldn't be seen.

New Terms:

data

hosts

host specific

malnourishment

manipulated variable

parasites

polyphagous

primary host

responding variable

2. Working together as a team, invent a skit (5 minutes or less!) around the subject of WOWBugs choosing from among different hosts. Present it to the class.

3. Share the results of your research with scientists who study *Melittobia*. They would love to hear from you! Write to Dr. Robert Matthews, Department of Entomology, The University of Georgia, Athens, GA 30602. Or e-mail your information to the Georgia WOWBugs Project (bugdoc@arches.uga.edu).

Mission: Entomological

Key Concepts: Life cycles; Insect behavior.

Prerequisites: None.

Time: One class period or less.

Getting Ready: Have a few general entomology texts on hand (for suggestions, see Chapter 7). If you are going to read it to the class, draw the map on the board or show it as a transparency.

Students can do this activity before or after they have actually observed or experimented with WOWBugs. However, you might need to talk with them about parasitic insects, if they have not observed the WOWBugs before.

Objectives: Solve problems by analyzing data; Consider the effects of temperature on insects; Think about parasitic insects.

This is an entertaining way to introduce key life cycle concepts in an investigative format. It is quite effective when read aloud, pausing at the appropriate places for student reactions. Alternatively, it can be used as a paper and pencil activity done by individual students, pairs, or teams — but there's always the temptation to peek ahead for clues as to the answers!

This activity is based on the fact that many animals are sensitive to changes in temperature. Some mammals hibernate when it gets too cold; most insects overwinter in a state of arrested growth called diapause. Extreme temperature, especially cold, often kills most adult insects, although the eggs they have laid usually survive.

Materials:

• this activity sheet, including map
• entomology sourcebooks

You are a famous research entomologist at a well-known university. One day, the president of the university calls you to his office. He tells you that there are problems at the university's research station located at the North Pole.

Last week, the scientists at the research station noticed a lot of small insects about the size of a fruit fly. The researchers are not entomologists. They say the insects do not seem to be dangerous to people, but the researchers are worried that these creatures might damage their equipment. If they just get rid of the insects without understanding what they are and how they got there, how can they be sure the same thing won't happen again? They need your immediate help!

You quickly pack your parka and fur-lined boots, and prepare for your trip to the North Pole. You are armed only with your knowledge of science and your ability to think like a scientist.

Good luck on your **Mission: Entomological!**

One of the key elements of scientific thinking is gathering data and evaluating them to try to solve a problem.

1. As soon as you arrive, you ask for a map of the research station. Where have they been finding the insects?

They are all in the kitchen area.

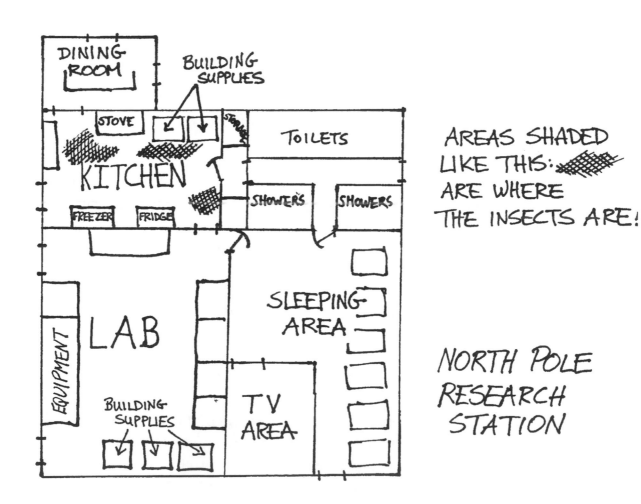

AREAS SHADED LIKE THIS: ARE WHERE THE INSECTS ARE!

NORTH POLE RESEARCH STATION

2. You ask the researchers if anything unusual happened last week, and discover an interesting fact. New building supplies were recently delivered to the laboratories, and some of the supplies were also brought to the kitchen.

3. Carefully inspecting the supplies and the crates they were sent in, you discover that a few of the crates have brown tubes of dry mud attached to the underside of the lid. Immediately, you recognize that these are nests of the mud dauber wasp. However, the small insects in the kitchen area are definitely not mud daubers.

4. You ask to see the insects. Borrowing a powerful microscope from one of the researchers, you look carefully. The insect has four wings with relatively few veins. The hind wings are smaller than the front wings, and are hard to see. Between the thorax and abdomen, the insects look squeezed together. You can see the tip of a tiny stinger at the end of their abdomens. As a good entomologist, you know what scientific **order** of insects they are. What order is it? What kind of insects are they?

If students haven't yet studied WOWBugs, provide some simple entomology guidebooks (see Chapter 7 suggestions) and help them decide that they must be Hymenoptera, and are probably wasps.

5. What possible connections could there be between the little insects and the mud dauber nests?

The smaller wasps could be parasites of the mud daubers. They also could be insects that are only using the mud tubes for shelter without having any biological interaction at all with the mud daubers.

6. How could you test your ideas to see if they are correct? (Remember to consider every life stage in the mud dauber life cycle.)

Look inside the nests for mud daubers themselves, and see if they have any evidence of parasitism. Be sure to check what-

ever stages you find, including breaking open cocoons.

7. You break open a nest from a crate in the research laboratories. The mud dauber cocoons are full of tiny pupae too small to be mud dauber offspring. Immediately, you know the small insects' role. What is it?

They are parasites on the immature mud daubers.

8. Only one problem, though. You look at the map again. Hmm. Where are the crates? And where are the insects? Hmm. What could be the reason for this?

The crates are in both the kitchen and the laboratory. The little parasitic wasps are only in the kitchen. Something must be different about the two rooms or about the two groups of crates.

9. When you go back and forth between the laboratories and the kitchen, you notice that the labs seem quite a bit cooler. With a thermometer, you check out the **ambient temperature** — that is, the temperature of the air and surroundings. The ambient temperature in the labs is about 10 degrees Celsius (50 degrees Fahrenheit). The kitchen, with the stoves and ovens on, is about 27 degrees Celsius (80 degrees Fahrenheit). What do you think is going on with the small insects and the temperature?

The lower temperature in the labs is like spring outdoors. It is too cool for the pupae to develop into adults, and the activity of any adults already present is reduced to a minimum. Because the temperature in the kitchen is more like summer, the life cycle is continuing. In the warm air, the adult wasps are emerging, moving around, and generally thriving.

10. How could you find out whether your idea is correct?

Lots of ways. One way is to raise the lab temperature and see if wasps emerge there. Or put the nests in different temperatures and see whether wasps emerge.

11. Now that you know what is going on, the researchers need your advice. They don't really want to have the

insects around and in the way, but they also don't want to kill them. How can they control them? What could they do to be sure this doesn't happen again?

They really don't need to do anything with the adults now around because they'll only live for a few weeks. To keep it from happening again, they could inspect incoming materials for mud nests and remove them. As a second line of defense, they could reduce the kitchen temperature and continue to keep the temperature low in the laboratories.

12. The researchers thank you for your help in resolving their problem. You return to the university with a sample of the insects. Looking them up in the entomology books, you find that their scientific name is *Melittobia digitata*, and that some people call them WOWBugs.

The university president gives you a big raise.

You write an article about your research.
The reviewers love it!

Another success for the Mission: Entomological team!

Concept Application And Elaboration:

1. Write your own "Mission: Entomological" mystery about some other insect's life cycle or about another aspect of WOWBug biology.

2. Write a skit based on this activity. Present it to students in another class.

3. Learn more about insect diapause and the hibernation of mammals. How are they alike? How are they different?

New Terms:

ambient temperature

order

A Life Cycle Mystery

Objectives: Describe changes that occur during the life cycle of an insect.

Materials (per student or team)

- *WOWBug immatures on host, in numbered container*
- *dissecting microscope, Magiscope®, or lighted magnifying glass*
- *composition book (or, at least 12 sheets of lined and 12 sheets of unlined paper, punched and placed in a loose-leaf binder)*
- *pencil*
- *millimeter ruler*

One of the most interesting things about WOWBugs is their life cycle. An entire generation develops and grows to adulthood in a very short while. Additionally, they do all this in a container that fits in the palm of your hand, a tiny, self-contained "world" that doesn't require any maintenance.

What is the nature of this life cycle? What do its stages look like? How long do they last? These are things we're going to find out.

First Day of Observations

1. If you're not using a composition book for your lab manual, construct a notebook using the lined and unlined paper and loose-leaf binder. Put the paper in the binder so that each two page spread has unlined paper on one side for drawings and lined paper on the other side for notes.

2. Write today's date in the upper right corner of the first lined page of your notebook. Write the date in this location on a new page each time your make observations.

3. Get a culture container with a **host** and a female WOWBug. Carefully check to find the identification number of your container. Write this number in your lab notebook, below the date.

4. Keep the container closed to avoid contaminating it. Working slowly and carefully, try to find clusters of eggs on the yellow skin of the host. On the lined page, write a paragraph that describes their appearance. How large are they compared to the host? What

color are they? Are they shiny or dull? Do they move? About how many are there?

5. Use the ruler to measure the host and to estimate the size of the eggs. Write these numbers down in your notebook.

6. On the unlined paper, draw a sketch of the host and the eggs. Label your sketch. If you are using a microscope to see them, write down the magnification. Using the ruler, draw a **scale bar**, to show how large they actually are.

7. When you are finished, return the culture to its storage area. Your teacher will tell you where to put it.

Days Three and Beyond

1. Examine your container every other school day for three weeks. Use a different two-page spread in your laboratory notebook each day. Be sure to write the date and container number in the corner of your notebook page.

2. Ask the same questions you did on the first day. Describe what you see on the lined page and draw what you see on the unlined page. Label all your sketches, and include magnification and a scale bar.

3. At the end of this study, you should have lots of insects. Try to estimate how many are in your vial. Later, your teacher may give you the chance to find out if your guess is accurate.

Final Day

Label the final page in your notebook "Results and Discussion." On that page, write the answer to the following questions.

1. Remember that the female insect was put in the vial a few days before you started your observations. How many days total did it take before the eggs hatched? How did you know when they had hatched?

2. What did the insect that hatched from the egg look like? When and how did it move?

3. What was the yellow-brown, curly material that appeared in the vials (probably between days 7 and 9)? What did it indicate?

4. When did the insects begin to move off their host? What did they do then? What did the host look like at this point?

5. What was the next change in appearance that you saw? When did it happen? Did all the insects change in the same way?

6. Your culture started with one fertilized female insect. About how many were there in the vial at the end?

7. How many different life cycle stages did the WOWBugs go through?

8. Is this life cycle more like that of grasshoppers or butterflies? Why?

9. How could the entire WOWBugs life cycle be diagrammed? Use the data collected in your laboratory notebook to draw a diagram that shows the different stages of the life cycle. Be sure to put how many days each stage took.

Time-Lines, Cylinders, And The Cycle Of Life

In biology, we often speak of the **life cycle** of an organism — that is, the genetically programmed sequence of events by which individuals of a species are produced, grow, develop, and themselves reproduce.

Life history information can be presented in many different ways. This activity introduces three: tables, time-lines, and time cylinders.

What does the WOWBug life cycle look like, based on our own experimental data?

Procedure:

1. Working in pairs or small groups, review the information in your laboratory notebooks. Make a list of events you think were important milestones in the life of your population of *Melittobia digitata.*

2. Make a chart or table that includes each event, its data, and a column to indicate the number of days between events. Use the calendar to determine how to fill in the last column. How long did the complete WOWBug life cycle take?

3. Measure the length of the poster board strip in centimeters. Divide this length by the total days in your WOWBug life cycle to figure out your time-line scale. Round your number down to the next half-centimeter. Use the ruler to draw a line along the length of the poster board strip, and mark it at the proper intervals. It's all right to have some extra space at the ends.

4. Plot, label, and illustrate events on the time line.

5. To show the repeating life cycle, roll the time-line into a cylinder. Overlap the ends so that the life cycle time-line becomes a continuous loop. Fasten the edges with clear tape.

Objectives: Develop time-lines to encourage class comparisons, discussions, and evaluations of life history data; Turn time-lines into cylinders to produce visual models that reinforce the concept of the repeating cycle of life.

Materials (per student or team)

- *Long poster board strip or length of adding-machine tape*
- *Pencil*
- *Colored markers*
- *Transparent tape*
- *Meter stick*
- *Small individual calendars or a few large calendars posted where they can be easily seen*
- *Student laboratory notebook with data on the WOWBug life cycle*

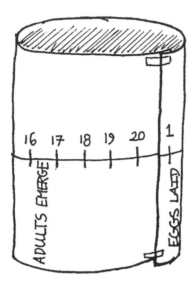

Discussion:

1. Compare your time-line with that of others. Are the life cycle events all on the same days? To the same scale? Why or why not?

_____

_____

_____

_____

_____

_____

_____

_____

2. In nature or under different classroom conditions, how might the time-line you draw be different? What variables might be changed?

_____

_____

_____

_____

_____

_____

_____

Effects of Diet on Development

Insects are one of the most successful classes of animals. They have survived, adapted, and expanded until there now are more different kinds of insects on our planet than different kinds of any other creature. There are many reasons for this success, but a very important one is the wide range of dietary habits.

Many insects are **host specific**, meaning they live on, or off of, one particular species of animal or plant. For the insects that are strictly host specific, absence of the host means death. Not surprisingly, many other insects are able to expand their possibilities when their primary host is not available. An insect or animal that eats a variety of foods is described as being **polyphagous**.

People are polyphagous. We can eat lots of different kinds of food and still survive, even if we don't like the food very much. You might prefer to eat pizza, for example, but you could survive if the only things you had to eat were broccoli, asparagus, and eggplant.

Are WOWBugs host specific or polyphagous? The surprising answer is both! Normally, they live off of one particular species of animal or host, the mud dauber wasp larva. If they find other kinds of larvae, however, they can use them instead. WOWBugs have been successfully reared from over 20 different insect host species, from cockroaches and caterpillars to flies to honeybees.

If we humans don't get to eat the food that we like and need, our bodies can suffer from **malnourishment**. This means we don't have enough of a particular vitamin, or nutrient, or something else our body needs from the food. We might be slow to mature. We might not grow very big, and we might be pretty weak or sick.

Objective: Determine the effects of altered host quantity and quality on parasite growth by examining WOWBugs development on various alternative hosts.

Materials (per team):

- *resource materials on insects and parasites*
- *diet possibilities*
- *unmated female WOWBugs*
- *one male WOWBug*
- *magnifying lens, stereo microscope, or Magiscope®*
- *several test tubes or vials*
- *small watercolor brush or pipe cleaner*
- *cotton*

Does the same thing happen with WOWBugs? When they must use a different host than the mud dauber larvae they prefer, what kinds of effects might it have on their life cycle and development? Scientists don't know. This is what we will be trying to figure out in this activity.

Part A. Getting Background Information

Before you design your research project, what does your group need to know? The questions below will help you decide. Some of this information you might already know from earlier studies or observations. You will need to get the rest from the books and articles your teacher has available, and by observing and asking questions.

a. What are **parasites** and **hosts**? Give definitions and examples.

_____

_____

_____

b. What kind of insect is the WOWBugs' **primary host** (the one they prefer or use most often)? What stage of life are the hosts in? Why is this a good time for WOWBugs to parasitize them?

_____

_____

c. If WOWBugs were to parasitize a different insect, what kind of problems might develop? Brainstorm with other group members, and see how many ideas you can think of.

_____

_____

_____

_____

Part B. Designing An Original Research Study

Now it's time to create your own experiment to test some of the ideas you've been thinking about.

1. First, you need to ask a question that has a **manipulated variable** and a **responding variable**. It also needs to be a question that you can answer by experimentation. This question should have to do with WOWBugs' diet and with their development. It also should include something that can be measured to show a change or difference. (For example, suppose you were studying humans. You might ask, "Do babies fed nothing but pizza gain the same amount of weight as babies that are fed milk?")

A good idea here is for your group to brainstorm a lot of different ideas and questions. Write them down. Circle the one that is the most interesting to you. (Make sure it is one that you can test).

Our Questions Are:

_____

_____

_____

_____

_____

_____

In our most interesting question, the manipulated variable is:

_____

In our most interesting question, the responding variable is:

_____

2. Next, you need a hypothesis. In answer to your circled question, what do you think will happen? How will you measure it? Write a statement that includes the words "if" and "then" and gives your prediction in measurable terms. Be as specific as possible. (For example, your human-babies nutrition question might become the hypothesis "If human babies are fed nothing but pureed pizza for the first six months of their life, then they will gain less weight than babies that are fed nothing but milk.")

Our Hypothesis Is:

_____

_____

_____

3. At the beginning of this activity, some basic supplies were listed. What additional materials would you need in order to do your specific experiment? Are they obtainable? If not, then you'll need to go back to step 1 and choose another question.

Our Materials:

_____

_____

_____

4. What are the exact steps you would need to take to test your hypothesis? Try to be very specific.

Our Procedures:

_____

_____

_____

_____

5. Remember that it is very important to control all your variables other than the one to be manipulated! Identify all the variables you can. Indicate how you will control each.

_____

_____

_____

_____

6. What sort of **data** (information) will you gather? How will the data be recorded? As numbers of days, sizes, colors, numbers of insects, or something else?

Kind Of Data We Are Collecting:

_____

_____

Part C. Carrying Out The Experiment

Talk with your teacher about the experiment you have designed. After your teacher okays your procedures, it is time to actually carry out your experiment.

Gather together the supplies you will need, from the list you wrote. Paying attention to your hypothesis and your variables, go through the steps of the Procedure that you created. In your laboratory notebook or other permanent record, write down all your data and your results as they occur. Then summarize them below:

Summary Of Our Data And Results:

_____

_____

_____

_____

Now you need to analyze or look at your data and results and decide what they mean. What did you learn as a result of this study?

Our Analysis:

_____

_____

_____

_____

_____

How did your results relate to your hypothesis? Did your data support your hypothesis? Or not?

Our Conclusions:

_____

_____

_____

Think about the experiment you designed and what you learned from it. If you wanted to do your experiment again, but better, how would you change it?

_____

_____

_____

What kind of a follow-up experiment could you do? What other related questions could you test?

_____

_____

_____

_____

_____

_____

_____

Mission: Entomological!

You are a famous research entomologist at a well-known university. One day, the president of the university calls you to his office. He tells you that there are problems at the university's research station located at the North Pole.

Last week, the scientists at the research station noticed a lot of small insects about the size of a fruit fly. The researchers are not entomologists. They say the insects do not seem to be dangerous to people, but the researchers are worried that these creatures might damage their equipment. If they just get rid of the insects without understanding what they are and how they got there, how can they be sure the same thing won't happen again? They need your immediate help!

You quickly pack your parka and fur-lined boots, and prepare for your trip to the North Pole. You are armed only with your knowledge of science and your ability to think like a scientist.

Good luck on your **Mission: Entomological!**

1. As soon as you arrive, you ask for a map of the research station. Where have they been finding the insects?

_____

2. You ask the researchers if anything unusual happened last week, and discover an interesting fact. New building supplies were recently delivered to the laboratories, and some of the supplies were also brought to the kitchen.

3. Carefully inspecting the supplies and the crates they were sent in, you discover that a few of the crates have brown tubes of dry mud attached to the underside of the

Materials:

- *this activity sheet, including map*
- *entomology sourcebooks*

lid. Immediately, you recognize that these are nests of the mud dauber wasp. However, the small insects in the kitchen area are definitely not mud daubers.

4. You ask to see the insects. Borrowing a microscope from one of the researchers, you look carefully. The insect has four wings with relatively few veins. The hind wings are smaller than the front wings, and are hard to see. Between the thorax and abdomen, the insects look squeezed together. You can see the tip of a tiny stinger at the end of their abdomens. As a good entomologist, you know what scientific **order** of insects they are. What order is it? What kind of insects are they?

_____

5. What possible connections could there be between the little insects and the mud dauber nests?

_____

_____

_____

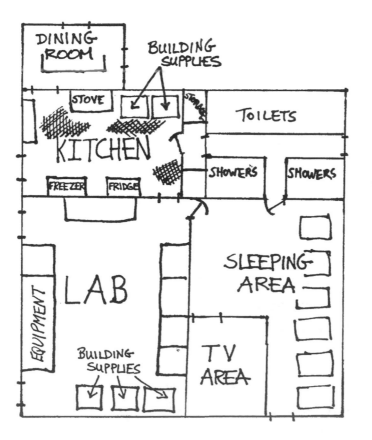

AREAS SHADED LIKE THIS: ▨ ARE WHERE THE INSECTS ARE!

NORTH POLE RESEARCH STATION

6. How could you test your ideas to see if they are correct? (Remember to consider every life stage in the mud dauber life cycle.)

_____

_____

_____

7. You break open a nest from a crate in the research laboratories. The mud dauber cocoons are full of tiny pupae too small to be mud dauber offspring. Immediately, you know the small insects' role. What is it?

_____

_____

_____

8. Only one problem, though. You look at the map again. Hmm. Where are the crates? And where are the insects? Hmm. What could be the reason for this?

_____

_____

_____

9. When you go back and forth between the laboratories and the kitchen, you notice that the labs seem quite a bit cooler. With a thermometer, you check out the **ambient temperature** — that is, the temperature of the air and surroundings.

The ambient temperature in the labs is about 10 degrees Celsius (50 degrees Fahrenheit). The kitchen, with the stoves and ovens on, is about 27 degrees Celsius (80 degrees Fahrenheit). What do you think is going on with the small insects and the temperature?

_____

_____

_____

_____

10. How could you find out whether your idea is correct?

_____

_____

_____

_____

11. Now that you know what is going on, the researchers need your advice. They don't really want to have the insects around and in the way, but they also don't want to kill them. How can they control them? What could they do to be sure this doesn't happen again?

_____

_____

_____

_____

12. The researchers thank you for your help in resolving their problem. You return to the university with a sample of the insects. Looking them up in the entomology books, you find that their scientific name is *Melittobia digitata*, and that some people call them WOWBugs.

The university president gives you a big raise.

You write an article about your research. The reviewers love it!

Another success for the Mission: Entomological team!

Chapter Five.
Sensory Responses:
Experimental Design
And Control Of
Variables

What would it like to eat?" "Can it see me?" "Can it hear me when I talk?" Such questions are among the first that young children ask about a new animal. That more sophisticated versions of the same questions still intrigue working scientists hints at sensory responses' universal appeal.

Developing the ability to explain and predict the world requires a great many experiences over a long period of time. Insect sensory responses have proven especially fertile ground for such experiences. This chapter includes five student favorites that have been used successfully both as full open-ended inquiries and as shorter guided inquiry lessons.

Decisions, Decisions...
An Overview of All Five Investigations

These experiments utilize a common experimental design: individual organisms are given the opportunity to choose between discrete conditions of a manipulated variable, each of which is presented in a separate arm of a choice apparatus. By their behavior (moving toward one or the other, or failing to do so), the organisms tell us something about their sensory world.

Students may work as pairs or as teams. Each different exercise can be run by all students over several class periods, or each group can test a different stimulus during the same period. The same data chart may be used by all; a sample "Sensory Response Choice Test Data Chart" appears in Chapter 8. Each team will need two per activity (one for part A, another for part B). Rather than making multiple photocopies, you may wish to project the chart for students to copy.

For these experiments, each team of students will need to make **choice tunnels** using clear plastic straws and a "Y" connector. We recommend using a 5/16" outside-diameter polypropylene or Nalgene "Y" connector. You can get these from biological supply catalogs. Make sure that the brand of straws you use fits snugly over, or in, the "Y" connector. If the straw is too big to fit, make a short (1 cm or 1/2 inch) cut in one end first, and try again, using a twisting motion. With some straws, cutting one end at a slight angle may ease insertion into the connector.

Key Concepts: Sensory systems and behavior; Experimental design.

Prerequisites: Students should have some practice handling and moving WOWBugs. They should also understand the concept of controlling variables.

Time: One class period to run each different exercise. Up to one more class period to analyze the results.

Getting Ready: Use adult female WOWBugs, since males will not really move around much. Decide how you want students to use these activities. Some teachers have allowed student teams to choose between them, then run several types of choice tests concurrently. For guided inquiries, use the activity sheets. For full inquiry, substitute steps figured out by students themselves.

Objectives: Test the effects of stimuli on insects. Determine whether Melittobia digitata are attracted to or repelled from such stimuli as temperature, smell, taste, sound and light.

Also make sure your cotton swabs fit snugly into the straws. If they do not, you might try fluffing the end of the cotton a bit first.

The instructions for making and using the choice tunnel, given here with commentary, are repeated in a transparency master in Chapter 8, which also could be copied for student use.

Directions For Making And Using A WOWBug Choice Tunnel

1. Using the ruler and scissors, cut a straw into two equal pieces. These will be the two paths the insects can choose from. Put one end into the two branches of the tubes of the "Y" connector. The length of the straw arms is not critical, but both should be the same length.

2. From another straw, cut a piece about 4 cm long. After you use it to collect the WOWBugs (step 4, below), this piece will serve as the stem of the "Y". It is a little shorter so the students don't have to wait so long for the insects to choose between the branches. Vary its length if necessary.

3. Cut two double-ended cotton swabs in half with the scissors. (The "handles" do not have to be the same length.) Put the plump end of one swab in the end of each branch to keep the insects from escaping. (Occasionally a WOWBug may escape if the connection to the Y is not tight or if a swab fits too loosely. If this happens, fix the "leak" and have the students continue with the remaining insects.)

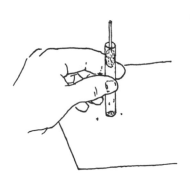

4. Use the 4-cm "stem" straw as a collecting tube. Plug its top end with a cotton swab. Then gently shake 6 to 10 WOWBugs from the culture onto a piece of paper. Quickly turn the straw straight up. Place it over the insects, one at a time, so they will crawl or hop up inside it. (While doing this, have someone else use the paintbrush or pipe cleaner to gently keep the remaining insects on the paper.)

5. After about 6 insects have entered the straw, they begin to fall or crawl out about as fast as another new one can be added. Pick up the tube and quickly plug the open end with another swab. When you are ready to begin your experiment, unplug one end and insert the straw into the "Y" connector stem.

Introducing These Experiments

Discuss with students how each kind of animal lives in a different sensory world. Furthermore, even when they are sensitive to the same environmental input, different creatures may react in different ways. Something that smells "nice" and thus is attractive to us might smell "awful" and repel an insect, and vice versa.

Some examples: A dog can hear whistles that are higher pitched than we can hear, and can smell where someone has been, but sees mostly in black-and-white. Honeybees are attracted to colors and patterns on flowers that are invisible to us unless we use special films and filters.

Talk also about the roles of different sorts of variables in scientific experiments. Discuss the concept that the presence or absence of a particular treatment really represents two different conditions of a **manipulated variable**.

To have any valid idea whether these two conditions make any difference, other factors that might affect the results must be cancelled out, neutralized, or otherwise controlled. **Control variables** are critically important to assure that there is only one possible cause for the observed result: the variable we are testing. For example, if you're investigating odor, you would need to control for differences in sound, light, length of choice tube, etc. The only two conditions you want to have influencing the result are the two odor choices.

When an animal moves in response to a stimulus such as an odor, a sound, or the presence of light, this behavior is called a **taxis**. An insect might exhibit positive **phototaxis**, moving towards light, or be negatively phototaxic, moving away from it. Similar terms include **geotaxis** for gravity; **thermotaxis** for temperature, etc. These directed responses are widespread in the animal world, and the stimuli that cause them represent major sorts of variables that must be controlled.

As a follow-up to these experiments, you may want to introduce the use of bioassay chambers (see Chapters 2 and 8), which give the organism four choices rather than two.

Discussion Questions

Since this chapter's activities are essentially all variations on the same theme, many of the questions for discussion are the same (although with different variables). Therefore, the first six questions for discussion are repeated here and at the beginning of the student pages at the back of this chapter. Any special teacher comments regarding the results or answers appear at the beginning of each activity's Discussion session. Each activity also has several additional questions specific to the particular variables tested.

1. In part A, what were the two conditions of the manipulated variable? Did the WOWBugs prefer to move toward either condition, or did they show no preference? What is your evidence?

Results will vary from activity to activity. In some cases, there is apparently no preference.

2. In part B, what were the two conditions of the manipulated variable? Did the WOWBugs prefer to move toward either condition, or did they not discriminate between them? What is your evidence?

Results will vary from activity to activity. In some cases, there is apparently no preference.

3. Did your results support the hypotheses you wrote down at the beginning?

This will obviously depend on the hypotheses!

4. Did all the WOWBugs choose the same branch? How

can you explain this?

Not all insects went into the same branch. In anthropomorphic terms, one could say that some needed more time to decide, or were content or confused or changed their mind.

5. Why do you think we did each test twice, putting the manipulated variable on the left and on the right?

To make sure no directional outside variable influenced the test results.

6. What other sorts of questions could you test using WOWBugs and choice tunnels?

There are, of course, the other tests in this chapter. Students should be encouraged to think of additional possibilities.

The Light At The End Of The Tunnel

Getting Ready: Be sure to read the introductory material earlier in this chapter.

Objectives: Determine the effects of white light and colored light on WOWBug location choices.

If you come to a fork in the road, how do you choose which route to take? If one of the ways looks rough and dark, you might choose the smoother, more brightly lit path. Would an animal necessarily choose a road the same way that you do? What about WOWBugs? How does light affect the way they react?

Materials (per team):

- clear straws (about 20)
- WOWBugs stock culture
- white paper
- cotton swabs (about 10)
- "Y" connector
- scissors
- millimeter ruler
- small paintbrush or pipe cleaner
- 2 identical small flashlights
- 3x5-inch index cards
- cellophane tape
- colored filters

These filters can be made of colored plastic, like that used for report covers. Colored cellophane, such as that which wraps candies like butterscotch or cinnamon ones, or colored plastic food wrap could also be used.

This experiment is designed to use white light, then to test one other color. Time permitting, students can test a variety of colored lights. This experiment could also be separated into two: one testing light vs. dark, one testing white vs. colored light.

Part A. Effects Of White Light On Female WOWBugs

For this experiment, we will be testing how light influences WOWBugs. When an animal moves towards light, we call this **positive phototaxis**. If it moves away from light, this is **negative phototaxis**.

We will have two choices for where the insects can go (the conditions of our manipulated variable). In one, we will put our extra bright light. In the other, we will not allow extra light. We will attempt to control for all other conditions, such as sound, temperature, etc.

1. To test which way the WOWBugs will go, we need to make sure they only have two choices. Each insect will go through a tube called a **choice tunnel**. (For obvious reasons, some biologists call it a Y-maze.) To construct one, follow the directions your teacher provides.

Show a transparency (master provided in Chapter 8) or dupli-cate those instructions and hand out to students.

2. If they are given the choice of going into the tube with the light or into the tube without the extra light, where do you think the WOWBugs will prefer to move? Or will they have no preference and move into both branches equally? Write down your hypothesis below.

3. Get the index card ready. You will need to hold it between the two branches to keep the light away from the control branch. Also, get your flashlight ready. One person should hold the index card in between the two branches. Another student should turn on the flashlight and point it only at the end of the <u>left</u> straw. Hold it steady, or set it on the table. Do not hold it so close that it heats up the straw.

The students will alternate putting the light onto the left and right branches during separate tests. This is to make sure that no directional variable is affecting the insects' choices.

Trial 1.

4. Look at your watch (or a clock), and write down the

exact time. Open one end of the "loaded" straw and quickly connect it to the stem of the "Y". Then lay the choice tunnel apparatus on the table and reposition the flashlight and index card.

Watch the WOWBugs carefully for 3 minutes. Keep a tally of the number of WOWBugs entering each branch, and write this total on the data chart. At the end of this time, remove each straw tube and plug the open end with a cotton swab piece. Then count how many insects are in the branch with the light, and write this number down. Count and record the number of insects that are in the branch with no extra light. Are there insects that did not choose either branch? (Check in the bottom and in the Y-tube connector.) How many?

Three minutes is long enough for this activity. You can have the students observe longer; this will give the insects more time to choose one path or the other. Of course, the students' attention may drift, too, if the time is longer!

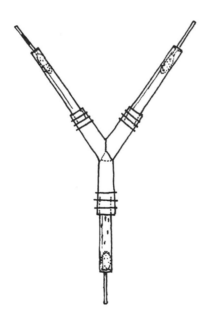

5. Take the WOWBugs out of all the parts of the choice tunnel and put them back in their container. Throw away the used straws and swabs. (Why not use them over? Think of a reason related to the experiment.)

Reusing them could introduce a new variable. For example, some kinds of insects will follow an odor trail left by others who went before them.

Trial 2.

6. Repeat the steps above, but instead of putting the extra light on the left straw branch, put it on the <u>right</u> branch. The other condition (no extra light) will then be the left branch. Why should you do this? What might happen if you didn't?

Reversing the branches controls for other variables such as compass direction, gravitational differences that might be caused by an uneven work table, etc.

7. Record the results of this second testing on the chart. Be sure to remember that the left and right branches have been reversed from the first testing!

8. Now, combine the results of both trials and record the totals on the data chart. What is the reason for this step?

Combining the results from two trials that are mirror images "cancels out" the effects of the possible directional variables that you were attempting to control.

Part B. Effects Of Colored Light

Run the same tests with a different condition of the manipulated variable. This time, instead of regular white light, use colored light. With a rubber band, fasten a colored filter over the end of the flashlight. The other condition of the manipulated variable will be a second flashlight without a filter, pointed at the other straw.

Before starting, write down your hypothesis for how the WOWBugs will react to this light. Then proceed as before. Be sure to write down which Y-arm received which condition of the manipulated variable.

If there is not enough time for each group to test both lights, you may want to have each group test only one color, but have different groups using different colors. If you have more time, the students can do more trials with the same color, or can test more different colors.

Discussion

Answer Questions 1 to 6 from the list provided by your teacher.

1. For white light, the insects should prefer to move towards it. The evidence is larger numbers recorded in the lighted branch.
2. For colored light, results may vary. Many insects do not respond to red or yellow light, but appear attracted to wave-

lengths closer to ultraviolet.

7. How could you change this test to have even bigger differences in the amount of light in each branch?

The control branch could be covered with something that would block all light.

New Terms:

choice tunnel

control variable

geotaxis

manipulated variable

phototaxis

stimulus

thermotaxis

variable

8. Why is it important to make sure the light does not heat up the branch?

Because temperature changes might influence the test results.

9. Why might it be important for WOWBugs to move toward light? How would their lives be different if they did not? (Hint: Think about where they normally would live.)

Since they normally are born inside a dark mud dauber nest, they need to move to light to find their way into the rest of the world.

Concept Application And Elaboration:

1. Many insects such as moths, cockroaches and June bugs (called May beetles in some parts of the country) become active at night. How might one of these species react to light? Design and use a larger choice tunnel apparatus to test your hypothesis.

2. Yellow light bulbs are marketed with the promise that they will attract fewer insects to your porches than white lights do. Does the evidence support such claims? Design and conduct an experiment to test your ideas.

3. Fireflies are beetles that react to the rhythm of flashes that the opposite sex produces. They usually flash their light in time intervals ranging from 1 to 4 seconds, depending on the species. Design an imaginary experiment that could use a choice tunnel apparatus to test firefly light attraction.

Odor Responses

If you come to a fork in the road, how do you choose which route to take? If one of the paths smelled awful and one smelled yummy, you might choose the sweet-smelling path. Would an insect choose a road the same way that you do?

Getting Ready: Be sure to read the introductory material earlier in this chapter.

For this experiment, we will be testing how **olfaction**, the sense of smell, influences WOWBugs. We will have two choices for where the insects can go. In one, we will put the "smelly" condition of the **manipulated variable** — something like perfume or vinegar. In the other, we will put water, which, although a liquid, doesn't have a smell (at least according to our own senses).

Objectives: Determine the effect of different smells on WOWBug behavior, and thus infer something about their sensory world.

How will these different olfactory conditions affect the way WOWBugs react?

Materials (per team):

- clear plastic straws (about 20)
- WOWBugs stock culture
- white paper or paper plate
- cotton swabs (about 10)
- "Y" connector
- scissors
- millimeter ruler
- small watercolor paintbrush or pipe cleaner
- 2 droppers
- 2 plastic film canisters (empty)
- vinegar, cologne, and other clear but odorous liquids
- water

Feel free to test other smelly liquids as well! Before conducting this experiment, you may want to brainstorm various ideas with your students.

Part A. Testing A Noticeable Odor And Water

1. To test which way the WOWBugs will go, we need to make sure they only have two choices. Each insect will go through a tube called a **choice tunnel**.

To make a choice tunnel, follow the instructions your teacher provides. Use new straws and swabs for each test. Give a reason why this might be important.

It's essential to make sure that the straws do not get contaminated by something different than what we want to test. This could be anything from traces of previous liquids to smells an insect itself might lay down.

2. From the choices available, pick an odor to test. Record it on your data sheet. Now we want to write a **hypothesis**. Do you think the WOWBugs will prefer to move into the tube with the smell or into the tube without it? Or will they have no preference and move into both branches equally? Write down your hypothesis.

Tips: To avoid spills and contamination, any liquid such as water, perfume, etc. should be given to the students in a small vial or film canister with its own dropper.

With young or inexperienced students, you may wish to provide extra practice using the droppers. One way is to draw small circles on blotter paper or construction paper. Give students a container with water tinted with food coloring. Have them place drops inside the circles..

3. Take a cotton swab and cut it into two pieces with the scissors. They do not have to be the exact same length. So that you will be able to tell the two pieces apart, put a black mark on the handle of one piece.

4. Put one small drop of the perfume you are testing onto the cottony end of the black-marked swab piece. This is the first condition of the manipulated variable. Then, stick the perfumed end into the <u>left</u> straw branch. Do not touch the swab end.

The students will alternate putting the "smelly" swab into the left and right branches. This is to make sure that no outside variable (such as the light source) is affecting the insects' choices.

5. Put one small drop of water onto the other piece of the swab. Stick it the same distance into the other straw branch. Do not touch the swab end.

6. As directed in "Making And Using A WOWBug Choice Tunnel," use the "stem" straw to move 6–10 WOWBugs from the culture container into the choice tunnel. Hold the filled choice tunnel vertically, with the two branches facing up in the air like a "Y."

Holding the two branches up will increase the speed of the insects' choice. They move toward light, so they will tend to crawl up to the branches of the "Y".

Trial 1.

7. Look at your watch (or a clock), and write down the exact time. Open one end of the stem straw containing the WOWBugs and quickly connect it to the stem of the "Y". Watch the WOWBugs carefully for 3 minutes. Count the number that enter each of the two branches of the choice tunnel (even if they later leave). Enter these tallies in the data summary sheet provided.

You can have the students observe longer than 3 minutes. This will give the insects more time to choose one path or the other. Of course, the students' attention may drift, too, if the time is longer!

8. At the end of this time, remove each tube and plug the open end with a swab. Then count how many insects are in the branch with the perfumed swab, and write this number down in the data summary chart. Count and record how many are in the branch with the watered swab. If there are insects that did not choose either branch, write this down too.

9. Tap the WOWBugs out of all the parts of the choice tunnel and put them back in the storage container. Throw away the used straws and swabs.

Trial 2.

10. Repeat your experiment with the same conditions of

the manipulated variable, but instead of putting the black-marked, odorous swab in the left straw branch, put it in the <u>right</u> branch. The water will now be in the left branch.

11. Record the results of this second testing. Be sure to remember that the left and right branches have been reversed from the first testing!

12. Now, combine the results of Test 1A and Test 1B, and record these numbers on the data sheet.

Part B. A Different Set Of Odor Conditions

If time permits, run new trials following the same procedure, but use a different pair of conditions for the manipulated variable. For example, if you used perfume as the odorous liquid for Part A, switch to vinegar. Before starting, write down your hypothesis for how the WOWBugs will react to this odor.

If there is not enough time for each group to test more than one odor, you may want to have each group test a different one and share results with the rest of the class. If you have more time, the students can do more runs with the same variable, or can test more different variables.

Discussion

Answer questions 1 to 6 from the list provided by your teacher.

7. Why was it important to use new straws and swabs for each different manipulated variable?

So that only the variable we wanted to test would be present.

8. Why did we put water on the control swab, instead of putting nothing on it?

To make sure factors like wetness or humidity did not influence the test results.

Concept Application And Elaboration:

1. Smell and taste are very closely related senses. To determine this for yourself, use pieces of peeled and cut raw potatoes and apples. Work with a partner. Take turns blindfolding each other and offering the two foods. Hold your nose closed with the fingers of one hand while you taste the sample your partner provides on a tooth-pick. Try to identify it without seeing or smelling it. Then breathe normally whle trying again.

New Terms:

choice tunnel

control

hypothesis

manipulated variable

olfaction

2. Chemical communication is the most thoroughly studied of all the insect sensory modes. Insects produce an awesome variety and complexity of odors, and insect odor receptors are no less complex and sophisticated. Find out more about one or more of the following:

a. sensilla (chemoreceptor cells found on the surface of insects' bodies)
b. odor-sensitive cells found on insect antennae
c. pheromones (substances that insect secrete that affect the behavior of others of their own species)
d. hairpencils (special scent-producing organs on the tip of many male butterflies' abdomens)

3. Draw a diagram of an insect antenna. Label its impor-tant parts. Write a caption for the diagram, explaining what each part does.

Tastes Good! Or Does It?

Getting Ready: Be sure to read the introductory and Getting Ready sections earlier in this chapter.

Objectives: Determine the effect of different tastes on WOWBug location choices, and in this way gain an insight into their sensory world.

If you are presented with a strange dish, what do you do? Probably you begin by looking it over and then cautiously smelling it. If it looks and smells all right, you might take a nibble. Only after the item passed all these tests would you proceed to eat it.

This is obviously a prudent way to behave. But you are a highly intelligent – and hungry! – animal, compared to a WOWBug. In the past, scientists said an adult WOWBug doesn't even need to eat! Recently, however, female WOWBugs have been observed sucking the fluid from their hosts, and males have been seen chewing on the bodies of dead male victims. With such strange appetites as these, what tastes good to a WOWBug?

Materials (per team of students):

• clear plastic straws (about 20)

• WOWBugs stock culture

• white paper or paper plate

• cotton swabs (about 10)

• "Y" connector

• scissors

• millimeter ruler

• small watercolor paintbrush or pipe cleaner

• droppers or pipettes

• water

• tonic water, sugar water, and other liquids with pronounced flavor but very little odor

Feel free to test other tasty things that dissolve in water as well! You may wish to brainstorm various possibilities with students before beginning this experiment.

To avoid spills and contamination, see tips for the previous activity.

Part A. What Tastes Good To A Female WOWBug?

For this experiment, we will be testing how taste influences WOWBugs' behavior. We will have two choices for where the insects can go. In one, we will put a liquid with a taste but no real identifiable smell (at least to our human senses!). In the other, we will put water, which doesn't have a special taste or smell (at least to us!).

As this paragraph implies, the bias introduced by our own sensory system is a major problem with any sensory response experiment.

With taste, the problem is particularly acute. Olfaction is in fact so difficult to separate from taste that some researchers call it "distance taste." However, we have included this activity because students ask for it, and we feel that it is important that students grapple with real-world limitations rather than experiencing only the parts of scientific inquiry that make it look easy.

1. To test which way the WOWBugs will go, we need to provide two choices. To make a **choice tunnel,** follow the instructions your teacher provides. To make sure that the straws and swabs do not get contaminated by something different than what we want to test, you will have to attach new straws and swabs for each different trial.

2. Choose a strong-tasting liquid to test. Record what it is. Do you think the WOWBugs will prefer to move into the tube with the strong taste (the first condition of the manipulated variable) or into the tube without the taste (the alternate condition of the manipulated variable), or will they have no preference and move into both branches equally? Write down your hypothesis.

3. Take a cotton swab and cut it into two pieces with the scissors. They do not have to be the exact same length. Put a black mark on the handle of one piece so that you

can tell them apart.

4. Put one drop of the test substance onto the end of the black-marked swab piece and insert it into the <u>left</u> straw branch. Do not touch the end of the swab with your fingers.

The students will alternate putting the control liquid into the left and right branches, to make sure that no outside variable (such as the light source) is affecting the insects' choices. If students have had relatively little practice with droppers or pipettes, you may want to have them do this step over a paper towel.

5. Put one drop of water onto the other piece of the swab. Poke it into the other straw branch to about the same distance as the black-marked swab.

Trial 1.

6. Follow the directions on "Making And Using A WOWBug Choice Tunnel" to move 6–10 WOWBugs into the stem piece of the choice tunnel. Hold the filled choice tunnel vertically, with the two branches facing up in the air like a "Y".

Holding the two branches up will increase the speed of the insects' choice. They move toward light, so they will tend to crawl up to the branches of the "Y".

7. Look at your watch (or a clock), and write down the exact time. For the next 3 minutes, keep a written tally of the number of times a WOWBug <u>touches</u> the cotton swab in each branch of the "Y." You'll need to work closely as a pair or team. Record your tally on the data chart.

Since by definition taste requires direct contact with the test substance, for this experiment it is essential that WOWBugs actually touch the cotton.

You can have the students observe longer than 3 minutes. This will give the insects more time to choose one path or the other, but students' attention may drift, too!

8. At the end of this time, remove each tube and plug the open end with a clean swab. Count how many insects are in the branch with the flavored swab, and write this number down on the data chart. Count and record how many are in the branch with the watered swab, and write this number down. If there are insects that did not choose either branch, write this down too.

Comparing the number of actual touches with the final counts in each branch is a control, of sorts, for the influence of olfaction on the results.

9. Take the WOWBugs out of all parts of the choice tunnel and put them back in the storage container. Discard the used straws and swabs.

Trial 2.

Repeat the experiment, with the same two conditions of the manipulated variable as the first time. However, instead of putting the (black-marked) flavored swab (the manipulated variable) in the left straw branch, put it in the <u>right</u> branch. The watered swab (our other condition) will now be in the left branch.

Write down the results of this second testing as before. (Be sure to remember that the left and right branches have been reversed from the first testing!) Then combine the results of Trial 1 and Trial 2. Record your combined results on the data chart.

Part B. Further Tests And Original Experimentation

If time permits, many additional possibilities can be tested. For example, you might run the same trials as Part A, but use male WOWBugs. Or you could compare different chemical solutions. Or look at the possibility of different responses from female WOWBugs before and after they have encountered (and thus have probably fed on) a host. This would all be new data. Scientists have never investigated such questions.

Whatever experimental question you decide to investigate, remember to carefully formulate your hypothesis, determine the conditions of your manipulated variable, and outline the steps you will take to control other possible variables.

Discussion

Answer Questions 1 to 6 from the list provided by your teacher.

Answers to 1. and 2. may vary, depending upon the substances tested. Probably the students will find no preference, as shown from about equal numbers in each tube.

7. How did measuring the results in terms of "touches" differ from measuring them in terms of "total final number in the branch"? What reasons might there be for obtaining both sorts of data?

Results may vary, depending upon the substances tested. Probably the students found few differences, with about equal numbers in each tube. Elicit the idea that if smell were involved, it could influence the final numbers that stayed in the tube, even if the insects couldn't taste any differences between the two substances.

8. Why was it important to use new straws and swabs for each different condition of the manipulated variable and each different trial?

So that only the variable we wanted to test would be present. Otherwise, we couldn't be sure the straws hadn't become contaminated with traces of previously used substances or by something the insects themselves had left behind.

9. If we had left the second swab dry rather than putting water on it, how might our results have differed?

Factors like wetness or humidity might have influenced the test results, or WOWBugs might have gone to the moist swab simply because they were thirsty.

10. What reasons can you suggest why might it be important for insects to be able to detect different flavors?

To find the right kind of food, to avoid eating poisonous items, to find an appropriate host, etc.

New Terms:

choice tunnel

Concept Application And Elaboration:

control

1. See ideas in "Odor Responses" activity in this chapter.

hypothesis

2. Just for fun, play Scrambled Spelling. Divide the class into teams of 4-6 people. Each team will need paper and a pencil. Have each team choose a recorder. The teacher calls out a series of letters which, when unscrambled, make a word. The recorder for each team writes them down. Then each team works together to try to reassemble them into a word.

manipulated variable

When the team has made the word, all the members raise their hands. The teacher calls on the first team to do so. If correct, they are awarded 2 points. If wrong, they lose 1 point and can't answer again during that round. The teacher then calls on the next team to raise its hands.

When a word is guessed, the teacher goes on to the next set of scrambled letters.

Some WOWBug word makers:

ssyoren (sensory), noitcafol (olfaction), chotu (touch), oomnetygol (entomology), nooocc (cocoon), eappu (pupae), etisrapa (parasite), tensnig (nesting), leam (male), ttboialemi (Melittobia).

Sound: Rockin' WOWBugs

Getting Ready: Be sure to read the introductory section earlier in this chapter. You will also need to modify the choice tunnel; see directions in Chapter 8.

Objectives: Determine the effects of sound on WOWBug location choices, and in this way gain an indication of their sensory world.

If you come to a fork in the road, how do you choose which path to take? If one of the trails had pleasant musical sounds or laughter, you might choose that path. Or you might use your other senses to smell or look. Would an insect choose a road the same way that you do?

Because music is important in their own world, students invariably want to test WOWBugs' reactions to various types. The concept of the relevance of such choices to insects seems to develop only much later, and with a fair amount of teacher guidance.

How does noise or sound affect the way WOWBugs react? For this experiment, we will give WOWBugs two choices. For the first condition of the manipulated variable, we will pipe in some type of recorded music. For the other, we will use a cotton swab to block sound. We'll attempt to control other variables such as light direction.

Materials (per team):

- clear plastic straws (about 10)
- WOWBugs stock culture
- white paper or paper plate
- cotton swabs (about 10)
- "Y" connector
- scissors
- millimeter ruler
- small watercolor paintbrush or pipe cleaner
- Walkman™ or other small tape player, with headphones
- 2 tapes with different music (for example, rock, classical, new age, country, lullabies)
- film canister modified into a sound chamber

Part A. Rockin' WOWBugs

1. Make a choice tunnel, following the directions your teacher provides.

See the instructions in Chapter 8 for making these sound chambers ahead of time.

2. Choose a type of music from those available. Do you think the WOWBugs will prefer to move into the tube with this sound (the first condition of the manipulated variable) or into the tube without any sound (the second condition), or will they have no preference and move into both branches equally? Write down your hypothesis.

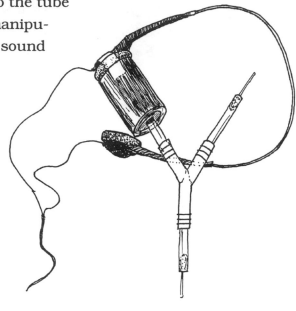

Help students appreciate that sound volume may be an important variable in this experiment. Encourage them to use a predetermined low volume setting.

3. Assemble the sound chamber if this hasn't already been done. Place it on the left branch of the choice tunnel. One person should help make sure the speaker stays securely on the branch during the rest of the experiment, and that the other earphone stays away from the other branch.

The students will alternate putting the control into the left and right branches. This is to make sure that no outside variable (such as the light source) is affecting the insects' choices.

4. Load the "stem" straw with 6–10 WOWBugs as directed in "Making And Using A WOWBug Choice Tunnel." Hold the filled choice tunnel up and down, with the two branches facing up in the air like a "Y."

Holding the two branches up will increase the speed of the insects' choice. They move toward light, so they will tend to crawl up to the branches of the "Y".

Trial 1.

5. Turn on the music <u>very softly</u>! Look at your watch (or a clock), and write down the exact time.

6. Watch the WOWBugs carefully for 3 minutes. Count how many enter each arm of the "Y" and record this tally on the data sheet provided.

You can have the students observe longer than 3 minutes. This will give the insects more time to choose one path or the other. Of course, the students' attention may drift, too.

7. At the end of this time, remove each tube and plug the open end with a cotton swab piece. Count how many insects are in the branch with the music, and write this number down. Count and write down how many are in the branch with the swab. If there are insects that did not choose either branch, write this down too.

8. Take all the WOWBugs out of the choice tunnel apparatus and put them back in their container.

Trial 2.

9. Repeat the experiment, with the same recording (first condition of the manipulated variable) as the first time. Instead of putting the music in the left straw branch, pipe it into the right branch. As you record your results, be sure to remember that the left and right branches have been reversed from the first testing!

10. Combine the results of Trial 1 and Trial 2, and record the totals on the data sheet. What is the reason for combining the trial results?

Reversing the directions helps control for directional variables such as light that might otherwise influence the results.

Part B. Different Musical Tastes?

If time permits, you might like to try a different kind of music. Before starting, write down your hypothesis for how the WOWBugs will react to this sound.

If there is not enough time for each group to test more than one kind of music, you may want to have each group test only one, then combine class results.

Repeat the procedures you used in Part A. There are two schools of thought about whether to use the same WOWBugs or a new set. What advantages and disadvantages might there be to either choice? Make a decision which you want to do, and record it.

Assuming all WOWBugs react the same, fresh insects might respond more promptly. However, if all WOWBugs do not react the same, they also might introduce more variation. This question could lead to discussion of the concept of adequate sample size for this, and in fact all WOWBug sensory experiments.

At this point, you can "innocently" ask students to look carefully at the experimental design and the apparatus. Oh no, there is an uncontrolled variable! What is it? How can we fix this problem?

Help students discover that the use of a dark film canister introduces a possible confounding variable. How does one know that the WOWBugs aren't avoiding the music simply because they don't want to go back towards the dark? One could run more trials, either substituting a clear film canister or putting an additional dark one on the opposite arm of the apparatus. This idea has more impact if you wait until after students have conducted the experiment before you point out your "discovery" of this "problem." If possible, allow interested students to conduct the additional trials, outside class if necessary.

Discussion

Answer Questions 1 to 6 from the list provided by your teacher.

1. Probably the insects did not care if there was music, and went to each tube in equal numbers.

7. What are some reasons why the music or sound should be very soft in this experiment?

So sound didn't come from all directions; so it was not so loud it might irritate them; because insects, like dogs, might be able to detect very soft sounds; so that other experiments and students weren't disturbed; etc.

8. Why might it be important for insects to be able to detect different sounds? What kinds of sounds might have meaning to a WOWBug?

New Terms:

acoustic

choice tunnel

control

hypothesis

manipulated variable

Possibly for location of food, home, mates, enemies, etc. They might respond to the buzzing of a mud dauber wasp or a blowfly, for example.

9. The word **acoustic** describes things pertaining to the sense of hearing. What do each of the terms below mean? Working together, figure out a simple definition for each. Name at least one more way "acoustic" is used.

acoustical tile: *soft-surfaced (often perforated) coverings used on ceilings, and sometimes on walls, to reduce the way sounds are reflected around the room.*
theater acoustics: *the qualities that determine how well sound can be heard in it.*
insect acoustic communication: *sounds given off by one insect that cause a behavioral change in another.*

Additional possibilities include acoustic guitar, acoustic channels in the ears, and acoustic assistive devices (hearing aids).

Concept Application And Elaboration:

1. Among the insects, "hearing" is best demonstrated in Orthoptera (grasshoppers, crickets, and their kin), Homoptera (cicadas), Coleoptera (beetles), and Diptera (flies). Produce an illustrated report on a sound-producing insect in one of these orders. Tell how it makes the sound and how it receives it.

Bennet-Clark, J.C. and A.W. Ewing. 1970. The love song of the fruit fly. *Scientific American* 233: 84-92 (July).

Cade, W. 1975. Acoustically orienting parasitoids: fly phonotaxis to cricket song. *Science* 190: 1312-1313.

2. Read one of the articles to the left, and present a brief oral summary to your class.

Temperature: Hot Stuff and Cold Feet

In your house in the winter, would you rather be in a room that is warm or one that is cold? What about during the summer? Would an insect choose the same way that you do? How does a change in temperature affect the way WOWBugs react?

For this experiment, we will be testing how temperature influences WOWBugs. We will have two choices for where the insects can go. In one, we will have the warm or cold temperature. In the other, we will not change the room temperature.

Most people think of insects as being purely "cold-blooded," passively reflecting the temperatures that surround them in their environment. The truth is more complex. Many have ways to change their body temperature. Some rely on physiology (such as metabolic heat). More common, however, are behavioral responses to perceived changes in external temperature. Some insects simply move away from heat or cold. Others seek it out.

Materials (per team):

- clear straws (about 20)
- WOWBugs stock culture
- white paper or paper plate
- cotton swabs (about 10)
- "Y" connector
- scissors
- millimeter ruler
- small watercolor paintbrush or pipe cleaner
- a small resealable bag *(Bags used to freeze food, such as Zip Loc™ brand, are most reliable.)*
- small thermometer
- pot-holder or insulated glove
- hot and cold water
- ice

Getting Ready: Be sure to read the introductory section earlier in this chapter. This experiment involves a few more calculations than the others. The results also are likely to vary with changes in the length of the experimental trials and differences in temperatures tested.

Objectives: Determine the effects of temperature on WOWBug location choices.

Part A. Effects of Heating

1. To test which way WOWBugs will go, we need to make sure they only have two choices. Make a choice tunnel, following the instructions your teacher provides.

2. Do you think the WOWBugs will prefer to be warmer than they presently are, or not? Or won't it matter to them? Write down your hypothesis.

This will vary depending on conditions; see teacher comments for discussion question no. 1.

3. To provide warmth for one arm of the choice tunnel, we'll be using a bag of hot water. The person from your group who is going to handle the hot water should use the pot holder or glove. This student needs to <u>carefully</u> put a little hot water into a resealable bag (until it is about 1/4 full). Squeeze it gently to get most of the air out, and zip it <u>completely</u> closed. It is very important to be careful with this step! Do not scald yourself or other students! Then, lay the bag flat on the table.

The water needs to stay hot for two runs of the experiment. Make sure it is not hot enough to scald the students or soften the bag!

4. Position the <u>left</u> straw so that it lays on the bag, touching it all along the straw's length. You may need to put pencils under the other straws to make the tunnels all level.

5. Look at the thermometer and record the temperature of the room. (This surrounding air temperature is called the **ambient temperature**.) Then, take the thermometer, and insert it into a piece of straw. Lay it on the bag as well.

Students will alternate the temperature of the left and right branches. This is to make sure that no outside variable, such as lighting, is affecting the insects' choices.

6. As directed in "Making And Using A WOWBug Choice Tunnel," use the "stem" straw to move 6-10 WOWBugs from the culture container into the stem piece of the choice tunnel.

Trial 1.

7. Adjust the apparatus on the bag. Look at your watch (or a clock), and write down the exact time. For the next 3 minutes, count how many WOWBugs enter each arm of the "Y" tube. Record this tally on your data chart.

8. At the end of 3 minutes, remove each tube and plug the open ends with a cotton swab piece. Then count how many insects are in the branch with the changed temperature, and write this number down on the data chart. Count and record how many are in the branch at room temperature. If there are insects that did not choose either branch, write this down too.

Students can observe longer than 3 minutes to give the insects more time to choose one path or the other. However, some students' attention may drift. Results may change (due to humidity changes) if the experiment is allowed to continue for 10 minutes or more. Time permitting, some students could try this.

9. Take the WOWBugs out of all parts of the choice tunnel and put them back in their container. Discard the straws and swabs that were used, and replace them with fresh ones. Why is this precaution necessary?

Reusing the straws might introduce new variables. For example, the insects might react to chemicals laid down by others.

Trial 2.

10. Repeat the same steps, but instead of putting the left straw branch on the warm-water bag, put the <u>right</u>

branch on it. Write down the results of this second testing. Be sure to remember that the left and right branches have been reversed from the first testing!

11. Now, combine the results of the two trials, and record these numbers on the data chart.

Part B. Effects of Cooling

12. Perform the same experiment, but with a different manipulated variable. This time, instead of warming the straw, cool it. Pour out the warm water in the bag. Put a few cubes of ice and a little cold water in the bag (to about 1/4 full), then close it tightly. Lay it down on the paper towel.

13. Before starting, write down your hypothesis for how WOWBugs will react to this temperature change. Do you think they will prefer to be cooler than ambient temperature, or not? Or won't it matter to them?

This will depend on the conditions of the experiments. See discussion question no. 2, below.

14. Run the trials as described for Part A. Do two trials, reversing left and right. Then combine your data.

If there is not enough time for each group to test both temperatures, you may want to have each group test only one manipulated variable, but have different groups using different temperatures. If you have more time, the students can do more runs with the same variable, or can test more different variables.

Discussion

Answer Questions 1 to 6 from the list provided by your teacher.

1. Part A tested additional warmth vs. ambient temperature. WOWBugs usually avoid the warmed branch, but since the intensity of the heat will vary, under some conditions the warmed branch might be quite attractive. You may want to correlate class results with the groups' mean temperatures of the water. This is a good opportunity to practice graphing skills.

2. Part B tested ambient temperature vs. cooler air. Usually, coolness is not attractive. However, especially when this test is allowed to run for about 10 minutes, most of the insects will probably be found in the cool arm straw. Because cold air promotes condensation of water, this may be the result of the increased relative humidity in the straw, rather than the cool temperature per se.

The evidence is the number of insects in each branch. Analyze data both in terms of numbers of entries and as final numbers. Help students recognize that the insects that enter the cool arm tend to become cooled and slow down. This makes them less likely to leave, since they're moving slowly.

7. How could you change this test to get more conclusive results?

The temperatures could be made even more extreme.

8. **Humidity** — the atmosphere's moisture content — is a primary element of climate. The amount of water vapor that air can hold changes with the temperature of the air. Thus, we speak of **relative humidity**, the ratio of the actual water-vapor content of the air to its total capacity at the given temperature. Does air hold more water vapor, or less, as it cools off? How does this affect the relative humidity?

Cooler air holds less water. Thus, even though the absolute amount of water in the air may be low, if the temperature is also low, the air may be nearly "full" or saturated. The relative humidity is therefore very high.

9. Why is it important to make sure the water does not drip from the bag into the straw? Do you think the absence of drips controlled completely for this variable? Why or why not?

To make sure factors like humidity or presence of water did not influence the test results. No. For the cool experiment, the cooler air probably had a higher relative humidity anyway.

10. How could you design an experiment to separate the effects of temperature and humidity?

Use a chemical agent to keep the air dry; test different relative humidity levels while keeping the temperature constant; etc.

New Terms:

ambient temperature

choice tunnel

humidity

hypothesis

manipulated variable

relative humidity

11. How might it benefit WOWBugs to be able to respond to temperature?

Because hosts are in sheltered areas, avoidance of heat and attention to cooler areas would tend to bring the WOWBugs in contact with potential hosts.

Concept Application And Elaboration:

1. How do insects stay warm? Do any insects shiver? How do scientists know? And:

2. How do insects stay cool? Do any insects sweat? Find and report on the answers by reading one of these:

Heinrich, B. 1993. *The hot-blooded insects: strategies and mechanisms of thermoregulation.* Cambridge: Harvard Univ. Press. 601 pp.

Matthews, R.W. and J.R. Matthews. 1978. "Regulation of heat gain," pages 105-106, in *Insect Behavior.* New York: Wiley.

3. Crickets chirp less and more slowly when the temperature drops. Many people think that by counting the number of chirps a cricket makes in 15 seconds, then adding 40, they will know the air temperature in degrees Fahrenheit. Is this really true? Design an experiment to research this question. Then get some crickets from a live-bait store, and actually perform your experiment.

This widely circulated formula is actually not based on common field crickets, but on the less well-known snowy tree cricket. Different cricket species have different chirp patterns.

Discussion Questions For Chapter Five Activities: Decisions, Decisions...

1. In part A, what were the two conditions of the manipulated variable? Did the WOWBugs prefer to move toward either condition, or did they show no preference? What is your evidence?

_____

_____

2. In part B, what were the two conditions of the manipulated variable? Did the WOWBugs prefer to move toward either condition, or did they not discriminate between them? What is your evidence?

_____

_____

3. Did your results support the hypotheses you wrote down at the beginning?

_____

_____

4. Did all the WOWBugs choose the same branch? How can you explain this?

_____

_____

5. Why do you think we did each test twice, putting the manipulated variable on the left and on the right?

_____

_____

6. What other sorts of questions could you test using WOWBugs and choice tunnels?

_____

_____

_____

The Light At The End Of The Tunnel

If you come to a fork in the road, how do you choose which route to take? If one of the ways looks rough and dark, you might choose the smoother, more brightly lit path. Would an animal necessarily choose a road the same way that you do? What about WOWBugs? How does light affect the way they react?

Part A. Effects Of White Light On Female WOWBugs

For this experiment, we will be testing how light influences WOWBugs. When an animal moves towards light, we call this **positive phototaxis**. If it moves away from light, this is **negative phototaxis**.

Objectives: Determine the effects of extra white light and colored light on WOWBug location choices.

Materials (per team):

- *clear straws (about 20)*
- *WOWBugs stock culture*
- *white paper*
- *cotton swabs (about 10)*
- *"Y" connector*
- *scissors*
- *millimeter ruler*
- *small paint brush or pipe cleaner*
- *2 identical small flashlights*
- *3x5-inch index cards*
- *cellophane tape*
- *colored filters*

We will have two choices for where the insects can go (the conditions of our manipulated variable). In one, we will put our extra bright light. In the other, we will not allow extra light. We will attempt to control for all other conditions, such as sound, temperature, etc.

1. To test which way the WOWBugs will go, we need to make sure they only have two choices. Each insect will go through a tube called a **choice tunnel**. (For obvious reasons, some biologists call it a Y-maze.) To construct one, follow the directions your teacher provides.

2. If they are given the choice of going into the tube with the light or into the tube without the extra light, where do you think the WOWBugs will prefer to move? Or will they have no preference and move into both branches equally? Write down your hypothesis below:

_____

_____

3. Get the index card ready. You will need to hold it between the two branches to keep the light away from the control branch. Also, get your flashlight ready. One person should hold the index card in between the two branches. Another student should turn on the flashlight and point it only at the end of the <u>left</u> straw. Hold it steady, or set it on the table. Do not hold it so close that it heats up the straw.

Trial 1.

4. Look at your watch (or a clock), and write down the exact time. Open one end of the "loaded" straw and quickly connect it to the stem of the "Y". Then lay the choice tunnel apparatus on the table and reposition the flashlight and index card.

Watch the WOWBugs carefully for 3 minutes. Keep a tally of the number of WOWBugs entering each branch, and write this total on the data chart. At the end of this time, remove each straw tube and plug the open end with a cotton swab piece. Then count how many insects are in the branch with the light, and write this number down. Count and record the number of insects that are in the branch with no extra light. Are there insects that did not choose either branch? (Check in the bottom and in the Y-tube connector.) How many? _____

5. Take the WOWBugs out of all the parts of the choice tunnel and put them back in their container. Throw away the used straws and swabs. (Why not use them over? Think of a reason related to the experiment.)

_____

_____

Trial 2.

6. Repeat the steps above, but instead of putting the extra light on the left straw branch, put it on the <u>right</u> branch. The other condition (no extra light) will then be the left branch. Why should you do this? What might happen if you didn't?

_____

_____

7. Record the results of this second testing on the chart. Be sure to remember that the left and right branches have been reversed from the first testing!

8. Now, combine the results of both trials, and record the totals on the data chart. What is the reason for this step?

_____

Part B. Effects Of Colored Light

Run the same tests with a different condition of the manipulated variable. This time, instead of regular white light, use colored light. With a rubber band, fasten a colored filter over the end of the flashlight. The other condition of the manipulated variable will be a second flashlight without a filter, pointed at the other straw.

Before starting, write down your hypothesis for how the WOWBugs will react to this light. Then proceed as before. Be sure to write down which Y-arm received which condition of the manipulated variable.

Hypothesis: _____

_____

Discussion

Answer Questions 1 to 6 from the list provided by your teacher.

7. How could you change this test to have even bigger differences in the amount of light in each branch?

_____

_____

8. Why is it important to make sure the light does not heat up the branch?

_____

_____

9. Why might it be important for WOWBugs to move toward light? How would their lives be different if they did not? (Hint: Think about where they normally would live.)

_____

_____

_____

Odor Responses

Objectives: Determine the effect of different smells on WOWBug behavior, and thus infer something about their sensory world.

Materials (per team):

- *clear straws (about 20)*
- *WOWBugs stock culture*
- *white paper*
- *cotton swabs (about 10)*
- *"Y" connector*
- *scissors*
- *millimeter ruler*
- *small watercolor paintbrush or pipe cleaner*
- *2 droppers*
- *2 plastic film canisters (empty)*
- *vinegar, cologne, and other clear but odorous liquids*
- *water*

If you come to a fork in the road, how do you choose which route to take? If one of the paths smelled awful and one smelled yummy, you might choose the sweet-smelling path. Would an insect choose a road the same way that you do?

For this experiment, we will be testing how **olfaction**, or smell, influences WOWBugs. We will have two choices for where the insects can go. In one, we will put the "smelly" condition of the manipulated variable — something like perfume or vinegar. In the other, we will put water, which, although a liquid, doesn't have a smell (at least according to our own senses).

How will these different olfactory conditions affect the way WOWBugs react?

Part A. Testing A Noticeable Odor And Water

1. To test which way the WOWBugs will go, we need to make sure they only have two choices. Each insect will go through a tube called a **choice tunnel**.

To make a choice tunnel, follow the instructions your teacher provides. Use new straws and swabs for each test. Give a reason why this might be important.

_____

_____

2. From the choices available, pick an odor to test. Record it on your data sheet. Now we want to write a hypothesis. Do you think the WOWBugs will prefer to move into the tube with the smell or into the tube without it? Or will they have no preference and move into both branches equally? Write down your hypothesis:

_____

_____

3. Take a cotton swab and cut it into two pieces with the scissors. They do not have to be the exact same length. So that you will be able to tell the two pieces apart, put a black mark on the handle of one piece.

4. Put one small drop of the perfume you are testing onto the cottony end of the black-marked swab piece. This is the first condition of the manipulated variable. Then, stick the perfumed end into the <u>left</u> straw branch. Do not touch the swab end.

5. Put one small drop of water onto the other piece of the swab. Stick it the same distance into the other straw branch. Do not touch the swab end.

6. As directed in "Making And Using A WOWBug Choice Tunnel," use the "stem" straw to move 6–10 WOWBugs from the culture container into the choice tunnel. Hold the filled choice tunnel vertically, with the two branches facing up in the air like a "Y."

Trial 1.

7. Look at your watch (or a clock), and write down the exact time. Open one end of the stem straw containing the WOWBugs and quickly connect it to the stem of the "Y". Watch the WOWBugs carefully for 3 minutes. Count the number that enter each of the two branches of the choice tunnel (even if they later leave). Enter these tallies in the data summary sheet provided.

8. At the end of this time, remove each tube and plug the open end with a swab. Then count how many insects are in the branch with the perfumed swab, and write this number down in the data summary chart. Count and record how many are in the branch with the watered swab. If there are insects that did not choose either branch, write this down too.

9. Tap the WOWBugs out of all the parts of the choice tunnel and put them back in the storage container. Throw away the used straws and swabs.

Trial 2.

10. Repeat your experiment with the same conditions of the manipulated variable, but instead of putting the black-marked, odorous swab in the left straw branch, put it in the right branch. The water will now be in the left branch.

11. Record the results of this second testing. Be sure to remember that the left and right branches have been reversed from the first testing!

12. Now, combine the results of Test 1A and Test 1B, and record these numbers on the data sheet.

Part B. A Different Set Of Odor Conditions

If time permits, run new trials following the same procedure, but use a different pair of conditions for the manipulated variable. For example, if you used perfume as the odorous liquid for Part A, switch to vinegar. Before starting, write down your hypothesis for how the WOWBugs will react to this odor.

_____

_____

Discussion

Answer Questions 1 to 6 from the list provided by your teacher.

7. Why was it important to use new straws and swabs for each different condition of the manipulated variable?

_____

_____

8. Why did we put water on the control swab, instead of putting nothing on it?

_____

_____

_____

Tastes Good! Or Does It?

Objectives: Determine the effect of different tastes on WOWBug location choices, and in this way gain an insight into their sensory world.

Materials (per team):

- *clear straws (about 20)*
- *WOWBugs stock culture*
- *white paper or paper plate*
- *cotton swabs (about 10)*
- *"Y" connector*
- *scissors*
- *millimeter ruler*
- *small watercolor paintbrush or pipe cleaner*
- *droppers or pipettes*
- *water*
- *tonic water, sugar water, and other liquids with pronounced flavor but very little odor*

If you are presented with a strange dish, what do you do? Probably you begin by looking it over and then cautiously smelling it. If it looks and smells all right, you might take a nibble. Only after the item passed all these tests would you proceed to eat it.

This is obviously a prudent way to behave. But you are a highly intelligent – and hungry! – animal, compared to a WOWBug. In the past, scientists said an adult WOWBug doesn't even need to eat! Recently, however, female WOWBugs have been observed sucking the fluid from their hosts, and males have been seen chewing on the bodies of dead male victims. With such strange appetites as these, what tastes good to a WOWBug?

Part A. What Tastes Good To A Female WOWBug?

For this experiment, we will be testing how taste influences WOWBugs' behavior. We will have two choices for where the insects can go. In one, we will put a liquid with a taste but no real identifiable smell (at least to our human senses!). In the other, we will put water, which doesn't have a special taste or smell (at least to us!).

1. To test which way the WOWBugs will go, we need to provide two choices. To make a **choice tunnel,** follow the instructions your teacher provides. To make sure that the straws and swabs do not get contaminated by

something different than what we want to test, attach new straws and swabs for each different trial.

2. Choose a strong-tasting liquid to test. Record what it is. Do you think the WOWBugs will prefer to move into the tube with the strong taste (the first condition of the manipulated variable) or into the tube without the taste (the alternate condition of the manipulated variable), or will they have no preference and move into both branches equally? Write down your hypothesis.

_____

_____

3. Take a cotton swab and cut it into two pieces with the scissors. They do not have to be the exact same length. Put a black mark on the handle of one piece so that you can tell them apart.

4. Put one drop of the test substance onto the end of the black-marked swab piece and insert it into the <u>left</u> straw branch. Do not touch the end of the swab with your fingers.

5. Put one drop of water onto the other piece of the swab. Poke it into the other straw branch to about the same distance as the black-marked swab.

Trial 1.

6. Follow the directions on "Making And Using A WOWBug Choice Tunnel" to move 6–10 WOWBugs into the stem piece of the choice tunnel. Hold the filled choice tunnel vertically, with the two branches facing up in the air like a "Y."

7. Look at your watch (or a clock), and write down the exact time. For the next 3 minutes, keep a written tally of the number of times a WOWBug <u>touches</u> the cotton swab in each branch of the "Y." You'll need to work closely as a pair or team. Record your tally on the data chart.

8. At the end of this time, remove each tube and plug the open end with a clean swab. Count how many insects are in the branch with the flavored swab, and write this number down on the data chart. Count and record how many are in the branch with the watered swab, and write this number down. If there are insects that did not choose either branch, write this down too.

9. Take the WOWBugs out of all parts of the choice tunnel and put them back in the storage container. Discard the used straws and swabs.

Trial 2.

Repeat the experiment, with the same two conditions of the manipulated variable as the first time. However, instead of putting the (black-marked) flavored swab (the manipulated variable) in the left straw branch, put it in the <u>right</u> branch. The watered swab (our other condition) will now be in the left branch.

Write down the results of this second testing as before. (Be sure to remember that the left and right branches have been reversed from the first testing!) Then combine the results of Trial 1 and Trial 2. Record your combined results on the data chart.

Part B. Further Tests And Original Experimentation

If time permits, many additional possibilities can be tested. For example, you might run the same trials as Part A, but use male WOWBugs. Or you could compare different chemical solutions. Or look at the possibility of different responses from female WOWBugs before and after they have encountered (and thus have probably fed on) a host. This would all be new data. Scientists have never investigated such questions.

Whatever experimental question you decide to investigate, remember to carefully formulate your hypothesis, determine the conditions of your manipulated variable, and outline the steps you will take to control other possible variables.

Discussion

Answer Questions 1 to 6 from the list provided by your teacher.

7. How did measuring the results in terms of "touches" differ from measuring them in terms of "total final number in the branch"? What reasons might there be for obtaining both sorts of data?

_____

_____

_____

8. Why was it important to use new straws and swabs for each different condition of the manipulated variable and each different trial?

_____

_____

9. If we had left the second swab dry rather than putting water on it, how might our results have differed?

_____

_____

10. What reasons can you suggest why might it be important for insects to be able to detect different flavors?

_____

_____

Sound: Rockin' WOWBugs

Objectives: Determine the effects of sound on WOWBug location choices, and in this way gain an indication of their sensory world.

Materials (per team):

- *clear plastic straws (about 10)*
- *WOWBugs stock culture*
- *white paper or paper plate*
- *cotton swabs (about 10)*
- *"Y" connector*
- *scissors*
- *millimeter ruler*
- *small watercolor paintbrush or pipe cleaner*
- *Walkman™ or other small tape player, with headphones*
- *2 tapes with different music (for example, rock, classical, new age, country, lullabies)*
- *film canister modified into a sound chamber*

If you come to a fork in the road, how do you choose which path to take? If one of the trails had pleasant musical sounds or laughter, you might choose that path. Or you might use your other senses to smell or look.

How does noise or sound affect the way WOWBugs react? For this experiment, we will give WOWBugs two choices. For the first condition of the manipulated variable, we will pipe in some type of recorded music. For the other, we will use a cotton swab to block sound. We'll attempt to control other variables such as light direction.

Part A. Rockin' WOWBugs

1. Make a choice tunnel, following the directions your teacher provides.

2. Choose a type of music from those available. Do you think the WOWBugs will prefer to move into the tube with this sound (the first condition of the manipulated variable) or into the tube without any sound (the second condition), or will they have no preference and move into both branches equally? Write down your hypothesis.

_____

_____

3. Assemble the sound chamber if this hasn't already been done. Place it on the left branch of the choice tunnel. One person should help make sure the speaker stays securely on the branch during the rest of the experiment, and that the other earphone stays away from the other branch.

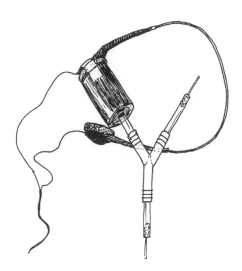

4. Load the "stem" straw with 6–10 WOWBugs as directed in "Making And Using A WOWBug Choice Tunnel." Hold the filled choice tunnel up and down, with the two branches facing up in the air like a "Y."

Trial 1.

5. Turn on the music <u>very softly</u>! Look at your watch (or a clock), and write down exactly what time it is.

6. Watch the WOWBugs carefully for 3 minutes. Count how many enter each arm of the "Y" and record this tally on the data sheet.

7. At the end of this time, remove each tube and plug the open end with a cotton swab piece. Count how many insects are in the branch with the music, and write this number down. Count how many are in the branch with the swab, and write this number down. If there are insects that did not choose either branch, write this down too.

8. Take all the WOWBugs out of the choice tunnel and put them back in their container.

Trial 2.

9. Repeat the experiment, with the same recording (first condition of the manipulated variable) as the first time. Instead of putting the music in the left straw branch, pipe it into the <u>right</u> branch. As you record your results, be sure to remember that the left and right branches have been reversed from the first testing!

10. Combine the results of Trial 1 and Trial 2, and record the totals on the data sheet. What is the reason for combining the trial results?

Part B. Different Musical Tastes?

If time permits, you might like to try a different kind of music. Before starting, write down your hypothesis for how the WOWBugs will react to this sound.

_____

_____

Repeat the procedures you used in Part A. There are two schools of thought about whether to use the same WOWBugs or a new set. What advantages and disadvantages might there be to either choice?

_____

_____

_____

_____

Make a decision which you want to do, and record it.

_____

Discussion

Answer Questions 1 to 6 from the list provided by your teacher.

7. What are some reasons why the music or sound should be very soft in this experiment?

_____

_____

_____

8. Why might it be important for insects to be able to detect different sounds? What kinds of sounds might have meaning to a WOWBug?

_____

_____

_____

9. The word **acoustic** describes things pertaining to the sense of hearing. What do each of the terms below mean? Working together, figure out a simple definition for each of them. Name at least one other way "acoustic" is used: _____

acoustical tile:

_____

_____

theater acoustics:

_____

_____

acoustic communication:

_____

_____

Temperature: Hot Stuff and Cold Feet

Objectives: Determine the effects of temperature on WOWBug location choices.

Materials (per team):

- *clear straws (about 20)*
- *WOWBugs stock culture*
- *white paper or paper plate*
- *cotton swabs (about 10)*
- *"Y" connector*
- *scissors*
- *millimeter ruler*
- *small watercolor paintbrush or pipe cleaner*
- *a small resealable bag*
- *small thermometer*
- *pot-holder or insulated glove*
- *hot and cold water*
- *ice*

In your house in the winter, would you rather be in a room that is warm or one that is cold? What about during the summer? Would an insect choose the same way that you do? How does a change in temperature affect the way WOWBugs react?

For this experiment, we will be testing how temperature influences WOWBugs. We will have two choices for where the insects can go. In one, we will have the warm or cold temperature. In the other, we will not change the room temperature.

Part A. Effects of Heating

1. To test which way WOWBugs will go, we need to make sure they only have two choices. Make a choice tunnel, following the instructions your teacher provides.

2. Do you think the WOWBugs will prefer to be warmer than they presently are, or not? Or won't it matter to them? Write down your hypothesis.

_____

_____

3. To provide warmth for one arm of the choice tunnel, we'll be using a bag of hot water. The person from your group who is going to handle the hot water should use the pot holder or glove. This student needs to <u>carefully</u> put a little hot water into a resealable bag (until it is about 1/4 full). Squeeze it gently to get most of the air out, and zip it <u>completely</u> closed. It is very important to be careful with this step! Do not scald yourself or other students! Then, lay the bag flat on the table.

4. Position the <u>left</u> straw so that it lays on the bag, touching it all along the straw's length. You may need to

put pencils under the other straws to make the tunnels all level.

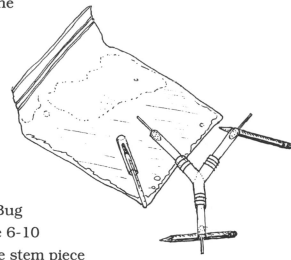

5. Look at the thermometer and record the temperature of the room. (This surrounding air temperature is called the **ambient temperature**.) Then, take the thermometer, and insert it into a piece of straw. Lay it on the bag as well.

6. As directed in "Making And Using A WOWBug Choice Tunnel," use the "stem" straw to move 6-10 WOWBugs from the culture container into the stem piece of the choice tunnel.

Trial 1.

7. Adjust the apparatus on the bag. Look at your watch (or a clock), and write down the exact time. For the next 3 minutes, count how many WOWBugs enter each arm of the "Y" tube. Record this tally on the data sheet provided.

8. At the end of 3 minutes, remove each tube and plug the open ends with a cotton swab piece. Then count how many insects are in the branch with the changed temperature, and write this number down on the data chart. Count and record how many are in the branch at room temperature. If there are insects that did not choose either branch, write this down too.

9. Take the WOWBugs out of all parts of the choice tunnel and put them back in their container. Discard the straws and swabs that were used, and replace them with fresh ones.Why is this precaution necessary?

_____

_____

Trial 2.

10. Repeat the same steps, but instead of putting the left straw branch on the warm-water bag, put the <u>right</u> branch on it. Write down the results of this second testing. Be sure to remember that the left and right branches have been reversed from the first testing!

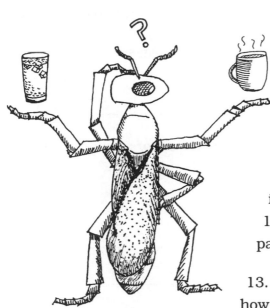

11. Now, combine the results of the two trials, and record these numbers on the data chart.

Part B. Effects of Cooling

12. Perform the same experiment, but with a different manipulated variable. This time, instead of warming the straw, cool it. Pour out the warm water in the bag. Put a few cubes of ice and a little cold water in the bag (to about 1/4 full), then close it tightly. Lay it down on the paper towel.

13. Before starting, write down your hypothesis for how the WOWBugs will react to this temperature change. Do you think they will prefer to be cooler than ambient temperature, or not? Or won't it matter to them?

_____

_____

14. Run the trials as described for Part A. Do two trials, reversing left and right. Then combine your data.

Discussion

Answer Questions 1 to 6 from the list provided by your teacher.

7. How could you change this test to get more conclusive results?

_____

8. **Humidity** — the atmosphere's moisture content — is a primary element of climate. The amount of water vapor that air can hold changes with the temperature of the air. Thus, we speak of **relative humidity**, the ratio of the actual water-vapor content of the air to its total capacity at the given temperature. Does air hold more water vapor, or less, as it cools off? How does this affect the relative humidity?

_____

_____

9. Why is it important to make sure the water does not drip from the bag into the straw? Do you think the absence of drips controlled completely for this variable? Why or why not?

_____

_____

10. How could you design an experiment to separate the effects of temperature and humidity?

_____

_____

_____

_____

11. How might it benefit WOWBugs to be able to respond to temperature?

_____

_____

_____

_____

Chapter Six. Populations And Communities: The Interdependence Of Organisms

Young students tend to interpret phenomena separately rather than as part of a larger system. By the middle grades, it's important to make explicit efforts to encourage a broader vision that not only sees how an individual organism lives, but also appreciates populations, communities, and the ways they interact with one another and with the environment.

Two single class-period activities and one long-term inquiry in this chapter center on various aspects of WOWBug population ecology. The final exercise explores the mud dauber ecosystem in which WOWBugs play a significant role.

Population Sex Ratios

From the two-by-two's of Noah's Ark to children's stories of "mommy and daddy" birds, bears, and elephants, we are conditioned to think of male and female animals as being roughly equal in number. We even tend to think that there are equal numbers of both sexes in people. In fact, statistics reveal that slightly more male than female humans are born each year. Similarly, not all animals have a 50:50 balance of the sexes. In some cases such as humans, this imbalance or "skew" is slight. In others it is much more extreme.

Most aphids (plant lice), for example, have almost entirely dispensed with males. By a type of sexless reproduction called **parthenogenesis**, females give birth to daughters and they in turn to granddaughters all summer long, entirely without males. In the fall, however, a few males are produced and after mating, the females produce eggs instead of giving birth to their young. These eggs then overwinter before hatching to start another all-female population.

Unmated female WOWBugs also are capable of parthenogenesis; see "Momma's Boys" for an activity based on it.

What sort of sex ratio occurs in a typical WOWBug population?

Materials (per student or team):
• Pipe cleaner or small paint brush
• WOWBugs culture at late red-eyed pupa stage
• One sheet of unlined white paper or index card
• Optional: magnifying lens (10x), dissecting microscope, or Magiscope®

Key Concepts: Determining sex ratios; Factors underlying skewed sex ratios.

Prerequisites: This activity can be used after observing the WOWBug life cycle, combined with other single-session activities, or used alone after showing the WOWBug Biology videotape and discussing the WOWBug life cycle with the class. Photocopy or make a transparency of the WOWBug pupae chart in Chapter 8.

Time: One class period.

Getting Ready: Begin new WOWBug cultures 12–15 days ahead. Alternatively, freeze pupae as a convenient way to ensure having a colony at the proper (late red-eyed pupa) developmental stage. Once thawed, the pupae will be fine for a day or so, but then will begin to decompose and should be discarded.

Objectives: Distinguish between the sexes of Melittobia digitata pupae. Determine the relative numbers of males and females in a typical WOWBug population.

Part A. Hypothesizing.

1. As a class, review what you know about the WOWBug life cycle. The container you will be receiving has the offspring that resulted when five mated female WOWBugs were placed on a single host larva. This situation closely mimics a natural infestation of WOWBugs on their mud-dauber host in early summer.

2. Before you start looking at your WOWBug population, make a guess. Do you think there will be about the same number of each sex? More males? More females? If 100 insects were in the container, how many do you think would be female? How many would be male? In the space below, or in your laboratory notebook, write your prediction of what you think will be the numbers of females and males in your container.

When a fertilized female WOWBug lays a large clutch of eggs on her host, the proportion of males and females that develops is not equal, as students might expect, but a ratio wildly skewed in favor of females — a discrepant event that makes a wonderful teaching opportunity.

Predicted number of females ___ and males____. Total: _____.

3. Since we don't yet know how many offspring are in the population, guessing the number of individuals of each sex in this way is difficult. We could, however, state the hypothesis in the form of a percentage. For example, if we predicted exactly the same number of females as males, our prediction would be 50% female, 50% male. This relationship would be the same whether the population actually contains 20 individuals, 200, or 2,000.

To change your prediction for female WOWBugs to a percentage, divide it by the total. Do the same for the males.

Predicted percentage of females = $\frac{\text{predicted no. females}}{\text{predicted total}}$ x 100 = ____%.

Predicted percentage of males   =   <u>predicted no. males</u>   x 100 = ____%.
                                        predicted total

If necessary, remind students that the percentages always need to add up to 100%. Suggest rounding to the nearest whole number.

4. Scientific researchers often use a **sex ratio** to express the number of males and females in a population. Writing a sex ratio is the same as writing the percentages, compared to each other. If written as numbers, the two numbers need to add up to 100 total, just as percentages do. (In numbers, an equal sex ratio would be expressed as 50:50.)

Write your hypothesis in the form of a predicted sex ratio. If your predicted ratio is different than 50:50, it doesn't matter which percentage comes first, as long as you specify what you are doing. For example, you could write "a 40:60 male:female sex ratio" or "a 60:40 female:male sex ratio." However, scientists generally give the larger number first.

Part B. Testing The Hypothesis

5. Gather the supplies you need to test your hypothesis. Place your sheet of white paper on the desktop. Let your teacher know you are ready to receive your culture of WOWBug pupae. Gently empty the container of insects onto the middle of the paper.

Depending upon available time and student skill levels, you can choose to have each student sort and count one culture (about 400 insects) or have students work as teams, dividing the culture so each is responsible for a portion of the contents and combines his or her data with those of classmates afterwards. Students should work individually on the sorting and counting, however.

Note: If a few living adults are present in your culture, try to determine their sex and include them in your counting. Trap them under a clear container if possible, and notify the teacher so the WOWBugs can be collected for further use.

If adult wasps are present in any of the cultures, you also will need to explain how to tell the difference with them. The first few adults to emerge are usually males. These can be used in a number of related activities. They will, however, need to be housed individually. See the "Darwinian Selection" activity.

6. To sort the pupae, you need to look for the ways the males and females are different. The outward appearance is also called **external morphology**. Examine a few individual WOWBug pupae and refer to the chart provided by your teacher. Use the microscope or magnifying lens if you need it.

As you become more aware of what you are looking for, you probably will no longer find magnification necessary. You'll begin to recognize the two sexes by their total appearance (what scientists call **gestalt**, a German word for overall shape and configuration).

Initially, you may have to help the students identify the different sexes. Consider using a microprojector to display an enlarged pupa of each sex on the screen and go over the characteristics listed in the chart with the class. Alternatively, use transparencies (see Chapter 8) or review the appropriate portion of the WOWBug Biology videotape. Also, because of developmental variation, some larvae may not have pupated yet; these can be ignored for this activity.

7. Using the brush or pipe cleaner, gently sort the pupae into two groups, males and females. Use the microscope or magnifying lens if you need it. Put one group on each

side of the paper. Don't worry about counting them right now.

8. After you have sorted all the pupae, count the number of male and female pupae. (You may find it easiest to brush pupae into piles of ten to keep from losing track of where you are.) Write the numbers in your notebook or in the spaces below. Then add the two numbers together to get the total number of WOWBugs in your culture.

Females _____ + Males _____ = Total _____.

9. Put away the pupae as your teacher instructs. Do not mix your male and female pupae. Place the males in one pile or container and the females in another. Clean up and return all laboratory materials to their proper places.

Set up separate containers to collect the separate male and female pupae at the end of the activity. You can save them for related activities or store them in a refrigerator for a few days. At room temperature, they will complete their development.

Part C. Analysis

10. Determine the percentage of females in your culture. As before, divide the number of females you counted by the total number of pupae (male and female combined), then multiply your answer by 100 to get the percentage of females: _____%

Example: 301 females/309 total x 100 = 97.4% females.

Now, do the same thing for the percentage of males. Record your answer. Males = _____%. Do the percentages add up to 100%?

Suggest rounding to the nearest whole number.

11. Express your results as a sex ratio. Give the larger percentage first. Specify which number refers to which sex.

Discussion:

1. What WOWBug sex ratio did you predict at the beginning of the activity? How close was your prediction to the ratio you actually found?

Ratios predicted will generally be close to 50:50. Actual ratios are generally about 95:5 female:male. Advanced students could be encouraged to run a chi-square analysis, which compares expected and observed results (see Chapter 8).

2. If you were a scientist looking at adult male and female WOWBugs for the first time and seeing their different morphology, what hypotheses might you make about their biology?

Encourage the entire class to discuss this together. On the basis of their appearance, you'd probably guess that males were blind, and that they couldn't fly. Inside the dark cocoon, they wouldn't need to see or fly, so you'd probably guess that's where they stay. You might also guess that they must find female WOWBugs by touch or smell.

You'd guess that females could both see and fly. Therefore they probably need to be able to do both, so you'd guess that they must leave the nest.

Since they are so small, you'd guess that WOWBugs would have a difficult time finding one another once they left the cocoon. Therefore, you might hypothesize that males and females mate inside the cocoon, and the fertile females leave soon afterward to find new hosts.

3. What is different about the risks in the life of a male and female WOWBug that might help explain why they have this unusually skewed sex ratio?

Answers will vary. However, because the winged female WOWBugs are the ones that leave the nest trying to find a new host, there is adaptive sense to producing great numbers of them. The life of a female WOWBug is a dangerous one, and most will die before they have the chance to successfully reproduce. Males, on the other hand, live their entire life in the shelter of the nest. For them, success in reproduction simply means being available to mate when females emerge from their pupae.

Concept Application And Elaboration:

1. Research and give a report on aphid (plant lice) reproduction, a complex system by which aphids build up tremendous populations in a relatively short period of time.

2. Investigate the mathematical advantages of a skewed sex ratio — in particular, one with a great many more females than males.

a. Assume that a single mated female WOWBug genetically programmed to have a 95:5 female: male sex ratio finds a mud dauber colony on June 1. She lays 500 eggs that all develop successfully to adulthood, then she dies. Each of her daughters does the same, and so on. By late August, when the fourth generation of offspring matures, how many female WOWBugs will there be?

95% of 500 is 475, so 4 generations of females would be 475^4, or over fifty billion wasps (50,906,640,625).

b. Assume by a genetic twist, the same female produces offspring and descendents with a 50:50 sex ratio. By late August, how many female WOWBugs will there be?

50% of 500 is 250, so 4 generations is 250^4, or over three billion wasps (3,906,250,000).

New Terms:

external morphology

gestalt

parthenogenesis

sex ratio

Momma's Boys: Sex Determination in WOWBugs

Key Concepts: Life cycles; Sexual and asexual reproduction; Haplo-diploidy; Genetics of reproduction.

Prerequisites: Basic understanding of WOWBug biology and life cycle.

Time: One class period, two 15-minute observation periods per week for three weeks, one period or less for final discussion.

Getting Ready: Be sure your WOWBug culture contains individuals at the late pupa stage (see Chapter 7). Set up separate labeled containers to collect pupae and adults at the end of the activity.

If possible, plan to project images of male and female pupae for the class or view the WOWBug Biology videotape.

Objectives: Discover the biological determinant behind production of males and females in Melittobia digitata *(and in fact, all Hymenoptera), and examine its genetic implications.*

All organisms need to reproduce, or **propagate** their own kind. If cats, for example, stopped having kittens, soon there would be no more cats at all. If oaks made no acorns, soon there would be no more oaks.

In many organisms, about half of the offspring develop into males, and the other half become females. This makes sure there are enough males and females for the next generation to reproduce again. Other organisms may produce more individuals of one sex than of another, but have developed elaborate ways to bring males and females together.

If students have completed the "Population Sex Ratios" and/or "Courtship Communication" activities, you may wish to go into more detail.

But one can't attract what is simply not there. What if the members of the opposite sex simply can't be found? Or if males and females are not produced in the same place at the same time? Or if all the males die? Surely, most of the population will die. But the rare individual that develops a way to cope has an incredible advantage.

Thus, it's not too surprising to find that a great many solutions have arisen to deal with the possibility of the sexes being isolated from each other. Some of these solutions are so common we tend to take them for granted. Many plants, for example, can reproduce either sexually (through pollinated flowers producing fruits or seeds) or asexually, developing new plants from runners, bulbs or other parts.

Other solutions can seem quite strange from our point of view. Certain kinds of fish that live in coral reefs can change from being female to being male, or vice versa, depending on conditions. Tapeworms have become **hermaphrodites**. Each individual tapeworm has both male and female reproductive organs, so that a lone parasite can fertilize itself.

> *According to experts, the oyster*
> *In its shell, or crustacean cloister,*
> *May frequently be*
> *Either he or a she*
> *Or both, if it should be its choice ter.*
> — Berton Braley

What about WOWBugs? With their very unbalanced sex ratio, some females in every parasitized cocoon probably do not mate before leaving. Yet WOWBugs have spread around the world. Do unmated females simply die without reproducing? Or is something else going on?

Materials (per student or team):

• Six (2-dram) shell vials or similar containers
• Cotton balls to use as stoppers
• Host cocoons or blowfly puparia, two per student
• Pipe cleaner or small watercolor paint brush
• Magnifying lens (10x), dissecting microscope, or Magiscope®
• Fine point permanent marker pen
• White unlined index card
• Poster putty
• Small plastic storage box or petri dish
• For entire class: One *Melittobia digitata* culture at late pupa stage (red eye)

Part A. Setting Up The Experiment

To learn how mating affects the reproduction of female WOWBugs, we need two groups: mated and unmated females. Because mating takes place very quickly, the best way to be sure that females are unmated is to isolate them while they are still pupae.

1. Gather your supplies, including two shell vials. With the marker, label one vial "unmated females." Label the other, "mated females." Gently add a host to each vial. Place two pieces of poster putty in the bottom of the plastic box or petri dish. Rest the vials on the putty to keep them from rolling about.

If students have not previously opened mud dauber cocoons, demonstrate the procedure (see Chapter 8). Remind students to be careful in handling hosts. Any liquid inside the vial is a sign the host larva has been ruptured and must be discarded.

Suggest that students only write near the end of the vial (near its opening), so as to permit easier observation of vial contents.

2. Let the teacher know you are ready to receive pupae from the *Melittobia digitata* stock cultures. After they are shaken onto your index card, use the brush or pipe cleaner to gently spread them out.

WOWBug pupae are fairly durable. Simply shake them gently from the stock culture vial. Female pupae progressively change from entirely creamy white to yellowish with red eyes and then to jet black just prior to becoming adults. Reliably separating male and female WOWBugs is easiest at the red-eyed stage. Each student or team will need at least ten red-eyed pupae. The number of pupae you need to provide to obtain these will depend, of course, on the developmental age of the culture.

3. Look for pupae with red eyes. (Use magnification if you need to.) Will these be males or females? How do pupae of the other sex look? (Remember what you know about the appearance of adult WOWBugs.)

All of the red-eyed pupae will turn into females. Only female WOWBugs have eyes. Male pupae are honey- or amber-colored and lack eyes. Refer to the chart in the previous activity.

Initially, you may have to help the students identify the different sexes. Consider using a microprojector to display an enlarged pupa of each sex on the screen and go over the characteristics listed in the chart with the class. Alternatively, use transparencies (see Chapter 8) or review the videotape of WOWBug biology.

4. Sketch a red-eyed pupa in your laboratory notebook or in the space on the chart on the next page *(of student version)*. Label and date the drawing, and provide some indication of the pupa's size.

Encourage students to sketch what they see; it is a good laboratory habit. Have them also make a habit of including a size reference, e.g., a scale bar or an indication of the magnification used.

5. With the brush or pipe cleaner, carefully transfer 5 red-eyed pupae to the vial marked "unmated females." Close the vial securely with a tight cotton plug. Set it down in its poster putty cradle inside the box or dish.

Emphasize that the cotton plug must be very snug to prevent escape by the adult wasps later.

6. Place another 5 red-eyed pupae in the vial marked "mated females." Add a male pupa or adult. Mating will occur soon after the females emerge.

Males develop faster, but they are few in number. Usually a few males can be found crawling among the female pupae by the time cultures reach the red-eye stage. Provide them to students, or allow students to look through the stock culture vial remains to find the more reclusive males.

7. With the fine-tipped marker, label the plastic box or dish with your name, class period, and the date. Set it aside where your teacher directs.

Part B. Life Cycle Observations

8. Over the next three weeks, regularly check and observe your two vials under the magnifying lens or low power dissecting microscope. Record each observation in your laboratory notebook. Write the date and sketch whatever changes you observe. Watch newly emerged adults for signs of stinging the host, feeding, and egg laying. In the "mated female" vial you may also observe mating and courtship activity.

Encourage students to use magnification and carefully examine the host, looking for small clusters of tiny translucent eggs which grow into tiny rice-like larvae. Eggs and larvae are found only on the outside of the host, but can be difficult to see.

Keep observation periods relatively brief and infrequent (about twice a week for about 15 minutes). Students may show some impatience or apparent boredom, as changes can seem slow to occur. Reassure students that patience is a necessary part of doing real science.

9. After 10 days, use the brush to gently remove all adult insects from both vials. Transfer them into a new empty shell vial. Close it with a tight cotton plug, then return it to your teacher. Why is this step necessary?

The purpose of this step is to avoid confounding the results. If they were not removed, some of the original adults could (and probably would) live long enough to still be alive by the time their offspring emerge as adults.

If you don't want to save them, a simple alternative is to just let them go outdoors.

Part C. Concluding The Experiment

10. During the third week (14-21 days), new adults should begin to emerge. In your laboratory notebook, construct a table that has columns to compare the numbers of new adults of each sex from each rearing container.

11. Get three new shell vials. Label one "new adults." Label the other two "male pupae" and "female pupae." Then open the box or dish with your experimental vials.

12. Unplug the "mated females" vial. Use the brush to remove any living adults, one at a time. Determine the sex of each, record it in the appropriate column in the table, then place the WOWBug in the "new adults" vial, and set it aside.

If there are just a few, they will probably be males, since males tend to emerge a little sooner than females. Often, some males will be found dead and possibly dismembered (see the "Darwinian Selection" activity).

13. Shake out the rest of the contents of the vial onto an unlined index card. Use the brush or pipe cleaner gently to sort the insect pupae into two groups, males and females. Use the microscope or magnifying lens if you need it. Put one group on each side of the card. Don't worry about counting them yet.

14. After you have sorted all the pupae, count them. (You may find it easiest to brush pupae into piles of ten to keep from losing track of where you are.) Write the numbers in your notebook. Then add the two numbers together to get the total number of WOWBugs in your "mated females" culture.

15. Put away the pupae in the labeled vials. Do not mix your male and female pupae. Place the males in one container and the females in another.

Several related activities can be conducted with these unmated individuals. They can be saved in a refrigerator for a few days, if necessary. At room temperature, they will complete their development.

16. Open your "unmated females" vial. Repeat steps 12 to 15. (When you have finished with the adults and pupae, place them in the labeled vials as before. At this point, it is all right to mix individuals from both cultures. However, be sure not to mix male and female pupae with one another.)

This container will have far fewer (about 3-30) adults and pupae, and the original host will still be largely untouched. All adults and pupae will be males, unless females were not removed before any new adults emerged.

Discussion:

1. Compare the total number of individuals produced in both cultures. What did you find? What differences in numbers of each sex? What differences in development time? What differences in host appearance?

Results should be clear. In the unmated female container only male Melittobia digitata *should result, and there will be only a few of them. Typically they will have completed development somewhat sooner than those in the mated vial (2-4 adult males may appear after 14-16 days). Most of the host will appear unchanged. The container with the mated females, in contrast, will have large numbers (>200) of individuals (almost all female) and the host will be completely used.*

2. Another way to compare the two cultures is to look at the <u>percentage</u> of females and males in each.

a. For your "mated females" culture, divide the number of females you counted by the total number of individuals (male and female combined). Multiply your answer by 100 to get the percentage of females. Do the same thing for the percentage of males. Record your answers. Do the percentages add up to 100%?

<u>Example</u>: 301 females/309 total x 100 = 97.4% females.

Specify the number of digits (significant figures) students should write down, and whether or not they should round the answers.

b. Determine the percentage of males and females in your "unmated females" culture. How do they compare with the percentages for the "mated females" culture?

3. With only one vial of each, how can you be sure the differences you found are not just due to chance? Compare your percentage results to those of classmates. Are they the same?

Scientists distinguish between **raw data** (observations in their natural, unaltered state) and **transformed** (or "cooked") **data** (information that has been altered by mathematics). Combine everyone's results by adding together the raw data (the actual numbers of individuals everyone counted) for all the cultures in the class. Recalculate the percentages. How does this affect the results? How does it affect your confidence in the results?

Actual numbers of offspring will vary, as will percentages. All of us, scientists and nonscientist alike, can be more confident of results based on larger samples. With more advanced classes, you may wish to extend this discussion to include some elementary statistical analysis, such as the chi-square test (Chapter 8).

4. What do these sex ratio findings suggest about sex determination in *Melittobia digitata*? What about its mother determines whether an individual develops into a male or a female? What is different about the eggs that become females and those that become males?

The mating status of the mother determines the sex of her offspring. If she is unmated, all of her offspring will be males. Mated females produce mostly female offspring, but a few of their eggs remain unfertilized and produce males.

5. What is there about the WOWBug life cycle that favors such an unusual form of sex determination?

After a relatively short time inside the host cocoon (during which mating usually, but not always occurs), female WOWBugs disperse from the nest. Females cannot expect to find a mate at a new host, because males never leave the cocoon where they were born. However, unmated females that find a new host can live long enough to produce a few male offspring. Then they can mate with these sons and produce a full, largely female generation on the same host.

6. What are the genetic implications of this way of determining sons and daughters? As a class, review what you know about what happens to genes during sexual reproduction.

*Review at least the following, reintroducing the bold terms. A typical case of **sexual reproduction** involves two parent organisms, each with two genes for every trait. Both parents pass on one of each gene to offspring by way of **gamete** (sex cells – egg and sperm) formation. Because the egg or sperm has only half of each pair of genes, it is called **haploid**.*

*In mating, sperm made by the male unite with the female's eggs, pairing up the genes from each parent. Thus, in the first cell of a new individual (and all the body cells that develop from it), there are two genes for every trait — half from one parent, and half from the other. When a cell has its genes in pairs, it is said to be **diploid**.*

If you could look at WOWBug genes, how many of each kind would you expect to find?

Because males develop from unfertilized eggs, male body cells have only one set of chromosomes (haploid) and hence only a single gene for each trait. Females result from fertilized eggs, so females have two sets (diploid), or two genes for each trait.

7. Look up the term **haplo-diploidy**. (It's sometimes spelled without the hyphen.) How does it relate to WOWBug reproduction? In what animals does it occur?

Haplo-diploidy is the method of sex determination in which males develop from unfertilized eggs (and thus male body cells are haploid) and females result from fertilized eggs (so female body cells are diploid). Haplo-diploidy occurs in all Hymenoptera — the ants, bees, and wasps — and sporadically elsewhere in the arthropods.

8. Some organisms (bacteria, for example) divide by fission, a type of **asexual reproduction**. A single parent passes on to offspring a duplicate of all of its genes. Unless a mutation occurs, the offspring can only be genetically identical copies, or **clones**, of the parent. How is a WOWBug male like an asexually produced clone? How is it different?

Male WOWBugs receive all of their genes from a single parent. However, since their mother gives them only one gene of every

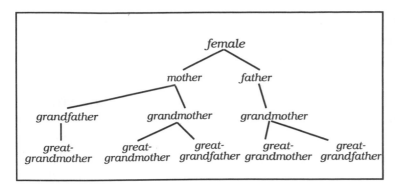 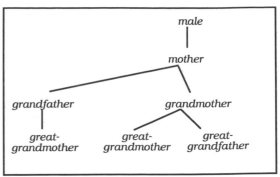

pair that she has, they are not true clones. Brothers receive different mixtures of these unpaired genes, so they are not identical. Sisters have pairs of genes, one of each pair coming from their fathers, so they are even less like their brothers. (These facts provide an interesting backdrop that has significance in related activities such as "Darwinian Selection.")

9. The WOWBug sex determination system results in a very strange **pedigree**, or chart of family relationships. On the back or in your notebook, draw a "family tree" showing four generations for a female WOWBug. Do the same for a male WOWBug.

See the family tree pedigree chart, above.

Use these pedigrees to identify the sex of the following individuals:

I have two parents and three grandparents: *Female.*
I have twice as many great-grandmothers as great-grandfathers: *Male.*
I have only daughters: *Male.*
I have a grandfather but no father: *Male.*
I have only one grandfather: *Female.*

Concept Application And Elaboration:

1. Draw your own family tree for 3 or 4 generations. Write a set of questions about your relatives that can be answered by looking at the tree. Working in pairs, exchange copies and see if you can figure out the identity of the person described in each of your partner's questions.

New Terms:

asexual reproduction

clones

diploid

gamete

haplo-diploidy

haploid

hermaphrodite

pedigree

propagate

raw data

sexual reproduction

transformed data

Mud Dauber Nest Ecology*

Key Concepts: Life cycles; Nesting biology; Parasitism; Sample sizes; Food webs; Use of a dichotomous key.

Prerequisites: None beyond some knowledge of basic ecological concepts.

Time: Two to three class periods.

Getting Ready: Photocopy (and laminate, if desired) the keys and relevant illustrations in the transparency masters section in Chapter 8. Read the background material in Chapter 7, then dissect a nest yourself. Identify the organisms. Save representatives for a class reference collection. Although written for use with organ pipe mud dauber nests, this activity can be used equally well with nests of other mud dauber species.

Objectives: Describe, measure, and sketch a mud dauber nest; Identify contents via a simple dichotomous key; Construct a food web for the nest inhabitants; Explore nest structure, contents, and relationships; Determine the incidence of parasitism.

Mud dauber nests, which may persist on building walls for years, are familiar sights to most people. To the casual observer, they look like shelters made to live in. You may have noticed the maker — a relatively large, non-aggressive wasp. However, if you had stayed to watch her work for several days during the summer, you might have been surprised to find that as soon as the nest was finished, she flew off, and never returned.

If she's not going to live in it, why does a wasp go to all this trouble? In fact, the nest serves as a well-stocked nursery for her offspring. When all goes well, within its walls, each of the wasp's young is presented with fresh meat to feed upon, separated from hungry siblings, and protected from enemies. But how well does the system work?

Most of your class will probably have seen a mud dauber nest at some point, and a few may have knocked them down. However, it's rare that a student knows what to expect inside the nest. To set the stage and heighten the suspense, some teachers weave an introductory scenario in which the students are scientists from Mars, travelers in the uncharted rain forest, or early North American explorers. They have come upon the mud structures for the first time and, knowing nothing about them, decide to carefully describe and dissect them.

Materials (per student, pair, or group):

• One mud dauber nest in a plastic resealable bag
• Individual laboratory notebooks
• A white paper plate
• One pair of forceps
• About 6 vials or small jars with stoppers
• 10x magnifying lens, dissecting microscope, or Magiscope®
• Permanent fine-point marking pen
• Metric ruler

*Some of this appears in slightly different form in *The American Biology Teacher* (1997); for citation, see p. 259.

• One empty egg carton
• Key to mud dauber nest inhabitants

Part A. The Nest Exterior

*After students have sketched and
measured the external dimensions of
the nest from both sides, the nests
may be placed in labeled plastic bags
and stored in the refrigerator until the
next class session.*

exterior   interior

1. Working in teams or pairs,
assemble your materials.

2. Remove the nest from its bag and place it carefully on
the paper plate. Do all of your work on this plate, which
will contain the dirt for later disposal.

*When students first receive their nests, some will want to
immediately break them open. Strongly discourage this. Instead, encourage students to work slowly and to use care to
avoid breaking nests during the exterior nest analysis. Attention
to detail at this point will help them draw meaningful comparisons with the data they gather from inside the nest later.*

Above:
*The nest of the organ pipe mud
dauber, Trypoxylon politum,
consists of one or more parallel
mud tubes typically 10 to 12
cm in length. Note the surface
texturing, a series of chevron-
shaped mud strips. The
absence of large emergence
holes indicates that this is a
current year nest. The reverse
of the same nest shows mud
dividers which partition each
tube into individual cells.*

3. Observe the exterior of the nest. Which side was
attached to the wall? Describe the surface texture and
colors of the mud. Which end faced up? How can you
tell?

*The flat side of the nest was attached to the building. Often the
contents of the cell compartments are partly visible, because the
wasp uses the wall surface as the fourth side of her nest,
conserving materials and energy.*

4. Trace the nest outline in your notebook. Measure and
record the nest dimensions and the size and location of
any holes.

*Holes in the nest wall, if present, may be of two sizes. The
larger holes (2-5 mm diameter) spaced at about 20 mm intervals*

represent places where offspring chewed out sideways to escape their cells. Occasional smaller holes (about 1 mm diameter) most likely were exits made by pirate flies.

5. Find a section where textured mud arches or **chevrons** are clearly visible. Count the number of chevrons present along one centimeter of the tube's length. Multiply this number by the total length of the tube. What might each chevron represent? What does the total quantify?

Each of the chevrons, about 1 mm wide, results from two trips for mud, applied to alternate sides of the tube. Different colors reflect more than one source of mud. The total number of chevrons represents half the number of trips the wasp took.

6. Is each tube a continuous tunnel? Turn the nest over. Observe and sketch the nest as it appears from the flat side. Count the number of compartments (called **nest cells**). Measure and record their dimensions. Include inside tube widths and lengths.

Later, you will be asking students to compile data for the entire class and compare it with published dimensions.

Why would nest cells be needed? What functions might they serve?

The main purpose of the nest is to protect the offspring from intruders and (since they are carnivores) from one another.

7. Measure the thickness of the mud wall at five different points along the exterior wall, and obtain an average. Do the same for the cross-partitions between cells. Which is thicker? Why? What advantages might a thick exterior wall serve? What disadvantages might it have? What physical and biological factors might limit its thickness? Why might a relatively thin or non-existent back wall be advan-

tageous?

A thick exterior wall protects the mud dauber offspring better. However, beyond a certain thickness, it could present a problem when they try to emerge. Physical properties of the construction material (mud, water, and wasp saliva) probably also constrain the architectural possibilities.

Using the substrate as a back wall saves time, energy, and materials, but in locations with a great many mud nests, the wasps will sometimes build new tubes right on top of old ones. The flat surface of the substrate may, however, be important in orienting emergence. One research team (Cross et al., 1975) has noted that emergence holes of wasps exiting from tubes built upon other tubes rather than upon a flat surface show a high proportion of disorientation.

Part B. Mud Dauber Nest Dissection

Devote the second class period to dissecting each cell, identifying and tabulating the contents.

8. With the marker, number the compartments in the egg carton. Then, beginning at one end of the nest, carefully use your fingers to break into the first nest compartment. Switch to the forceps to gently remove the cell contents. Place them into compartment number 1 in the egg carton. Repeat for each of the cells of your nest. How many cells did your nest contain? What are the large, long cylindrical objects? Did every cell contain one? Did any cell with spiders also contain one of these?

The cylinders are cocoons constructed by the mud dauber larvae. A cell in which the offspring has died for one reason or another will not have one. Because the larva does not begin to pupate until after it has eaten all the spiders in its cell, finding a cell with both spiders and a cocoon would be highly unlikely.

9. In your notebook, construct a table in which to list and quantify the contents of each cell. Then use the key to identify and classify them. Do not break open any of the **cocoons** at this time. Based on the key, how many different organisms did **your nest** contain?

Answers will vary. At this point, you may wish to project the key and provide some information on the roles of the different inhabitants.

Note: You may wish to require the use of safety goggles during activities that involve breaking open mud nests.

10. Examine the intact cocoons. Are both ends the same? Sketch and describe one in your notebook. Can you guess which is the anterior (head) end? Measure each cocoon. Calculate average cocoon length. Record the average and the range in cocoon sizes in your notebook. How might the range differ if nests had no cells? What other factors might cause sizes to vary?

Normal prudence dictates washing hands before and after handling living organisms or their remains.

In the organ pipe species, the anterior end is bumpy and rough where sand grains have been incorporated into it. (The reason for this is unknown.) In the black and yellow mud dauber, cocoons are more transparent and papery, with a mass of hard, dark material at the posterior end.

Cocoons generally range from 12 mm to 25 mm long. Some of the size variation is nutritional. If nests had no cells, the larger larvae would probably eat more. Assuming the smaller ones survived at all, the variation in size might be even greater. Another factor affecting size is gender. Male mud daubers tend to be slightly smaller than females.

11. Do all of the cocoons really contain mud daubers? Construct a data table in your laboratory notebook. Provide spaces to indicate the cell identification number, the type of cell contents, and the number of organisms found in the cell.

To view the inhabitants as adults, see the 35-mm slides in the Organ Pipe Mud Dauber Wasp Slide Set. *Additional life history data about the nest inhabitants can be found in the booklet,* "What's Inside A Mud Dauber's Nest? *See Chapter 8 for sources.*

a. Grasp a cocoon in your fingers and hold it under the hand lens or microscope. Examine it carefully for anything unusual, such as a tiny hole or a spot of mud.

b. Use your fingernail or forceps to carefully break off one end of the cocoon. Gently tip out the contents onto a piece of paper. Consult the key to identify the contents. Record your findings.

Help students relate their findings to pictures of the nest inhabitants as adults. Copies of the key provided in Chapter 8 can be laminated for use by several classes.

c. Repeat for each cocoon. Record your results.

Your data will be unique and new to science, for many factors affect the population dynamics at a particular locality. See Chapter 7 for comparative data.

Discussion:

The final class period should be spent analyz-ing and discussing class results. The unexpected presence of a variety of other inhabitants in the nests offers students an opportunity to gain first-hand appreciation of the diverse connections and interactions of this microcommunity. Food chains and webs differ from one nest to the next.

This is an appropriate time to show the videotape, "Organ Pipe Mud Dauber Biology." (See Chapter 8 for sources.)

Above: An opened mud dauber cocoon that has been parasitized by WOWBugs.

1. Construct a data table for the whole class results from Part A. (Each team should enter the data for their nest's architecture.) Calculate the average, and determine the range, for each measurement for the sum of all nests in your class. Compare these with your own team's results. What similarities do you find? What differences? What factors might be involved in this variation?

Answers will vary. Nest architecture varies with locality, type of mud, and probably many other factors. Help students look for patterns, rather than absolute numbers. For example, partitions generally are thinner than outer nest walls. Interestingly, there is some evidence that mother wasps construct larger cells for their female-producing eggs.

Advanced classes should be encouraged to perform some elementary statistical analyses, such as a chi-square test (Chapter 8), on various architectural measurements.

2. Many of your nests had various holes in the mud walls. Was there any relationship between hole size and cell contents?

Yes. The larger holes (2-5 mm diameter) represent places where mud dauber offspring chewed out to escape their cells. Smaller holes (about 1 mm diameter) most likely were exits made by pirate flies. Downing (1995) discusses methods of escape from mud nests.

3. Construct a data table for the whole class results from Part B. Each team should enter the data for their nest's inhabitants. Calculate the average, and determine the range, for the numbers of each inhabitant. How did the range compare from one type of inhabitant to another?

Scientists studying mud daubers have found that some parasites are quite numerous at one site, but may be essentially absent or relatively unimportant at another nearby site. Other parasites seemingly exist in about the same number everywhere. If students want to follow up on possible reasons, the paper by Cross et al. (1975) is a good place to begin.

4. From most to least common, what were the causes of death of mud dauber offspring in your nest? How did overall class results compare to yours? What sample size do you think would be necessary to reflect the natural situation accurately?

How much variation is acceptable? What criteria guide a scientist in deciding that he or she has gathered enough information for it to be published? These issues have real relevance to the world of working scientists, and there is no single "correct" answer.

5. Did any of your cocoons contain *Melittobia*? Did anyone else's nest have them? What variable might help explain your results?

Your class may find high levels, low levels, or no Melittobia *parasitism at all. Published studies have shown that WOWBugs may overcome much of the mud dauber population at one site, but may be absent from other sites in the same nesting season.*

Various explanations are possible. A favored one points out that once they have found a suitable area, mud daubers usually nest repeatedly in the same location. Because WOWBugs have a very high rate of population increase but a relatively limited ability to disperse very far, the most likely explanation is that different levels of parasitism reflect different nesting site ages. As mud daubers nest year after year in the same area, WOWBugs gradually build up populations able to saturate the site.

6. What percentage of the cells would have produced living mud dauber offspring? Based on your own nest, if a female mud dauber could make 12 cells in her lifetime, how many offspring would survive to become part of next year's population? Compare your results with those of others in the class. What similarities can you find? How might you account for differences?

Answers will vary. If you know where the nests came from, this would be a perfect opportunity to explore variation from one site to another. For example, a large sample of mud dauber nests from nine localities in Missouri and Missisippi found that mortality from all causes averaged 36%, but ranged all the way from 1% to 57%. Because mud dauber nests tend to be built in the same location, year after year, parasite populations can gradually build up.

7. The data collection in this activity is no different from what entomological researchers are doing. How do your class findings compare with theirs? Review data which have already been published for other parts of the country.

Either share the review in Chapter 7, or have the photocopies of the actual publications on hand. You may want to encourage publication of student results. By keeping careful records and combining results of several classes and/or successive years into a master data set, your classes could obtain information of sufficient scientific value to merit publication. Nesting habits of the organ pipe mud dauber vary with a number of environmental factors (see Barber and Matthews, 1979; Brockmann, 1980). Data like those of Cross and coworkers (1975) and Molumby (1995) would be particularly valuable for comparative purposes, especially if obtained from new locations.

8. Working in pairs or teams, construct a web or concept map that depicts the relationships between each of the organisms you found.

A typical web of interactions between mud dauber nest inhabitants is given as a transparency master in Chapter 8. Talk with students about what the arrows represent (the direction of energy flow). Because both spiders and mud dauber wasps are predators, at least two trophic levels exist outside of the nest habitat. Producers (plants) and consumers (herbivores) underpin the entire micro-community found in the nest.

Additional relationships are not unusual. For example, WOWBugs may parasitize the other parasites, a phenomenon termed hyperparasitism. If the mud dauber's egg fails to hatch or dies, spiders may serve instead as food for scavengers such as carpet beetles and book lice, both of which feast on dried insect remains. Pirate fly larvae can live only on freshly paralyzed spider prey; they enter the nest during the provisioning phase, when spiders are added, and confiscate the prey for themselves, perhaps by destroying the mud dauber's egg.

New Terms:

chevron

cocoon

nest cell

parasite

Concept Application And Elaboration:

1. Use library or classroom references to research and report on the habits of various nest inhabitants.

2. Try to rear various nest inhabitants to adulthood. Record information such as sex ratios, development times, etc.

3. Make artificial homes to attract other harmless solitary bees and wasps that normally nest in hollow stems. Plug one end of a number of drinking straws with modeling clay. Tape them together in a bundle with some facing each way. Attach them to the underside of a window sill. Check them at least once a week during fall or late spring. Remove filled straws and carefully slit them open to reveal their contents.

Darwinian Selection

About a century ago, the young naturalist Charles Darwin put together a line of reasoning that was to turn the field of biology on its head — making the study of life both simpler, and at the same time more complex. It came to be called the **theory of evolution by natural selection**. In simplest form, it went like this:

1. Any population tends to outgrow its resources by producing more offspring than can survive.

2. Normal variations between individuals in local populations of a species include differences in the ability to acquire those limited resources.

3. Members of the population compete with one another and because of these differences, some individuals have a better chance of surviving and reproducing.

4. Because the population will come to have more of these successful individuals' offspring, slowly over generations it will shift. There will be more individuals that resemble the successful ones in various inherited traits.

In the years since Darwin's explanation, evolutionary biologists have also pointed out that among sexually reproducing animals, other members of one's species create some of the greatest obstacles to reproductive success.

Competition between males is a case in point. Males of all species compete for needed resources such as food and mates, of course. Male WOWBugs are no different,

Key Concepts: Male competition; Natural selection.

Prerequisites: Understanding of WOWBug life cycle.

Time: One class period.

Getting Ready: If male pupae have not been isolated as part of another exercise, set up unmated female cultures 18 days prior to this activity (see Chapter 8). For best results, males must be young, have had recent mating experience, and be isolated from other males for at least 24 hours. Remove males as late pupae or new adults. Isolate them in a plastic well slide with 2–3 mature female pupae (black stage). They can stay in the well slide for 3–4 days without problems if necessary.

Objectives: To determine how male WOWBugs compete among themselves.

though their world is limited to the dark inside of a host cocoon. Here they are born and live and die, never leaving. Everything they need is available here, but only for a short time and not in unlimited supply. Females mate only once, and as soon as they mate, they immediately try to leave the cocoon to find a new host. Thus, in this tiny closed world, inter-male competition takes on an incredible urgency.

Materials (per pair):

• Pipe cleaner or small brush
• Plastic well slide with cover
• Stop watch or wrist watch that shows seconds
• 10x magnifying lens, dissecting microscope, or Magiscope®
• Laboratory notebook

1. Get the materials you need. When ready, ask your teacher for your male.

Provide each male in a separate plastic well slide, along with one or two females.

Carefully observe and examine both your own male and your partner's male, using the hand lens or microscope. Try to learn to tell them apart by appearance (relative size, slight coloration differences, etc.).

Usually this is possible.

2. If you can recognize anything distinctive about your male, set up a table in your notebook to record your notes in two columns, one describing "your" male's actions, and the other column describing the opponent male's actions. If individual recognition/identification of the two males is uncertain, you'll need to record your notes as a continuous narrative of events. In either case, leave space to provide as much detail as you can, including regular notes as to the clock time elapsed since the start of any interactions.

*Stress the importance of good journal note taking as the basis
of all scientific research. In this activity, results are unpredict-
able, which increases the need for careful observation and
description.*

3. Working in pairs, use the pipe cleaner or brush to
gently transfer your male and your partner's male into
the empty clean plastic well slide together. When both
males are in the well slide replace the cover. Under
magnification, observe their interactions. How did the
males react to each other in their first contact?

*Answers will vary. Generally, as soon as they make contact
they will vigorously attempt to climb onto each other and to try
to bite each other somewhere. Usually, it appears that each
male prefers to be on top.*

4. Under magnification, continue to observe their interactions over the next several minutes. Keep careful notes
of everything that occurs.

*Generally, males will begin to interact within minutes of being
placed together. Fights are tumbling contests in which each
male attempts to grab his opponent in a vulnerable spot. If
successful, one male may bite into his opponent; bites can result
in wounds to any part of the body, in loss of parts of antennae
or legs, or even in death, particularly if it is a neck bite. There is
no "typical" sequence of behaviors. Each contest will be unique.
Students may predict that the larger males will win, but this is
not always the case. If you have video projection capability,
consider having the class share bouts. A fight sequence is also
included in the "WOWBug Biology" videotape.*

*In most cases fights will ultimately end with death to one or the
other (occasionally both) of the males. (You may wish to give
students the option of separating combatants before fatal
wounds are delivered.) Stress that fighting that often results in
dismemberment or death is normal in Melittobia digitata, and
that a single surviving male is capable of mating with all the
available females. It really is a case of "winner takes all."*

5. If time permits, pair the survivor with the winner
WOWBug from another pair of students and stage an-

other match. How does this combat compare with the first one?

Results will vary.

Discussion:

1. Combine the results for the entire class in a single table. What were the various outcomes of male combat? How many fights ended in one male mutilating or killing the other? In how many cases was no fighting at all observed? How might such variation be explained?

Variation in any behavior trait — including aggression — is normal, and to be expected. Since male age and experience were not uniform, this could play a role in the results.

2. Recall that males lack eyes and therefore can't see their opponent. How might they find each other?

Touch may accidentally work in the close confines of the plastic well slide. It is also likely that odor (smell) may be involved, but this question has never been investigated experimentally.

3. Males in a single culture will most likely be brothers. Why should brothers fight so violently?

Answers will vary, but should bring out the peculiarities of the WOWBug life cycle. First, each male produces enough sperm to fertilize all of the females in the cocoon. Second, males are trapped inside the host cocoon, unable to find other females to mate with. Thus, even though there may be hundreds of females, they are a limited resource. Because females mate only once, the only way a male can increase his own reproductive success is by eliminating the competition.

4. Did anything you observed suggest how males might obtain food to supply the energy needed for combat?

Winning males often "chew" for long periods on their victims. It is likely that they ingest the blood and nutritious body fluids in this way. Essentially it appears that they may cannibalize their brothers.

Concept Application And Elaboration:

1. How many males in a cocoon meet their death in combat? Stock WOWBug cultures that have died can be saved and carefully examined. Count the number of decapitated or dismembered males versus the number of intact male bodies. Relate the findings to the class results from this activity.

New Terms:

theory of evolution by
     natural selection

2. Read "Horned Beetles," by W.G. Eberhard (*Scientific American*, March 1980, 242 (3): pp. 166-182). Write a report about what you learned.

3. Draw a poster that shows examples of combat between male mammals.

Well-known examples are deer (where antlers can inflict serious injury), bull elephant seals, and bighorn sheep.

Population Sex Ratios

From the two-by-two's of Noah's Ark to children's stories of "mommy and daddy" birds, bears, and elephants, we are conditioned to think of male and female animals as being roughly equal in number. We even tend to think that there are approximately equal numbers of both sexes in people. In fact, statistics reveal that slightly more male than female humans are born each year. Similarly, not all animals have a 50:50 balance of the sexes. In some cases such as humans, this imbalance or "skew" is slight. In others it is much more extreme.

Most aphids (plant lice), for example, have almost entirely dispensed with males. By a type of sexless reproduction called **parthenogenesis**, females give birth to daughters and they in turn to granddaughters all summer long, entirely without males. In the fall, however, a few males are produced and after mating, the females produce eggs instead of giving birth to their young. These eggs then overwinter before hatching to start another all-female population.

What sort of sex ratio occurs in a typical WOWBug population?

Objectives: Distinguish between the sexes of Melittobia digitata *pupae. Determine the relative numbers of males and females in a typical WOWBug population.*

Materials (per student or team):
• *Pipe cleaner or small paint brush*
• *WOWBugs culture at late red-eyed pupa stage*
• *One sheet of unlined white paper*
• *Optional: magnifying lens (10x), dissecting microscope, or Magiscope®*

Part A. Hypothesizing.
1. As a class, review what you know about the WOWBug life cycle. The container you will be receiving has the offspring that resulted when five mated female WOWBugs were placed on a single host larva. This situation closely mimics a natural infestation of WOWBugs on their mud-dauber host in early summer.

2. Before you start looking at your WOWBug population, make a guess. Do you think there will be about the same number of each sex? More males? More females? If 100 insects were in the container, how many do you think would be female? How many would be male? In the space below, or in your laboratory notebook, write your prediction of what you think will be the numbers of females and males in your container.

Predicted number of females ___ and males___. Total: _____.

3. Since we don't yet know how many offspring are in the population, guessing the number of individuals of each sex in this way is difficult. We could, however, state the hypothesis in the form of a percentage. For example, if we predicted exactly the same number of females as males, our prediction would be 50% female, 50% male. This relationship would be the same whether the population actually contains 20 individuals, 200, or 2,000.

To change your prediction for female WOWBugs to a percentage, divide it by the total. Do the same for the males.

Predicted percentage of females = $\underline{\text{predicted no. females}}$ x 100 = _____%.
                                                    predicted total

Predicted percentage of males = $\underline{\text{predicted no. males}}$ x 100 = ___%.
                                                    predicted total

4. Scientific researchers often use a **sex ratio** to express the number of males and females in a population. Writing a sex ratio is the same as writing the percentages, compared to each other. If written as numbers, the two numbers need to add up to 100 total, just as percentages do. (In numbers, an equal sex ratio would be expressed as 50:50.)

Write your hypothesis in the form of a predicted sex ratio. (It doesn't matter which percentage comes first, as long as you specify what you are doing. For example, you could write "a 40:60 male:female sex ratio" or "a 60:40 female: male sex ratio." However, scientists generally give the larger number first.)

Predicted sex ratio: _____.

Part B. Testing The Hypothesis

5. Gather the supplies you need to test your hypothesis. Place your sheet of white paper on the desktop. Let your teacher know you are ready to receive your culture of WOWBug pupae. Gently empty the vial of insects onto the middle of the paper. **Note:** If a few living adults are present in your culture, try to determine their sex and include them in your counting. Trap them under a clear container if possible, and notify the teacher so the WOWBugs can be collected for further use.

6. To sort the pupae, you need to look for the ways the males and females are differ-ent. The outward appearance is also called **external morphology**. Examine a few individual WOWBug pupae and refer to the chart provided by your teacher. Use the microscope or magnifying lens if you need it. As you become more aware of what you are looking for, you probably will no longer find magnification necessary. You'll begin to recognize the two sexes by their total appearance (what scientists call **gestalt**, a German word for overall shape and configuration).

7. Using the brush or pipe cleaner, gently sort the pupae into two groups, males and females. Use the microscope or magnifying lens if you need it. Put one group on each side of the paper. Don't worry about counting them right now.

8. After you have sorted all the pupae, count the number of male and female pupae. (You may find it easiest to brush pupae into piles of ten to keep from losing track of where you are.) Write the numbers in your notebook or in the spaces below. Then add the two numbers together to get the total number of WOWBugs in your culture.

Females _____ + Males _____ = Total _____.

9. Put away the pupae as your teacher instructs. Do not mix your male and female pupae. Place the males in one pile or container and the females in another. Clean up and return all laboratory materials to their proper places.

Part C. Analysis

10. Determine the percentage of females in your culture. As before, divide the number of females you counted by the total number of pupae (male and female combined), then multiply your answer by 100 to get the percentage of females: _____%

Now, do the same thing for the percentage of males. Record your answer. Males = _____%. Do the percentages add up to 100%? _____

11. Express your results as a sex ratio. Give the larger percentage first. Specify which number refers to which sex, _____

Discussion:

1. What WOWBug sex ratio did you predict at the beginning of the activity? How close was your prediction to the ratio you actually found?

_____

_____

2. If you were a scientist looking at adult male and female WOWBugs for the first time and seeing their different morphology, what hypotheses might you make about their biology?

_____

_____

_____

3. What is different about the risks in the life of a male and female WOWBug that might help explain why they have this unusually skewed sex ratio?

_____

_____

_____

_____

Momma's Boys: Sex Determination in WOWBugs

Objectives: Discover the biological determinant behind production of males and females in Melittobia digitata *(and in fact, all Hymenoptera), and examine its genetic implications.*

Materials (per student or team):

• *Six (2-dram) shell vials or similar containers*
• *Cotton balls to use as stoppers*
• *Host cocoons or blowfly puparia, two per student*
• *Pipe cleaner or small water-color paint brush*
• *Magnifying lens (10x), dissecting microscope, or Magiscope®*
• *Fine point permanent marker pen*
• *White unlined index card*
• *Poster putty*
• *Small plastic storage box or petri dish*
• *For entire class: One* Melittobia digitata *culture at late pupa stage (red eye)*

All organisms need to reproduce, or **propagate** their own kind. If cats, for example, stopped having kittens, soon there would be no more cats at all. If oaks made no acorns, soon there would be no more oaks.

In many organisms, about half of the offspring develop into males, and the other half become females. This makes sure there are enough males and females for the next generation to reproduce again. Other organisms may produce more individuals of one sex than of another, but have developed elaborate ways to bring males and females together.

But one can't attract what is simply not there. What if the members of the opposite sex simply can't be found? Or if males and females are not produced in the same place at the same time? Or if all the males die? Surely, most of the population will die. But the rare individual that develops a way to cope has an incredible advantage.

Thus, it's not too surprising to find that a great many solutions have arisen to deal with the possibility of the sexes being isolated from each other. Some of these solutions are so common we tend to take them for granted. Many plants, for example, can reproduce either sexually (through pollinated flowers producing fruits or seeds) or asexually, developing new plants from runners, bulbs or other parts.

Other solutions can seem quite strange from our point of view. Certain kinds of fish that live in coral reefs can change from being female to being male, or vice versa, depending on conditions. Tapeworms have become **hermaphrodites**. Each individual tapeworm has both male and female reproductive organs, so that a lone parasite can fertilize itself.

What about WOWBugs? With their very unbalanced sex ratio, some females in every parasitized cocoon probably do not mate before leaving. Yet WOWBugs have spread around the world. Do unmated females simply die without reproducing? Or is something else going on?

Part A. Setting Up The Experiment

To learn how mating affects the reproduction of female WOWBugs, we need two groups: mated and unmated females. Because mating takes place very quickly, the best way to be sure that females are unmated is to isolate them while they are still pupae.

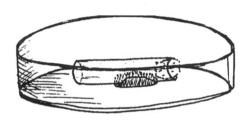

1. Gather your supplies, including two shell vials. With the marker, label one vial "unmated females." Label the other, "mated females." Gently add a host to each vial. Place two pieces of poster putty in the bottom of the plastic box or dish. Rest the vials on the putty to keep them from rolling about.

2. Let the teacher know you are ready to receive pupae from the *Melittobia digitata* stock cultures. After they are shaken onto your index card, use the brush or pipe cleaner to gently spread them out.

3. Look for pupae with red eyes. (Use magnification if you need to.) Will these be males or females? How do pupae of the other sex look? (Remember what you know about the appearance of adult WOWBugs.)

_____

_____

4. Sketch a red-eyed pupa in your laboratory notebook or in the space on the chart on the next page. Label and date the drawing, and provide some indication of the pupa's size.

5. With the brush or pipe cleaner, carefully transfer 5 red-eyed pupae to the vial marked "unmated females." Close the vial securely with a tight cotton plug. Set it down in its poster putty cradle inside the box or dish.

6. Place another 5 red-eyed pupae in the vial marked "mated females." Add a male

---

Observable Characteristics (External Morphology)
of WOWBug Pupae

Female Pupae

Black body color

Red or pink eyes

My drawing of a female pupa:

Male Pupae

Amber (golden) body color

Clear coloration where eyes should be

My drawing of a male pupa:

---

pupa or adult. Mating will occur soon after the females emerge.

7. With the fine-tipped marker, label the plastic box with your name, class period, and the date. Set it aside where your teacher directs.

Part B. Life Cycle Observations

8. Over the next three weeks, regularly check and observe your two vials under the magnifying lens or low power dissecting microscope. Record each observation in your laboratory notebook. Write the date and sketch whatever changes you observe. Watch newly emerged adults for signs of stinging the host, feeding, and egg laying. In the "mated female" vial you may also observe mating and courtship activity.

9. After 10 days, use the brush to gently remove all adult insects from both vials. Transfer them into a new empty shell vial. Close it with a tight cotton plug, then return it to your teacher. Why is this step necessary?

Part C. Concluding The Experiment

10. During the third week (14-21 days), new adults should begin to emerge. In your laboratory notebook or on a blank sheet of notebook paper, construct a table with col-

umns to compare the numbers of new adults of each sex from each rearing container.

11. Get three new shell vials. Label one "new adults." Label the other two "male pupae" and "female pupae." Then open the box or dish containing your experimental vials.

12. Unplug the "mated females" vial. Use the brush to remove any living adults, one at a time. Determine the sex of each, record it in the appropriate column in the table, then place the WOWBug in the "new adults" vial, and set it aside.

13. Shake out the rest of the contents of the vial onto an unlined index card. Use the brush or pipe cleaner gently to sort the insect pupae into two groups, males and females. Use the microscope or magnifying lens if you need it. Put one group on each side of the card. Don't worry about counting them yet.

14. After you have sorted all the pupae, count them. (You may find it easiest to brush pupae into piles of ten to keep from losing track of where you are.) Write the numbers in your notebook. Then add the two numbers together to get the total number of WOWBugs in your "mated females" culture.

15. Put away the pupae in the labeled vials. Do not mix your male and female pupae. Place the males in one container and the females in another.

16. Open your "unmated females" vial. Repeat steps 12 to 15. (When you have finished with the adults and pupae, place them in the labeled vials as before. At this point, it is all right to mix individuals from both cultures. However, be sure not to mix male and female pupae with one another.)

Discussion:

1. Compare the total number of individuals produced in both cultures. What did you find? What differences in numbers of each sex? What differences in development time? What differences in host appearance?

_____

_____

_____

_____

2. Another way to compare the two cultures is to look at the <u>percentage</u> of females and males in each.

a. For your "mated females" culture, divide the number of females you counted by the total number of individuals (male and female combined). Multiply your answer by 100 to get the percentage of females. Do the same thing for the percentage of males. Record your answers. Do the percentages add up to 100%?

_____

_____

b. Determine the percentage of males and females in your "unmated females" culture. How do they compare with the percentages for the "mated females" culture?

_____

_____

3. With only one vial of each, how can you be sure the differences you found are not just due to chance? Compare your percentage results to those of classmates. Are they the same?

_____

_____

Scientists distinguish between **raw data** (observations in their natural, unaltered state) and **transformed** (or "cooked") **data** (information that has been altered by mathematics). Combine everyone's results by adding together the raw data (the actual numbers of individuals everyone counted) for all the cultures in the class. Recalculate the percentages. How does this affect the results? How does it affect your confidence in the results?

_____

_____

_____

4. What do these sex ratio findings suggest about sex determination in *Melittobia digitata*? What about its mother determines whether an individual develops into a male or a female? What is different about the eggs that become females and those that

become males?

_____

_____

_____

5. What is there about the WOWBug life cycle that favors such an unusual form of sex determination?

_____

_____

_____

6. What are the genetic implications of this way of determining sons and daughters? As a class, review what you know about what happens to genes during sexual reproduction.

_____

_____

_____

_____

If you could look at WOWBug genes, how many of each kind would you expect to find?

_____

7. Look up the term **haplo-diploidy**. (It's sometimes spelled without the hyphen.) How does it relate to WOWBug reproduction? In what animals does it occur?

_____

_____

8. Some organisms (bacteria, for example) divide by fission, a type of **asexual reproduction**. A single parent passes on to offspring a duplicate of all of its genes. Unless a mutation occurs, the offspring can only be genetically identical copies, or **clones**, of the parent. How is a WOWBug male like an asexually produced clone? How is it different?

_____

_____

9. The WOWBug sex determination system results in a very strange **pedigree**, or chart of family relationships. On the back or in your notebook, draw a "family tree" showing four generations for a female WOWBug. Do the same for a male WOWBug.

10. Use these pedigrees to identify the sex of the following individuals:

I have two parents and three grandparents: _____

I have twice as many great-grandmothers as great-grandfathers: _____

I have only daughters: _____

I have a grandfather but no father: _____

I have only one grandfather: _____

Mud Dauber Nest Ecology

Objectives: Describe, measure, and sketch a mud dauber nest; Identify contents via a simple dichotomous key; Construct a food web for the nest inhabitants; Explore nest structure, contents, and relationships; Determine the incidence of parasitism.

Materials (per student, pair, or group):

• *One mud dauber nest in a plastic resealable bag*
• *Individual laboratory note-books*
• *A white paper plate*
• *One pair of forceps*
• *About six vials or small jars with stoppers*
• *10x magnifying lens, dissecting microscope, or Magiscope®*
• *Permanent fine-point marking pen*
• *Metric ruler*
• *One empty egg carton*
• *Key to mud dauber nest inhabitants*

Mud dauber nests, which may persist on building walls for years, are familiar sights to most people. To the casual observer, they look like shelters made to live in. You may have noticed the maker — a relatively large, non-aggressive wasp. However, if you had stayed to watch her work for several days during the summer, you might have been surprised to find that as soon as the nest was finished, she flew off, and never returned.

If she's not going to live in it, why does a wasp go to all this trouble? In fact, the nest serves as a well-stocked nursery for her offspring. When all goes well, within its walls, each of the wasp's young is presented with fresh meat to feed upon, separated from hungry siblings, and protected from enemies. But how well does the system work?

Part A. The Nest Exterior

1. Working in teams or pairs, assemble your materials.

2. Remove the nest from its bag and place it carefully on the paper plate. Do all of your work on this plate, which will contain the dirt for later disposal.

3. Observe the exterior of the nest. Which side was attached to the wall? Describe the surface texture and colors of the mud. Which end faced up? How can you tell?

_____

_____

_____

_____

4. Trace the nest outline in your notebook. Measure and

record the nest dimensions and the size and location of any holes.

5. Find a section where textured mud arches or **chevrons** are clearly visible. Count the number of chevrons present along one centimeter of the tube's length. Multiply this number by the total length of the tube. What might each chevron represent? What does the total quantify?

_____

_____

_____

6. Is each tube a continuous tunnel? Turn the nest over. Observe and sketch the nest as it appears from the flat side. Count the number of compartments (called **nest cells**). Measure and record their dimensions. Include inside tube widths and lengths.

Why would nest cells be needed? What functions might they serve?

_____

_____

7. Measure the thickness of the mud wall at five different points along the exterior wall, and obtain an average. Do the same for the cross-partitions between cells. Which is thicker? Why? What advantages might a thick exterior wall serve? What disadvantages might it have? What physical and biological factors might limit its thickness? Why might a relatively thin or non-existent back wall be advantageous?

_____

_____

_____

_____

_____

Part B. Mud Dauber Nest Dissection

8. With the marker, number the compartments in the egg carton. Then, beginning at one end of the nest, carefully use your fingers to break into the first nest compartment. Switch to the forceps to gently remove the cell contents. Place them into compartment number 1 in the egg carton. Repeat for each of the cells of your nest. How many cells did your nest contain? What are the large, long, cylindrical objects? Did every cell contain one? Did any cell with spiders also contain one of these?

_____

_____

_____

9. In your notebook, construct a table in which to list and quantify the contents of each cell. Then use the key to identify and classify them. Do not break open the **cocoons** at this time. Based on the key, how many different organisms did your nest contain?

_____

10. Examine the intact cocoons. Are both ends the same? Sketch and describe one in your notebook. Can you guess which is the anterior (head) end? Measure each cocoon. Calculate average cocoon length. Record the average and the range in cocoon sizes in your notebook. How might the range differ if nests had no cells? What other factors might cause sizes to vary?

_____

_____

_____

11. Do all of the cocoons really contain mud daubers? Construct a data table in your laboratory notebook. Provide spaces to indicate the cell identification number, the type of cell contents, and the number of organisms found in the cell.

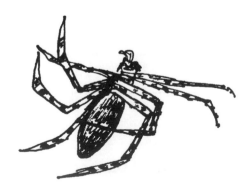

a. Grasp a cocoon in your fingers and hold it under the hand lens or microscope. Examine it carefully for anything unusual, such as a tiny hole or a spot of mud.

b. Use your fingernail or forceps to carefully break off one end of the cocoon. Gently tip out the contents onto a piece of paper. Consult the key to identify the contents. Record your findings.

c. Repeat for each cocoon. Record your results.

An opened mud dauber cocoon that has been parasitized by WOWBugs.

Discussion:

1. Construct a data table for the whole class results from Part A. (Each team should enter the data for their nest's architecture.) Calculate the average, and determine the range, for each measurement for the sum of all nests in your class. Compare these with your own team's results. What similarities do you find? What differences? What factors might be involved in this variation?

_____

_____

_____

2. Many of your nests had various holes in the mud walls. Was there any relationship between hole size and cell contents?

_____

_____

_____

3. Construct a data table for the whole class results from Part B. Each team should enter the data for their nest's inhabitants. Calculate the average, and determine the range, for the numbers of each inhabitant. How did the range compare from one type of inhabitant to another?

_____

_____

_____

4. From most to least common, what were the causes of death of mud dauber off-spring in your nest? How did overall class results compare to yours? What sample size do you think would be necessary to reflect the natural situation accurately?

_____

_____

_____

5. Did any of your cocoons contain *Melittobia*? Did anyone else's nest have them? What variable might help explain your results?

_____

_____

_____

6. What percentage of the cells would have produced living mud dauber offspring? Based on your own nest, if a female mud dauber could make 12 cells in her lifetime, how many offspring would survive to become part of next year's population? Compare your results with those of others in the class. What similarities can you find? How might you account for differences?

_____

_____

_____

7. The data collection in this activity is no different from what entomological research-ers are doing. How do your class findings compare with theirs? Review data which have already been published for other parts of the country.

8. Working in pairs or teams, construct a web or concept map that depicts the rela-tionships between each of the organisms you found.

Darwinian Selection

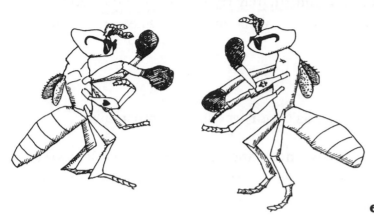

About a century ago, the young naturalist Charles Darwin put together a line of reasoning that was to turn the field of biology on its head — making the study of life both simpler, and at the same time more complex. It came to be called the **theory of evolution by natural selection**. In simplest form, it went like this:

Objectives: To determine how male WOWBugs compete among themselves.

1. Any population tends to outgrow its resources by producing more offspring than can survive.

2. Normal variations between individuals in local populations of a species include differences in the ability to acquire those limited resources.

Materials (per pair):

- *Pipe cleaner or small brush*
- *Plastic well slide with cover*
- *Stop watch or wrist watch that shows seconds*
- *10x magnifying lens, dissecting microscope, or Magiscope®*
- *Laboratory notebook*

3. Members of the population compete with one another and because of these differences, some individuals have a better chance of surviving and reproducing.

4. Because the population will come to have more of these successful individuals' offspring, slowly over generations it will shift. There will be more individuals that resemble the successful ones in various inherited traits.

In the years since Darwin's explanation, evolutionary biologists have also pointed out that among sexually reproducing animals, other members of one's species create some of the greatest obstacles to reproductive success.

Competition between males is a case in point. Males of all species compete for needed resources such as food and mates, of course. Male WOWBugs are no different, though their world is limited to the dark inside of a host cocoon. Here they are born and live and die, never leaving. Everything they need is available here, but only for a short time and not in unlimited supply. Females mate only once, and as soon as they mate, they immediately try to leave the cocoon to find a new host. Thus, in this tiny closed world, inter-male competition takes on an incredible urgency.

Procedure:

1. Get the materials you need. When ready, ask your teacher for your male.

Carefully observe and examine both your own male and your partner's male, using the hand lens or microscope. Try to learn to tell them apart by appearance (relative size, slight coloration differences, etc.).

2. If you can recognize anything distinctive about your male, set up a table in your notebook to record your notes in two columns, one describing "your" male's actions, and the other column describing the opponent male's actions. If individual recognition/identification of the two males is uncertain, you'll need to record your notes as a continuous narrative of events. In either case, leave space to provide as much detail as you can, including regular notes as to the clock time elapsed since the start of any interactions.

3. Working in pairs, use the pipe cleaner or brush to gently transfer your male and your partner's male into the empty clean plastic well slide together. When both males are in the well slide replace the cover. Under magnification, observe their interactions. How did the males react to each other in their first contact?

_____

_____

_____

4. Under magnification, continue to observe their interactions over the next several minutes. Keep careful notes of everything that occurs.

5. If time permits, pair the survivor with the winner WOWBug from another pair of students and stage another match. How does this combat compare with the first one?

_____

_____

Discussion:

1. Combine the results for the entire class in a single table. What were the various outcomes of male combat? How many fights ended in one male mutilating or killing the other? In how many cases was no fighting at all observed? How might such variation be explained?

_____

_____

_____

2. Recall that males lack eyes and therefore can't see their opponent. How might they find each other?

_____

_____

_____

3. Males in a single culture will most likely be brothers. Why should brothers fight so violently?

_____

_____

_____

4. Did anything you observed suggest how males might obtain food to supply the energy needed for combat?

_____

_____

_____

Just For Fun: A WOWBug Word Find Puzzle

```
M   Y   S   T   E   R   Y   H   B   G
I   A   E   W   O   W   B   A   U   I
N   Q   N   M   A   N   I   B   G   M
U   P   S   I   H   B   W   I   E   O
T   W   O   Y   P   O   T   T   H   C
E   S   R   A   W   U   S   A   Y   H
S   T   Y   E   L   N   L   T   P   O
D   R   Z   T   M   D   N   A   O   I
P   A   M   U   S   I   C   L   T   C
M   W   E   N   E   S   T   E   H   E
O   O   A   N   W   L   A   F   E   N
V   W   N   E   B   I   D   T   S   C
E   M   A   L   E   G   A   L   I   O
R   I   G   H   T   H   T   I   S   R
P   H   O   T   O   T   A   X   I   S
```

Find and circle these words: BOUND, CHOICE, DATA , LEFT, LIGHT, HABITAT, HOST, HYPOTHESIS, MALE, MANIPULATE, MAZE, MEAN, MINUTES, MOVE, MUSIC, MYSTERY, NEST, PHOTOTAXIS, RIGHT, SENSORY, STEM, STRAW, SWAB, TUNNEL, UP, WOWBUG.

(The answers are on page 112.)

Chapter Seven. WOWBug And Mud Dauber Biology

If this book has done its job properly, WOWBugs have whet your appetite for more information, not only about *Melittobia* and *Trypoxylon*, but about the rest of entomology, and indeed the whole biological world.

This chapter is a place to start. It provides answers to commonly asked questions about various aspects of the biology of WOWBugs and mud daubers. It also includes selected bibliographies of useful sources for further information on these and other insects.

More About Mud Daubers

Mud daubers are medium-sized, non-aggressive, solitary wasps classified in the family Sphecidae. In the United States, three species are common: the organ pipe mud dauber (*Trypoxylon politum*), the black and yellow mud dauber (*Sceliphron caementarium*) and the steel blue mud dauber (*Chalybion californicum*).

Any of these can be used to rear WOWBugs. However, the preferred species for class-room nest dissection activities is the organ pipe mud dauber, found throughout the eastern United States, from southern Maine to central Kansas and southeastern Texas. If the organ pipe mud dauber is not readily available in your geographic area, with slight modifications one of the other species can be substituted. Both are found throughout the entire United States and southern Canada, and have been widely introduced elsewhere.

The Mud Dauber Life Cycle

Unlike the perennial hives of honeybees, the nests of mud daubers are solitary, once-a-year undertakings. Although a single favorable location may have many nests, these are not a colony. Rather, they simply reflect common attraction to a favorable spot.

In early to mid-summer, mud daubers emerge from last year's nests. After mating, females begin to construct nests near a reliable source of water or mud and abundant spiders. Organ pipe mud daubers and black and yellow mud daubers pick up mud and carry it in their jaws. The steel blue mud dauber, however, carries only water, which it uses to soften and remove mud from pre-existing nests made by the other two species. After reusing others' nests, it reseals them with this recycled mud.

Each female organ pipe mud dauber begins by constructing a single mud tube, an activity that requires from three hours to a full day's labor. The female then switches to hunting spiders. Finding one, she stings it, then carries it back to the tube in her jaws and packs its paralyzed body inside. The wasp may gather from 3 to 18 spiders before she pauses. The number of spiders appears to be related to their size, a matter both of spider species and of seasonality, for spiders get larger as the summer progresses (Cross et al., 1975).

Finally the wasp lays an egg across the abdomen of one of the larger spiders, then seals off the prey and egg behind a mud partition. Repeating this entire process results in a linear series of cells within each tube.

Usually during construction the female is joined by a male who moves into the tube, mates repeatedly with her, and stands guard, defending the nest from insect intruders and competitors. However, he does not help in constructing the nest or in provisioning it.

Over the single season of her short adult life, a female mud dauber may construct several nests in various locations or add new tubes to preexisting nests. However, neither she nor her mate show any further interest in the completed nests or the offspring within. The other two mud dauber species have similar behavior, except for the absence of a guarding male.

Mud dauber development is an example of complete metamorphosis, in which the immature and adult forms are completely different creatures not unlike a caterpillar and butterfly. After about two days, the egg hatches into a young larva, which consumes the spider on which it rests. Moving freely about within its cell, the growing larva eats the remaining spiders over the course of about two weeks. In the now-empty compartment, it constructs a mesh cradle about itself, then fashions an elongate cylindrical cocoon, supported and suspended in the silk.

Inside, the larva enters diapause, a period of developmental delay. It remains a limp yellow prepupa for about nine months or for the duration of the winter. (In the southern United States, a part of the population may continue to develop without diapause late in the summer to produce a small second generation of adults.) When warm temperatures return, development resumes.

The larva molts into a pupa, acquires adult coloration gradually over the next six to eight weeks, then molts one last time into a winged adult wasp. Shortly afterward, the adult chews its way to freedom, first through the cocoon, then through the side wall of the nest. Interestingly, while larvae subsist on spider meat, adult mud daubers apparently feed upon nectar sipped from flowers, supplemented perhaps by the body fluids of spiders they have stung.

Several additional teaching aids about mud dauber wasps are available. A videotape from the "Working With WOWBugs" series is devoted to the biology of the organ pipe mud dauber. A set of twenty kodachrome slides, with a detailed guide, chronicles various nest inhabitants. For additional life history information about the inhabitants, see *What's Inside A Mud Dauber's Nest?: A Teachers' Guide With Identification Keys.* See Chapter 8 or the order form at the back of this book for information on obtaining these materials.

Additional Nest Dissection Background

Students may wish to compare their data with published measurements. In Alabama (Cross et al. 1975), the organ pipe mud dauber averaged 3.8 cell compartments per completed mud tube, with an inside tube width of 10.2 mm and average tube length of 106.2 mm (range 75-145 mm). The average cell length was 19.9 mm (range 7.4-28.0 mm). Interestingly, the mother wasp apparently constructed larger cells for her female-producing eggs: the average length of male-producing cells was 20.7 mm; for female-producing cells, 22.7 mm. Shafer (1949) describes the nesting of the black and yellow mud dauber.

Many factors affect the population dynamics at a particular locality. In a large sample of organ pipe mud dauber nests from nine localities in Missouri and Mississippi (Molumby 1995), mortality from all causes averaged 36% (range, 1-57%). *Melittobia* was the major cause of cell mortality, parasitizing an average of 23% of all cells (range, 0-35%). Carpet beetles accounted for 7% of failures, cuckoo wasps and bee flies for 3% each, and pirate flies for an additional 2%. Velvet ants occurred at only three of the sampled locations. Each mother wasp constructed an average of 12.27 cells in her lifetime, and half of these failed. Cross et al. (1975) obtained essentially similar results in Alabama.

Questions About WOWBug And Mud Dauber Biology

Do WOWBugs eat at all?

WOWBug larvae feed on their host, of course. Adult WOWBugs apparently don't need to eat to stay alive. However, females cannot mature their eggs unless they receive protein-rich fluids from a host. Once they find a suitable host, they sting it. Then they turn around and feed on the tiny droplets that flow from the sting wound.

Males were once thought not to feed, but over the years we've seen evidence that they might be cannibalistic, at least on occasion. Males often chew on the bodies of defeated competitors after a battle. In addition, males have sometimes been observed to begin what looks like normal courtship with a female. Part way through the ritual, they instead have begun to chew on the female's neck and thorax, fatally wounding her, after which they chew at these parts for an extended time.

For information on feeding a WOWBug culture in the classroom, see the next chapter.

What exactly is a parasitic wasp?

According to the dictionary **parasites** are plants or animals that live on or within another organism, taking enough nourishment to live and reproduce without killing or compensating this **host**. The term is derived from the Greek word *parasitos*, meaning one who eats beside or at the table of another. A flea on a dog, a tapeworm in the gut of an animal, or mistletoe growing on an oak tree are examples of parasites. A **predator**, on the other hand, kills another organism outright, and feeds upon one after another of this **prey**.

Like most folks, we have called WOWBugs parasites. However, in the purest sense, this isn't quite accurate. Most so-called **parasitic wasps** are neither parasitic nor predatory, but have a life style that is somewhere in between. Unlike true parasites, the wasps' larval stages invariably kill the organism on which they feed. Unlike predators, parasitic wasps require only one individual in order to complete their life cycle. Because they don't fit neatly into either category of parasite or predator, the parasitic wasps are more accurately termed **parasitoids** by entomologists. A further difference is that while many parasites and predators have the same food habits throughout life, parasitoid wasps often live a double life. The larvae are carnivorous, destroying their paralyzed host as they grow, but the adults may feed on sugars such as nectar or may not eat at all.

Parasitic wasps include a vast number of species. There are even parasites of parasites, called **hyperparasitoids** by entomologists. The life styles of parasitic wasps are diverse. Some attack insect eggs; others attack actively feeding larval stages like caterpillars. Still others specialize on adult or pupal stages of their hosts. Some develop entirely inside their host, and are called **endoparasitoids**. Others, like WOWBugs, develop externally, feeding through a lesion made in the host's cuticle; these are termed **ectoparasitoids**.

In some cases multiple individuals develop in groups on or in a single host. These **gregarious** parasitoids are thus distinctly different from those that develop singly in or on their host (**solitary** parasitoids).

Most parasitoid wasps tend to be **host specific** specialists, restricted to feeding on a single species of host. Some are able to attack any of several related species of hosts. Others are microhabitat-specific or **niche-specific generalists**. For example, a species that attacks only leaf-rolling caterpillars might encounter several unrelated kinds of caterpillars in this niche, any of which can serve as a suitable host.

WOWBugs, *Melittobia digitata*, are parasitoid wasps — technically, niche specific, gregarious ectoparasitoids. They can successfully attack almost any kind of solitary bee or wasp that constructs a nest, which means they can feed on a variety of unrelated host insects. They lay numerous eggs in groups on the outer surface of the host; when the eggs hatch the gregarious larvae feed through the host's skin and develop together.

Even though they are highly gregarious, we would not describe WOWBugs as social, however. This is because the essential ingredient of social behavior, such as occurs in honeybees or ants, is the existence of reproductive (queen) and sterile (worker) members in the group.

Where do mud daubers most often nest?

Nests can occur on nearly any building where there is a protective overhand. Productive sites include picnic shelters, underneath backyard decks and porches, on the interior walls of carports, barns, and other sheds and outbuildings, and under highway bridges over streams. Sites near permanent water sources are generally most productive, as water is needed to provide the mud used for nest construction.

When is the best time to collect their nests?

Any time of year will work, but we recommend the colder months of the year (roughly October to March). At this time, all nest contents will be dormant or in diapause. By keeping the nests refrigerated in plastic containers or sealed plastic bags, they can be kept ready for use at any time as needed. For a discussion of the merits of summer- and winter-collected nests for classroom use, see the following chapter.

What do the scientific names mean?

WOWBugs are technically *Melittobia digitata*. This is their **scientific name**, a Latinized moniker understood by scientists everywhere, regardless of their spoken language.

Every known species of animal plant or microbe has been bestowed with such a **binomial**, or pair of names, derived from Latin or Greek (or made to appear as though they were). The first name is always capitalized and is termed the **genus**. The second name in the binomial is the **specific epithet** and it is always written in lower case. Because the words are in a foreign language of sorts, every time the binomial appears, it is underlined or italicized; this sets it apart from the rest of the text. (Other levels of classification, such as the family name, don't get this special treatment. They are just printed in a normal typeface.)

Scientists usually use a name that denotes a characteristic of the species. The "digitata" in *Melittobia digitata* refers to a finger-like projection or "digit" that is prominently visible on the male's antenna. Sometimes a species may be named after its discoverer. *Melittobia evansi*, is named for Dr. David Evans, who first collected it. Species may also be named for the place they were discovered. *Melittobia australica* is an example.

When we began this project, *Melittobia digitata* had no common name (as is the case for the vast majority of all insects). Originally we called them just "parasitic wasps." Later they were christened "fast wasps," in reference to their rapid life cycle. However, it quickly became apparent that the name "wasp" caused unfounded concern among students, teachers, and parents, who wrongly assumed the "fast" had something to do with a quick sting. Thus the name WOWBug was invented. It properly reflects our awe and amazement at the incredible biological intricacies displayed by *Melittobia digitata*. Also, it was suggested that "WOW" could serve as an acronym for "Working on Wasps." So we've adopted and trademarked our invented name as a user-friendly descriptor of what's in store when you experience the wonders of WOWBugs through the activities in this book.

WOWBug Life Cycle At Room Temperature

Day Number

1

Place 5 Melittobia *females on mud dauber larva.* →

2

3

4

5

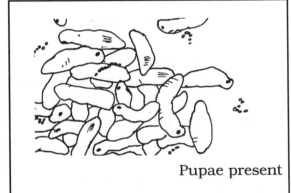

Eggs present

6

7

8

9

Larvae present

Hardiest point in life cycle.
This is the point at which diapause may occur. →

10

11

12

13

Pupae present

14

Pull out red-eye pupae (females) and place on a
new host, if a male-only culture is desired. →

15

16

17

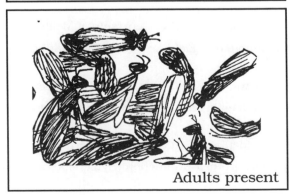

18

19

20

21

Adults present

Classroom-Useful References

It is our hope that the activities in this manual will stimulate teachers and students to want to further their understanding of insect biology. Many of the manual's activities will suggest additional questions and research topics to experienced teachers. Outside reference materials will in most cases facilitate these advanced studies. The brief listing below provides further background on WOWBugs, mud daubers and various topics suggested by this manual's activities.

A useful introduction to using insects in pre-college teaching that includes an extensive bibliography is "Insects as teaching tools in primary and secondary education," by R. W. Matthews et al., 1997 (*Annual Review of Entomology* 42: 269-289).

WOWBugs And Their Relatives

Dahms, E. C. 1984. A review of the biology of species in the genus *Melittobia* (Hymenoptera: Eulophidae) with interpretations and additions using observations on *Melittobia australica. Memoirs, Queensland Museum* 21 (2): 337-360.

Evans, D.A., and Matthews, R. W. 1976. Comparative courtship behaviour in two species of the parasitic chalcid wasp *Melittobia. Anim. Behav.* 24: 46-51.

Evans, H. E. 1966. "Parasitic Wasps, And How They Made Peyton Place Possible." Chap. 11, pp. 227-251. *Life on a Little-Known Planet.* New York: Dutton Press.

Freeman, B. E., and Ittyeipe, K. 1982. Morph determination in *Melittobia,* a eulophid wasp. *Ecological Entomol.* 7: 355-363.

Gonzalez, J. M., Matthews, R. W., and Matthews, J. R. 1985. A sex pheromone in males of *Melittobia australica* and *M. femorata* (Hymenoptera: Eulophidae). *Florida Entomol.* 68(2): 279-286.

Matthews, R. W. 1982. Courtship of Melittobia wasps. pp. 162-166 in *Insect Behavior. A Sourcebook of Laboratory and Field Activities,* J. R. Matthews and R. W. Matthews, editors. Boulder: Westview Press.

Matthews, R. W., Yukawa, J., and Gonzalez, J. M. 1985. Sex pheromones in male *Melittobia* parasitic wasps: female response to conspecific and congeneric males of 3 species. *J. Ethology* 3: 59-62.

Schmieder, R. G. 1933. The polymorphic forms of *Melittobia chalybii* Ashmead and the determining factors involved in their production (Hymenoptera, Chalcidoidea, Eulophidae). *Biol. Bull.* 65: 338-354.

Tumlinson, J. H., Lewis, W. J., and Vet, L. E. M. 1993. How parasitic wasps find their hosts. *Scientific American* 268(3): 100-106.

Vet, L. E., Van Lenteren, J. C., Heymans, M., and Meelis, E. 1983. An airflow olfactometer for measuring olfactory responses of hymenopterous parasitoids and other small insects. *Physiol. Entomol.* 8: 97-106.

Mud Daubers And Their Relatives

Barber, M. C. and Matthews, R. W. 1979. Utilization of trap nests by the pipe-organ mud dauber, *Trypargilum politum* (Hymenoptera: Sphecidae). *Annals Entomol. Soc. America* 72: 260-262.

Brockmann, H. J. 1980. Diversity in the nesting behavior of mud daubers *(Trypoxylon politum* Say; Sphecidae). *Florida Entomol.* 63: 53-64.

Coward, S., and Matthews, R. W. 1995. Tufted titmouse *(Parus bicolor)* predation on mud dauber wasp prepupae *(Trypoxylon politum). J. Kansas Entomol. Soc.* 68: 371-373.

Covillle, R. E. 1982. Wasps of the genus *Trypoxylon* subgenus *Trypargilum* in North America (Hymenoptera: Sphecidae). *Univ. Calif. Publ. Entomol.* 97: 1-147.

Cross, E. A., Stith, M. G., and Bauman, T. R. 1975. Bionomics of the organ pipe mud dauber, *Trypoxylon politum* (Hymenoptera: Sphecidae). *Annals Entomol. Soc. America* 68: 901-906.

Downing, H. 1995. Methods of escape for both fly parasites and wasps from the clustered pipes of *Trypoxylon politum* nests (Hymenoptera: Sphecidae). *J. Kansas Entomol. Soc.* 68: 473-476.

Irving, W. G., and Hinman, E. H. 1935. The blue mud-dauber as a predator of the black widow spider. *Science* 82: 395-396.

Landes, D. A., Obin, M. S., Cady, A. B. and Hunt, J. H. 1987. Seasonal and latitudinal variation in spider prey of the mud dauber *Chalybion californicum* (Hymenoptera, Sphecidae). *J. Arachnol.* 15:249 -256.

Matthews, R. W. 1997. Teaching ecological interactions with mud dauber nests. *American Biology Teacher* 59: 152-158.

Matthews, R. W. and Matthews, J. R. 1968. A note on *Trypoxylon (Trypargilum) arizonense* in trap nests from Arizona, with a review of prey preferences and cocoon structure in the genus (Hymenoptera: Sphecidae). *Psyche* 75: 289-293.

Molumby, A. 1995. Dynamics of parasitism in the organ-pipe wasp, *Trypoxylon politum*: effects of spatial scale on parasitoid functional response. *Ecological Entomol.* 20: 159-168.

Muma, M. H., and Jeffers, W. F. 1945. Studies of the spider prey of several mud-dauber wasps. *Annals Entomol. Soc. America* 38: 245-255.

Rau, P. 1935. The wasp, *Chalybion cyaneum* Fab., preys upon the black widow spider, *Latrodectus mactans* Fab. (Hymen., Araneae). *Entomol. News* 46: 259-260.

Shafer, G. D. 1949. *The Ways of a Mud Dauber*. Stanford: Stanford University Press. 78 pp.

Selected General Texts on Insect Biology

Adams, J., ed. 1992. *Insect Potpourri: Adventures in Entomology*. Gainesville: Sandhill Crane. 336 pp.

Berenbaum, M. R. 1989. *Ninety-nine Gnats, Nits, and Nibblers*. Urbana: Univ. Illinois Press. 254 pp.

Berenbaum, M. R. 1995. *Bugs in the System. Insects and their Impact on Human Affairs*. Reading: Addison-Wesley. 377 pp.

Brackenbury, J. 1994. *Insects: Life Cycles and the Seasons*. U. K.: Blandford. 160 pp.

Evans, H. E. 1984. *Life on a Little-Known Planet*. Chicago: Univ. Chicago Press. 2nd ed.

Farb, P. 1980. *The Insects*. N. Y.: Time-Life. 143 pp.

Imes, R. 1992. *The Practical Entomologist*. N. Y.: Simon & Schuster. 160 pp.

Matthews, R. W., and Matthews, J. R. 1978. *Insect Behavior*. N. Y.: John Wiley & Sons. 507 pp.

O'Toole, C. 1995. *Alien Empire: An Exploration of the Lives of Insects*. N. Y.: Harper-Collins. 224 pp.

Peters, M. 1988. *Insects and Human Society*. N. Y.: Van Nostrand Reinhold. 450 pp.

Romoser, W. S., and Stoffolano, J. G. 1994. *The Science of Entomology*. Dubuque: W. C. Brown. 552 pp. 3rd ed.

Stokes, D. W. 1983. *A Guide to Observing Insect Lives*. Boston: Little, Brown. 371 pp.

Suzuki, D. 1992. *Looking at Insects*. N. Y.: John Wiley & Sons, 96 pp.

Turpin, F. T. 1992. *The Insect Appreciation Digest*. Lanham: The Entomological Foundation. 144 pp.

Useful Identification Guides

Arnett, R. H., Jr., and Jacques, R. L., Jr. 1981. *Simon & Schuster's Guide to Insects*. N. Y.: Simon & Schuster.

Arnett, R. H., Jr, and Jacques, R. I., Jr. 1985. *Insect Life. A Field Manual for the Amateur Naturalist*. Englewood Cliffs: Prentice Hall. 354 pp.

Borror, D. J., and White, R. E. 1970. *A Field Guide to the Insects of America North of Mexico*. Boston: Houghton Mifflin. 404 pp.

Chu, H. F. 1992. *The Immature Insects*. Pictured Key Nature Series. Dubuque: W. C. Brown. 352 pp. 2nd ed.

Dunn, G. A. 1994. *The Insect Identification Guide*, 3rd ed. E. Lansing: Young Entomologists' Society. 70 pp.

Kaston, B. J. 1978. *How to Know the Spiders*. Pictured Key Nature Series. Dubuque: W. C. Brown. 272 pp. 3rd ed.

Leahy, C. 1987. *Peterson's First Guide to Insects of North America*. Boston: Houghton Mifflin. 128 pp.

Lehmkuhl, D. M. 1979. *How to Know the Aquatic Insects*. Dubuque: W. C. Brown. 168 pp.

Levi, H. W., and Levi, L. R. 1968. *Spiders and Their Kin*. N. Y.: Golden. 160 pp.

McGavin, G. C. 1992. *American Nature Guides: Insects*. N. Y.: Smithmark. 208 pp.

Walton, R. K. 1990. *The Audubon Society Pocket Guide to Familiar Butterflies and Moths of North America*. N. Y.: Knopf. 190 pp.

Wright, A. B. 1993. *A Simplified Field Guide to the Caterpillars of Common Butterflies and Moths of North America.* Boston: Houghton Mifflin. 128 pp.

Zim, H. S., and Cottam, C. 1987. *Insects: A Guide to Familiar American Insects.* N. Y.: Golden. 160 pp. rev. ed.

Selected References on Insect Rearing and Maintenance

Carolina Biological Supply. 1995. *Carolina Arthropods Manual.* Burlington: Carolina Biological Supply. 31 pp.

Dunn, G. A. 1993. *Caring for Insect Livestock: An Insect Rearing Manual.* E. Lansing: Young Entomologists' Society. 96 pp.

Hampton, C. H., Hampton, C. D., and Kramer, D. C. 1994. *Classroom Creature Culture: Algae to Anoles.* Arlington: National Science Teachers Association. 96 pp. rev. ed.

Kneidel, S. S. 1994. *Pet Bugs: A Kid's Guide to Catching and Keeping Touchable Insects.* N. Y.: John Wiley & Sons. 117 pp.

Kramer, D. C. 1989. *Animals in the Classroom: Selection, Care and Observations.* Menlo Park: Addison-Wesley. 234 pp.

Lutz, F. E., Welch, P. S., Galtsoff, P. S., and Needham, J. G. 1959. *Culture Methods for Invertebrate Animals.* N. Y.: Dover. 590 pp.

Silverly, R. E. 1962. *Rearing Insects in Schools.* Dubuque: W. C. Brown. 113 pp.

Singh, P., and Moore, R. F., eds. 1985. *Handbook of Insect Rearing*, vols. 1, 2. Amsterdam: Elsevier. 488 pp., 514 pp.

Smith, R. W. 1987. *Critters in the Classroom.* Grand Rapids: Instructional Fair. 96 pp.

Chapter Eight.
Teaching Aids

In the process of developing and testing the activities in this book, research scientists worked shoulder-to-shoulder with classroom teachers for almost three years. Along the way, these participants developed and shared a great many interesting ideas, useful suggestions, and insightful observations.

This chapter seeks to share many of these. It's our hope that as you proceed along your own WOWBug journey, you'll find that nothing that comes up will bug you!

Establishing And Maintaining A WOWBug Culture

WOWBug reproduction has been likened to a lottery in which few win, but those that do win really big! In nature, female WOWBugs must find hosts, a risky business. Due to small size and weak flying ability, the chance of an individual successfully dispersing beyond the immediate area is very small. However, there can be a huge payoff. Depending upon the size of the host, up to a thousand young may be produced by a single female. The fact that these tiny insects are found all over the world attests to the success of their strategy of consistently producing as many offspring as possible.

What practical implications does this have for the teacher using WOWBugs in the classroom? One, obviously, is that with hundreds of young emerging from a single host within a single rearing container, it takes very few cultures to have enough WOWBugs for several classes. To keep a culture going, a few newly emerged adults should be placed with fresh hosts on a regular basis (about once a month). The rest can be safely released outdoors to play in nature's lottery.

Another is that because the number of young that WOWBugs produce is related more to host size than to number of females, success can be made more consistent by putting several females in with a single host.

Still another is to remember that adult females "want" to escape. They are ready to find new hosts. If you do not keep their container tightly stoppered, they will quickly

Helpful Hints

- *Always set a few more cultures than you think you will need.*
- *If cultures must be refrigerated, do so in the prepupa (fully grown larva) stage, not as adults.*
- *Release adults outside when the study is complete.*
- *Label culture vials at one end or the other (either the bottom of the vial, or up near the cotton) to avoid obscuring the viewing area.*
- *Label baby food jars on their lids.*
- *Rest each vial on poster putty in a Petri dish or small plastic box, rather than having students handle individual vials. These containers are easier for students to handle and carry, and provide some protection against the host being rolled about inside the vial.*

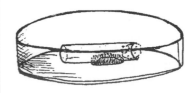

More Helpful Hints

• *Store the Petri dishes or boxes in a drawer or tub.*
• *For older students, vials can be easily stored along the side of a cabinet or chalkboard, stuck firmly in a small wad of poster putty.*
• *As an alternative, use clear view chambers. Label them on the end or side. Sixteen chambers will fit neatly into a single sandwich-size box. View chambers are excellent if you plan to photograph WOWBugs.*
• *Before setting up cultures, clean and disinfect culture tubes, jars, chambers, etc. to reduce the possibility of contamination by mold.*
• *Before any activity that involves the use of small numbers of adults, fill individual vials or other containers with an appropriate number of WOWBugs for each student or team. This will forestall students dumping out "twenty million" and wasting time rounding up the excess.*
• *View the videotape "Working With WOWBugs: Rearing and Maintenance" for additional tips.*

escape. Remember, also, WOWBugs' defensive trick. If you poke one as you are attempting to move it, it often will fall over as if dead. Don't be fooled. Moments later, it will get up and begin to run away again. With the bristles of a soft brush, scoop up the seemingly dead wasp while it's playing possum.

Starting Cultures With WOWBug Adults

Start the first culture as soon as possible after receiving your first batch of female WOWBugs. Your new adult WOWBugs do not need to be fed or watered. They will obtain their nourishment from their host.

If you are delayed, keep the adults in a cool but not cold place to slow down their metabolism. (Refrigeration is possible but risky, because they are less cold-tolerant than either their own pupae or those of their mud dauber hosts.)

At normal room temperatures of 72 to 78 degrees F (22-25 degrees C) the average WOWBug life cycle is 21 days. This can be shortened to between 14 and 17 days by keeping your cultures at 85 to 90 degrees F (30-32 degrees C) or extended by keeping the cultures somewhat cooler.

A continuous culture system is easy to set up, and will assure that you always have adults, larvae, and pupae when you need them. It's as simple as spending 5 minutes every week or two to place 4 to 6 adult female WOWBugs in a fresh container with a new host.

1. Start by setting up your rearing chambers. Assuring the cleanliness of these containers is crucial for success. The most common cause of culture failure is mold. Never

use a container that has not been washed, then rinsed with dilute bleach, alcohol, or other disinfectant. An inexpensive product called B-Brite, used by home brewers to sterilize bottles prior to bottling, works very well for sterilizing rearing containers, and has the advantage of being kinder to hands and clothing.

> **Classroom Safety**
>
> • *Practice safety with glass-ware. Use plastic instead whenever possible.*
> • *Protective eye wear is suggested during activities that involve breaking open mud nests.*
> • *Normal prudence dictates washing hands before and after handling living organisms or their remains.*

2. After opening the host cocoon as described below, carefully transfer the host from its cocoon into the rearing container. Avoid touching either the host or the inside of the container. This will minimize the second most common source of WOWBug culture contamination, microbes transferred during host handling.

3. Place the host on its side by tipping the container gently, if necessary. Use poster putty to keep the container in the same relative position throughout development for best viewing. If it is turned about, especially after adults have begun emerging, detritus will cover the inside, obscuring the view of the contents.

4. When released, adult female WOWBugs tend to crawl or hop rather than fly. Tip a few out of the shipping container onto a sheet of white paper. Pick them up gently in the bristles of a small brush or on the fuzz of a pipe cleaner. Tap them into the rearing container with the host. Add 4 to 6 adult female WOWBugs into the container in this way. Close the container with a tight-fitting lid or a tight plug of cotton. No special provision for air needs to be made. Air exchange through the cotton plug or around the edges of the lid is sufficient. Place it where it won't be jarred about.

5. Round up WOWBugs by placing a small clear vial over the top of each one in turn. They will crawl up into the vial. Plug the open end securely with cotton.

Starting Cultures With WOWBug Pupae

1. To begin a regular mixed-sex WOWBug culture from pupae, simply allow adults to emerge together. Mating occurs almost immediately upon emergence. Place females from this culture onto fresh hosts as described above.

2. To produce a culture that contains only males, remove several dark colored WOWBug pupae. Those with red eyes at this stage are females. Put 4 to 6 of them in a rearing chamber with a fresh host as described above. Because they will have no access to males when they emerge, all of their offspring will be male.

As the adult male offspring emerge, you may wish to transfer them into individual holding containers. They are extremely aggressive toward one another and if not isolated, only a few will survive. One or two unmated females will only produce 8 to 20 males on a mud dauber host. If you need more males for an activity, you might wish to start several simultaneous cultures with unmated females.

Long-term Storage of Cultures

For long-term storage, cultures are best refrigerated when WOWBugs are in the prepupa (fully fed larva) stage. This most closely mimics the situation in which they spend the winter outdoors. Should it be absolutely necessary to refrigerate adults, keep them cold for as short a time as possible, and store them in the dairy compartment on the refrigerator door where the temperature is slightly warmer. Don't be alarmed if they don't move right away when you take them out. It sometimes takes up to an hour for them to warm up enough to begin to act normally.

Using Natural Hosts

The most common natural hosts for WOWBugs are mud dauber wasp offspring which have just finished feeding and are resting in their cocoons. At this stage they are called prepupae. Mud dauber prepupae are fragile, limp, and harmless.

Prepupae can easily be tipped out of their brown cocoon. You can open either end. Insert your thumbnail slightly into the top, then pop off the end like a cap. Turn the open end down toward the open vial, and gently shake the prepupa out. If you need to move one, ease it onto a brush. It will hang over like a bag of jelly. Place it gently. If punctured, prepupae are useless as hosts and must be discarded.

Mud dauber nests collected during the cold winter months when mud daubers are not actively nesting will contain prepupae in cocoons. Because these are in a state of arrested development (diapause), they can be kept in plastic bags or containers in a refrigerator (not a freezer!) for years, either within the complete nests or as individual cocoons. If and when they are allowed to become warm again, they will resume development. On the average, at room temperature, adult mud daubers will emerge about two months after being taken out of cold storage. Unless you actually want adult mud daubers, keep prepupae in the refrigerator until needed for hosts.

Using Alternate Hosts

If mud daubers are in short supply, other hosts often prove suitable to keep the cultures going. WOWBugs have been reared successfully on immature stages of over 20 different insect host species, ranging from cockroaches to flies to honeybees. A bit of experimentation will be in order. They may be less satisfactory than mud dauber prepupae for student viewing of the life cycle.

Blow fly (*Sarcophaga bullata*) puparia purchased from a biological supply company make quite satisfactory hosts and are the preferred substitute. Keep extra fly puparia in the refrigerator in a covered container until needed. Occasionally, a puparium will die; you will usually recognize this by its unpleasant smell.

While it is not necessary to open an end of the blowfly puparium, carefully doing so exposes a bit of the white pupa inside and allows a visual check that the pupa is healthy. If you see any liquid oozing from an opened puparium, you have punctured the pupa; discard the puparium and try another.

To start a culture, put two or three puparia in a rearing chamber with 5 to 10 WOWBug females. Because blow fly pupae are smaller than mud dauber prepupae, you will raise proportionately fewer WOWBugs (on the order of 50 to 100) on each one.

Adults will chew out through the host puparium, However, if you have opened the puparium, as soon as pink-eyed WOWBug pupae appear, you can dump out the contents so they can be seen. Males tend to stay inside. Once adults begin to appear, you may need to break apart the puparium and chase them out with a soft brush.

Occasionally, seemingly good puparia are not successfully parasitized. Then after about two weeks, a large hairy fly will emerge. This is sufficiently interesting to students that you might consider rearing a host without allowing WOWBugs to have access to it.

Obtaining Mud Dauber Nests

Nests for classroom use should be collected during the cool months between September and April, when nests have been abandoned, and the nest contents are in diapause. You may wish to remove the nests yourself. Alternatively, students are often aware of places where mud dauber nests occur and eager to help collect nests. Consider extra credit or other suitable reward. In any case, collect wisely! Don't gather more nests than you need.

Bridges are particularly rewarding places to look for nests. Other good sites include old barns (look on the walls around entrances), golf course shelters near water holes, under decks and porches, and on carport walls.

Typically, favorable sites will have nests of various ages and conditions. **If you have a choice, collect current nests for these activities.** Old nests from previous nesting cycles characteristically have large holes in their sides where newly adult offspring chewed through to emerge. Sometimes a later occupant may have refilled these holes with mud of a different color. *Current year* nests — those completed during the most recent nesting season — lack these holes because the new generation of wasps is still inside. (Current nests may have an occasional small hole, however, if they have been parasitized.)

Nests attached to wood generally will be easier to remove than those attached to concrete or brick. Use a putty knife, paint scraper, or stiff spatula to pry off and dislodge nests. Remove nests from the top downward for less chance of cracking them. As they fall, catch them in a net or box. Place each in a separate clear plastic resealable bag. Label the bag with the data and locality, using a fine-tipped permanent marker.

> *There was a mud dauber from Gloucester —*
> *The scientist thought he had lost her,*
> *But he found her that night*
> *In the freezer, locked tight,*
> *And we all had to help him defrost her.*

Store the bags in a refrigerator — not the freezer! — until use. Refrigerate mud dauber nests in small units so as to be able to remove one section at a time. Like all arthropods, the nest inhabitants are cold blooded and can be kept refrigerated almost indefinitely.

Should you should need to collect nests during the summer, there is little risk from their makers. Unlike their social relatives the paper wasps, mud daubers are solitary nesters and do not defend their nests, even while constructing them. If disturbed during active nesting, the wasps simply fly away. They are not aggressive toward people.

Are mud dauber nests safe in the laboratory? Yes, particularly if collected from late fall to very early spring. Because of the wasp's life cycle, an adult would never lurk in a nest collected in fall, winter, or spring. The insects within the cocoons are helpless grub-like immatures. Unless they are kept at room temperature for weeks, they will not complete their development to adulthood.

Because mud daubers collect spiders, some teachers have expressed concern about the possibiity of spider bites. The spider prey have been stung and paralyzed. If still alive at all, they cannot move except for an occasional leg twitch. The steel blue mud dauber, *Chalybion californicum,* has been reported to capture black widow spiders as prey (see Irving and Hinman, 1935; Rau, 1935; Landes et al., 1987, in the references in Chapter 7). This species often nests in the "blob" type mud nests originally made by the black and yellow mud dauber, *Sceliphron caementarium.* However, the black and yellow mud dauber and the organ pipe mud dauber (the preferred species for the nest dissection activity) have never been reported to prey on black widows or brown recluse spiders. (See Muma and Jeffers, 1945; Matthews and Matthews, 1968.)

However, because nests are, after all, made of mud, and contain various living organisms, including microbes, simple prudence dictates that you require students to wash their hands after handling nests.

Safe Collecting Practices

• Mud dauber nests are often located in habitats shared by other wildlife. Dress appropriately when collecting nests, and watch out for other animals, both small (paper wasps) and large (snakes).

• Location of mud dauber nests may require climbing. Follow appropriate supervision and safety practices.

• Collecting tools may have sharp edges. Use caution.

• Nests may crumble during collection. Protect eyes and face by wearing goggles.

• Collect nests only from late fall to very early spring. Late spring and summer nests may contain adult wasps.

• Although adult mud daubers usually are not aggressive, they are capable of stinging. If one should be brought into the classroom, capture it quickly in a container and release it outside.

Questions About WOWBugs And Mud-Daubers In The Classroom

What should I feed the WOWBugs in my classroom?

Some scientists who work with other parasitic wasps routinely add bits of a soaked raisin to their cultures. They feel the adult insects benefit from such a carbohydrate source. The soaked raisin bits must be replaced at least every other day, or they become fermented and begin to mold. We don't recommend this, because the effects of this feeding regimen on WOWBug health or longevity has never been systematically investigated. It could, however, make an interesting question for a science fair project or other independent investigation.

Some of my WOWBug cultures molded. Why? How can I keep it from happening again?

Contamination by molds most often results from one of two sources: use of non-sterile rearing containers, and/or touching the host larva with one's hands during its transfer from the cocoon to the rearing container.

Review the steps for setting up a WOWBug culture. Make it a rule never to use second-hand containers as rearing chambers without first washing, then rinsing them with dilute bleach, alcohol, or a B-Brite solution. When transfering host larvae, dump the larva from the cocoon into the rearing chamber without handling it directly.

In spite of such precautions, hosts sometimes mold. Spores may have been introduced on the bodies of the parent WOWBugs. There is really nothing that can be done to stop contamination that occurs in this manner. To assure an ample supply of developing cultures, always set up some extras.

Moldy hosts present interesting teaching opportunities. They can be used to get students thinking about the processes of decomposition and recycling, and ways in which molds are an important part of the natural scheme of things. The class can be encouraged to determine whether there is more than one kind of mold represented. They also can be led to consider possible reasons why moldy larvae are almost never found inside intact cocoons.

What if, when a mud dauber cocoon is opened, it already has a parasite?

Immediately place it in a covered container and save it for "Show and Tell" time! After you have identified it using the key in the "Mud Dauber Nest Dissection" activity and shared it with students, take it outside and dispose of it, well away from your hosts and healthy cultures so that there is no chance for contamination. Alternatively, rear them to see what the adults look like, and then release the adults outside.

Several other species of *Melittobia* are known to attack mud daubers. These are often encountered when dissecting mud dauber nests. One common parasite is *Melittobia femorata*. It is difficult to distinguish it from the WOWBug, *Melittobia digitata*. While the biology of the other *Melittobia* species is very similar to that of *Melittobia digitata*, there are some important differences that make the other species less suitable for use in the activities in this book. It is best to isolate and dispose of other unknown species of *Melittobia* in order to keep your WOWBug colonies pure.

Can we safely use summer-collected nests for classroom activities?

We don't recommend it as a whole-class activity. However, if you plan to start the school year with mud dauber nest dissection, it can be interesting to open some freshly collected nests. These nests may still have newly made cells stuffed with live but paralyzed spiders. Other cells may have developing parasites and predators which are impressive to see. Note that summer-collected nests also may have adult mud daubers. While not aggressive, they are still capable of stinging. Use care, and be ready to corral whatever you may find into a secure container. Chilling the nest for a couple of hours before you begin the dissection will slow down whatever arthropods are within. However, longer refrigeration will kill any larvae not yet inside cocoons.

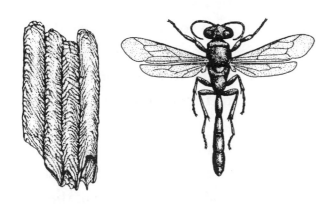

An organ-pipe nest, and a female Trypoxylon *(adapted from Borrer et al., 1981.* An Introduction to the Study of Insects, *Saunders College Publishing).*

Won't collecting a lot of mud dauber nests for my classroom reduce local mud dauber populations?

Of course you should be responsible and not collect more nests than you really need. However, because mud daubers prefer to nest in protected places, many nests are hidden. Even if you collect a great many, there will be a refuge population.

My students are bringing in a different type of mud nest. It resembles a blob of mud thrown against a wall. Can these be used for the dissection activity? What about for WOWBug rearing?

This is another species of spider-hunting wasp, the black and yellow mud dauber, *Sceliphron caementarium*. The last part of its name refers to the cement-like nature of its nest. As this would suggest, the nests are more difficult to remove and break open.

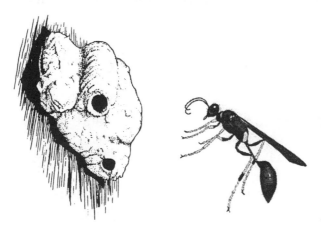

However, they are completely suitable otherwise.

The cocoons of the black and yellow mud dauber are elongate, light brown, papery thin, and tear easily. The larva is visible through the cocoon. If both mud dauber species are available, a comparison of the contents of their nests could be undertaken.

A nest of the black and yellow mud dauber (adapted from Little, 1957. General and Applied Entomology, *Harper & Row), and the* Sceliphron *female.*

Statistical Analysis: Chi-Square Tests

In today's world, we are continually bombarded by claims based on statistical probabilities. Whenever it is possible and appropriate to do so, students should be given opportunities to become acquainted with the basic procedures underlying such claims. Particularly for intermediate and advanced students, these opportunities can arise in the context of analysis of their own data and experimental results.

Statistical inference is an orderly means for drawing conclusions about a large number of events on the basis of observations collected on a sample of them. Some statistical tests make many (sometimes stringent) assumptions about the nature of the larger population from which the sample was drawn. Since population values are called "parameters" these techniques are called parametric. A commonly used parametric test is the Student's t test.

Other statistical techniques do not require these strict assumptions. Called "nonparametric" tests, they tend to be relatively quick and easy to compute. They may be used on small samples, and their power can be increased simply by increasing the size of the sample. For such reasons, nonparametric tests have found special popularity among biologists.

Chi square tests provide an excellent way to introduce intermediate and advanced students to the world of inferential statistics. These are a whole family of nonparametric tests that look at how often different categories of outcomes occur after samples are treated in different ways. The frequencies with which these outcomes happen are then compared with the situation that would occur if the treatments made no difference at all. When the frequencies are so very different that there's very little likelihood that chance variation could explain the difference, they are said to be "statistically significant."

Probably the most popular and widely applied statistical test among biologists is the chi square (2x2) test. It's also one of the simplest. The chi square (2x2) test gets its name from the 2x2 "contingency table" which is set up to classify individuals in 2 directions with 2 categories in each classification. A "contingency" is simply a possible event.

The samples might be any two independent groups (treated and controls, males and females, etc.). The categories might be any two mutually exclusive classifications or attributes (successes and failures, yes and no, above and below the median, locations A and B, etc.). The test determines whether the two sample groups differ in the proportion with which they fall into the two classifications. (The steps involved are outlined below. With a calculator, they aren't difficult.) Then the result is compared with the hypothetical distribution of values that would be expected if the treatments made no difference. A published table shows how often a particular chi square value would be expected to occur by chance alone. We've provided an abbreviated table that is sufficient for this case of only two groups and two classifications.

The chi square statistic that you calculate from your experiment becomes larger in value with greater observed differences. At some point, it becomes so large that it would be expected to occur only 5% (or .05), 1% (or 0.01) or even 0.1% (or .001) of the time by chance alone. Statisticians call this percentage the "alpha" or "level of significance." Alternatively, they specify the "p" (for "probability") level. When your results are so different they would occur less than, for example, 5% of the time, you can say that there is "a statistically significant difference" between the variables "at the $p<.05$ level." Sampling variation alone is unlikely to have made the difference you found — in fact, it is expected to do so less than .05 (or 5%) of the time.

As a final note about the chi-square test, it should be said that statistically it is best suited for sample sizes of 40 or more, and expected frequencies all larger than 5. In practice, these conditions are usually met in classroom experiments where the students' data are pooled.

Procedure:

A. Determine your hypothesis. How do you think the things you are measuring might be related? The automatic alternative (or "null hypothesis") in most cases is, of course, that they aren't related at all.

B. Conduct your experiment. Gather data in the form of number of times one or the other of two mutually exclusive things happens. (Note that observations can't be in the form of percentages or proportions. Data also must be independent of each other,

The basic formula for chi square for a 2x2 table looks like this:

$$\chi^2 = \Sigma\ (0\text{-}E) - 0.5)^2/E$$

It looks scarier than it is. This is simply mathematical shorthand for the steps outlined here in words.

which generally precludes taking more than one measurement from a single individual.)

B. Set up a contingency table like the one below. (The letters in and beside the boxes are just to make the steps easier to keep track of.)

C. Find out what frequency would be expected in each of the four cells of the table if the treatment made no difference. (To keep track, you'll probably want to put the numbers into another contingency table. It could be labeled "expected by chance" or "null hypothesis.")

For each cell, use the formula: expected frequency (E) = (row total x column total)/grand total

That is, in each case we multiply the two marginal totals common to a particular cell, and then divide this product by the total number (n) to obtain the expected frequency.

D. Since chi square is a measure of how different the expected and observed values are, we need to find the difference between the observed and expected value for each cell.

	Categories		
Group	(one)	(the other)	
I	a	b	a+b=
II	c	d	c+d=
	a+c=	b+d=	

n=a+b+c+d=

If the two are very similar, the differences will of course be small, and consequently the value of chi square will be small. If some or many are large, chi square's value will be also.

If your sample sizes were relatively small, after you obtain each difference, statisticians suggest that you substract 0.5 from each. This is simply a "correction factor" which they say improves the accuracy of the test.

E. Square each corrected value (this is where the "square" part of the name "chi square" comes in). Then divide each of these corrected values by the expected value for that cell. Add these four resulting numbers together, and you now have your very own chi square value!

F. Compare your calculated chi square value with published theoretical values and reach a conclusion. For convenience, we've provided an abbreviated table below. (More comprehensive chi square tables have many rows, and to find the appropriate comparison one must know the "degrees of freedom" or d.f. Happily, for simple 2x2 tables, this is always 1.)

Thus for $\alpha = 0.05$ (5% significance level or p = .05), any value greater than 3.841 would indicate a significant difference or significant association of the factors being compared. That is, the observed differences would be greater than expected by pure chance. Values of χ^2 less than 3.841 would be considered non-significant; the observed differences would be possible due to chance alone.

Abbreviated table of critical values of chi square:

d.f.	$\alpha = 0.9$	$\alpha = 0.5$	$\alpha = 0.2$	$\alpha = 0.05$	$\alpha = 0.01$	$\alpha = 0.001$
1	0.016	0.455	1.642	3.841	6.635	10.827

An example of chi square test use:

A biologist took several samples of *Melittobia* from two different mud dauber nest locations. She found that the *Melittobia* belonged to two different species, and wondered whether the proportions of the two species were the same near the lake as they were near the stream. Set into a 2x2 contingency table, her data looked like this.

	Species A	Species B	
# By lake	42	96	row total = 138
# By stream	12	104	row total = 116
	column total = 54	column total = 200	

total number of insects = 254

The biologist calculated chi square by these steps:

1. Find out what frequency would be expected in each cell of the table if the treatment made no difference. To do this, use the formula:

$$\text{expected frequency (E)} = (\text{row total} \times \text{column total})/\text{grand total}$$

a. Instead of 42, the expected frequency would be $(138 \times 54)/254 = 29.3$

b. Instead of 96, the expected frequency would be $(138 \times 200)/254 = 108.7$

c. Instead of 12, the expected frequency would be $(116 \times 54)/254 = 24.7$

d. Instead of 104, the expected frequency would be $(116 \times 200)/254 = 91.3$

These numbers sure look different than what she got! But is the difference real, or just random luck? To find out, she had to go on with the chi square calculation.

2. Find the difference between the observed and expected value for each cell. Then substract 0.5 from each difference (absolute value), and square the result. (This 0.5 is simply a "correction factor" which improves the accuracy of the test.)

a. $42 - 29.3 = 12.7$, then 0.5 from that makes it 12.2. Squared, it becomes 148.84.

b. $96 - 108.7 = -12.7$, then 0.5 from the absolute value makes it 12.2. Squared, it becomes 148.84

c. $12 - 24.7 = -12.7$, then 0.5 from the absolute value makes it 12.2. Squared, it becomes 148.84.

d. $104 - 91.3 = 12.7$, then 0.5 from that makes it 12.2. Squared, it becomes 148.84.

3. Divide each of these corrected values by the expected value for that cell.

a. $148.84 / 29.3 = 5.08$

b. $148.84 / 108.7 = 1.37.$

c. $148.84 / 24.7 = 6.03.$

d. $148.84 / 91.3 = 1.63$

4. Add these numbers for all four cells. $5.08 + 1.37 + 6.03 + 1.63 = 14.11$ to get chi square.Compare it with the published theoretical values. Since 14.11 is considerably greater than the $\alpha = 0.05$ critical value of 3.841 from the table, the biologist concluded that the association between the type of species and the location was highly significant, and not likely to be the result of chance alone.

WOWBugs On A Shoestring

Special kits from biological supply companies make life simple, but assembling your own materials can save money. The choice is yours.

Here are some favorite tips shared by teachers attending the Georgia WOWBug Workshops. Also included are detailed instructions for constructing some of the simple homemade equipment used in activities outlined in earlier chapters.

Displaying Insect Specimens

Most teachers like to save representative mud dauber nest inhabitants for a class reference collection, for use with the mud dauber nest ecology activity. This can be done in several ways. A relatively expensive but quite attractive option is to purchase Rikker display mounts from a biological supply company. These are like stationery boxes with glass or plastic fronts. The insect (and label) rest on a cotton backing.

For a durable, attractive, inexpensive homemade mount, place cotton batting inside a plastic petri dish or between a pair of clear food container lids such as those found on some yogurt containers (e.g., Dannon™). Center the nest inhabitant and an identifying label on the cotton, close the mount, and secure the sides with cellophane tape.

Inexpensive WOWBug Slides

To make your own slides for student viewing of WOWBugs, place a drop of clear nail polish on a blank commercial slide. (This is also a good use for dead WOWBugs!) Alternatively, any strip of heavy clear plastic (such as that used for transparencies) will do, as long as it is relatively stiff. Drop a dead WOWBug onto the nail polish. When the polish dries, the slide is ready.

Rather than trying to position the WOWBugs in the gluey polish, make up several of these slides at one time. Then look at them under a microscope and discard the ones that have problems or are positioned poorly.

Some teachers have found that using two drops of nail polish side by side, one for a male and the other for a female, provides a ready way for students to compare the anatomical differences between the sexes.

Pipe Cleaners As Transfer Tools

At the second WOWBugs Workshop, teacher David Zvonar shared his discovery that pipe cleaners (also called chenille craft sticks) easily pick up WOWBugs and are useful for transferring them to other containers. Pipe cleaners are much less expensive than the traditional alternative, camel's hair or small watercolor paint brushes. They also are more uniform. (Brush bristles vary in coarseness and density, and some types are less satisfactory.)

Any of the lighter colored pipe cleaners (white or yellow are especially good) make the black WOWBugs easier to see than on the paint brush. Longer pipe cleaners can be cut into three or four shorter sections which are easier for younger students to manipulate.

Sealable Plastic Bags For Observing WOWBugs

Teacher Linda Pollack discovered that sealable plastic bags work well to house student WOWBug colonies. Leave the hosts inside their opened cocoons, and the cocoon will provide support to keep the plastic bag from crushing the developing *Melittobia*. A potential problem is that adult WOWBugs may be able to chew through the plastic to gain their freedom. Various brands and styles of bags may differ in the ease with which WOWBugs can do this (a potential science fair project!).

For ease of student handling, bags need to remain flat on a rigid surface such as a small tray covered with white paper. Otherwise the cocoon tends to roll about the bag. When the adult WOWBugs emerge, they will crawl around inside the bag and can be easily seen and counted against the white background. The bag can be placed on an overhead projector and the WOWBugs projected onto a screen to share with the entire class.

The bags have also been used successfully following mud dauber nest dissection activities, to hold cocoons parasitized by other insects until those parasites emerge as adults.

Baby Food Jars As Culture Containers

Teacher Sarah Paul says for an inexpensive and easy way to store WOWBug stock cultures, consider using clean baby food jars. Punch a hole in the top of the lid the proper size for a drinking straw. Complete the rearing container by inserting a straw, or a piece of one, and stopper with a cotton swab or a piece of cotton.

Put your host and mated WOWBug females inside. Later, when adults are needed, unstopper the straw and allow them to crawl out into a vial.

A Simple Bioassay Chamber

For each chamber, you will need:
- Clear plastic straw
- Film can
- 16-penny common nail
- Pliers
- Bunsen burner or other heat source
- Millimeter ruler
- Scissors
- Poster putty
- Permanent fine-tip marker

Take a film container and mark a cross on the end. At each of the four points of the cross, extend the line up the side of the container as a guide. Use pliers to hold the nail head in the heat source until red-hot. Use the heated nail head to poke holes in the side of the container at the guidelines, as close to the bottom as possible.

From this point forward, the students can assemble the chambers following the instructions (also summarized in the transparency masters section).

Using the millimeter ruler and scissors, cut the clear plastic straw into 4 sections, each 4 cm long. Take a very small piece of poster putty and stretch it between your hands like a taffy pull until you have made a narrow ribbon of putty. Wrap the putty ribbon carefully around one end of each straw piece.

Insert the wrapped end just barely into one of the holes in the film container with a slight twisting motion to ensure a tight juncture between the straw and the film can. Repeat with each of the other three straws.

Peer inside the film can to be certain that the straws are nearly flush with the inside walls and that you can see no light coming in around the outside of the straws. Use your fingers to mold the putty to cover any leaks. Replace the lid and invert the film can. Check to see that the straws are more or less level, parallel with the table top.

With the permanent marker, number the straws consecutively, 1 to 4. Your bioassay chamber is now ready for use.

A Simple Sound Choice Tunnel

For the "Rockin' WOWBugs" activity in Chapter 5, you can construct a straightforward modification of the standard choice tunnel used for other activities in Chapter 5. A short version of these instructions is included in the transparency masters section.

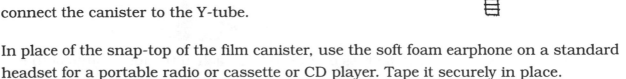

Take an empty plastic film canister. Carefully poke a straw-sized hole in the bottom of the canister with a sharp object like a skewer or a screwdriver. Alternatively, use a heated nail as described for the bioassay chamber. during the activity, students will put a straw through the poked hole to connect the canister to the Y-tube.

In place of the snap-top of the film canister, use the soft foam earphone on a standard headset for a portable radio or cassette or CD player. Tape it securely in place.

An Alternative Choice Tunnel

Aquarium tees, translucent plastic tubing, and cotton swabs make an inexpensive and reusable choice apparatus. These are more expensive than the standard straw and Y-tube apparatus explained in the activities for Chapter Five, but the tees and tubing are readily available at most pet shops and may be cleaned and reused indefinitely.

To provide enough setups for a class of 24 students, purchase a dozen 1/4 inch brass tees and 3 feet of 1/4-inch diameter clear aquarium air supply tubing. (Don't forget to ask about the possibility of an educational discount!)

Cut the tubing into 3-inch pieces. Attach two pieces on either end of the aquarium tee. (Use cotton swab pieces to close the ends, just as with the "Y"-tube apparatus.) The third piece can be "loaded" with a number of WOWBugs and plugged at both ends with the ends of another cut swab until time to begin the experiment.

Enlisting Cooperation From Schools And Parents

Teachers who have used WOWBugs in their classes pass along the following additional helpful hints, drawn from their own experiences:

• Ask school custodians to let you know about mud dauber nests that they find on school grounds and —please! — not destroy them.

• Learn which school administrators or others are involved with decisions about school fumigation or spraying for such insects as cockroaches or ants. Ask them to let you know in advance when they are spraying.

• Ask that spraying NOT take place in your room if you have living mud daubers, WOWBugs, or other cultures.

• With younger students or an extended unit on WOWBugs, you may wish to send home an information letter explaining the project and the harmless nature of the insects to be studied. Be very explicit; in the past, hearing "wasps," parents have inquired if their children would need allergy tests and sting kits. WOWBugs can not sting humans.

• In the same letter, or in place of it, request materials that would be helpful during the project, such as cotton balls or swabs, small paper cups, baby food jars with lids, clear straws, tweezers, and toothpicks.

Teacher Planning Time Line

Here's how one teacher successfully combined several WOWBug activities for her classes. As you choose activities from this book, you may find constructing a similar time line to be a convenient planning tool.

Activities:

Inquiry Activity: Mystery Life Cycle

Mud Dauber Nest Ecology

Population Sex Ratios

Momma's Boys: Sex Determination

Hoppin' Bug Connect-a-Dot; Speedy WOWBugs; Insect Olympics

Advanced class: Inquiry activities: Decisions, Decisions

Conclusion of sex determination activity

Phase I — 21-day life cycle

Phase II — 23 days

Phase III — 21 days

Notes:
To begin phase I, we need to have a large number of mud dauber larvae and a culture of WOWBug females to parasitize the larvae

In this 21-day period, students (individuals or in groups) will each receive a vial containing a mud dauber larva that has been parasitized (no adults in vial - eggs only). They are to observe the vials daily or every other day, and list observations and reflections in their journals (10-15 min. per session).

To end activity, spend time at end of 21-day period to discuss what was observed.

Allow time between phases I and II for students to collect mud dauber nests. (Could be as long as a month or two to get enough; if this is case, reculture monthly to keep some WOWBug colonies going for phase II activities).

Use mud dauber larvae collected by students to set new cultures. Put 5 females from phase I culture on each mud dauber larva for new observations of egg laying and life cycle.

These activities use adult wasps.

During this time, students can be doing previous activities started at end of Phase II.

Sources For Supplies

The following information is offered not as an endorsement or advertisement, but rather to facilitate teachers in assembling the materials they need to do the activities in this book.

WOWBug Educational Series

Three videotapes, a kodachrome slide set, and a newsletter supplement this manual. All include teacher's guides with discussion questions, concept application and extension activities, and reproducible activity masters. See the order form at the back of this book.

Riverview Press, LLC
P.O. Box 5955
Athens, GA 30604-5955
800-847-6540

Living Cultures

Living cultures of *Melittobia digitata* (# B3-L1162) are available commercially at about $10.00 for 50-100 individuals. You can also order *Sarcophaga* pupae (# B3-17-3480), the most convenient host for rearing them. Ten dollars buys about 100 pupae.

Carolina Biological Supply Co.
2700 York Road
Burlington, NC 27215
800-334-5551

B-Brite Cleaner

Mixed at 1 tablespoon per gallon of water, B-Brite will sterilize the surfaces of WOWBug rearing containers before they are used. An 8-ounce container will last a long time. Composed of sodium carbonate and sodium silicate, it is much easier to use than chlorine-based disinfectants. Because home brewers use B-Brite to sterilize their bottles, it is often available from local brewery supply stores for a couple of dollars.

Crosby & Baker
Westport, MA 02790

Deep Well Projection Slides (#60-3730F)

These clear plastic slides are ideal chambers for viewing the behavior of individual WOWBugs. A set of twenty slides is under $50.00. They are reusable indefinitely and can serve in other biology contexts.

Carolina Biological Supply Co.
2700 York Road
Burlington, NC 27215
800-334-5551

Discovery Scope, Inc.
3202 Echo Mountain Drive
Kingwood, TX 77345
800-398-5404

Clear View Chambers

These small (1"x2"x3/4") rectangular boxes are excellent for rearing and viewing WOWBugs. The minimum order is 100 boxes for $35.00.

TriState Plastics
P.O. Box 6, Hwy. 41A, N
Dixon, KY 42409
502-639-9142

Plastic Boxes

The sandwich-sized boxes make excellent storage containers for WOWBug cultures, as one box will compactly hold 16 of the clearview chambers. "The" source for plastic containers of all sizes and shapes. Request their catalog.

Ward's Biological Supply Co.
P.O. Box 92912
Rochester, NY 14692-9012
800-962-2660

Shell Vials and Plastic Y Tubes (#18W4720)

Many different types of rearing containers may be used successfully with WOWBugs, but we've found these straight-sided glass vials work very well. Substitute tight-fitting cotton plugs for the corks, however, as WOWBugs will chew through cork and escape. A dozen vials sell for just under $4.00, or they can be ordered in bulk. The plastic Y tubes will take a standard soda straw as an insert, or accept 3/16 inch aquarium tubing. They cost about $1.00 apiece.

Brock Optical, Inc.
P.O. Box 940831
Maitland, FL 32794
800-780-9111

Magiscopes®

These durable, simple to operate microscopes magnify just the right amount for optimal WOWBug viewing. They require no external light source. Magiscopes sell for about $150 each. Quantity discounts are available.

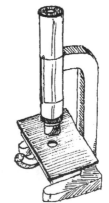

Watercolor Brushes, Straws, Pipe Cleaners, Etc.

These miscellaneous materials are easily found at major retailers such as SAM's Club, Big Lots, Walmart or K-Mart. Inquire about an educational discount.

Transparency Masters

On the following pages, we provide a set of illustrations, photographs, and charts which will serve to facilitate teaching and learning about WOWBugs. Teachers are hereby granted permission to make photocopies and transparencies from these masters for classroom use.

How To Herd A WOWBug

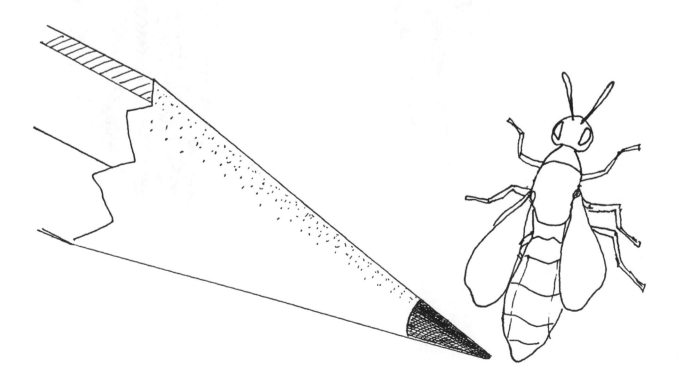

The organ pipe mud dauber
(Trypoxylon)

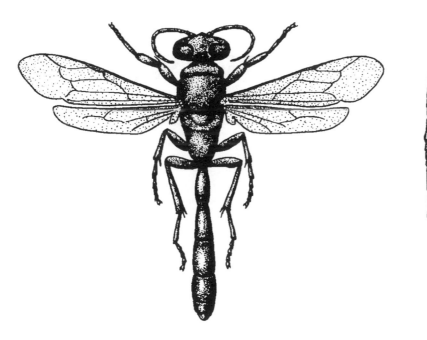 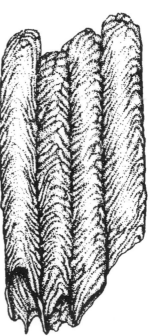

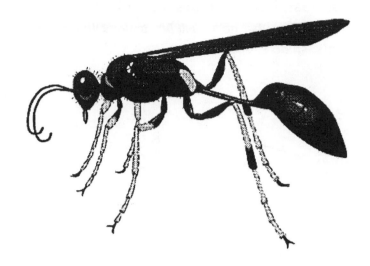

The yellow and black mud dauber (Sceliphron)

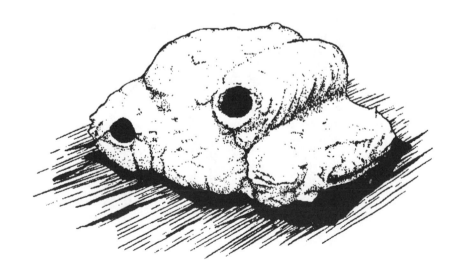

A key to the most common arthropod inhabitants of a current-year organ pipe mud dauber nest, Part A (before dissecting any cocoons).

Inhabitants of other kinds of mud dauber nests will be similar. Older nests may also have other solitary bees and wasps, ants, spiders, and beetles.

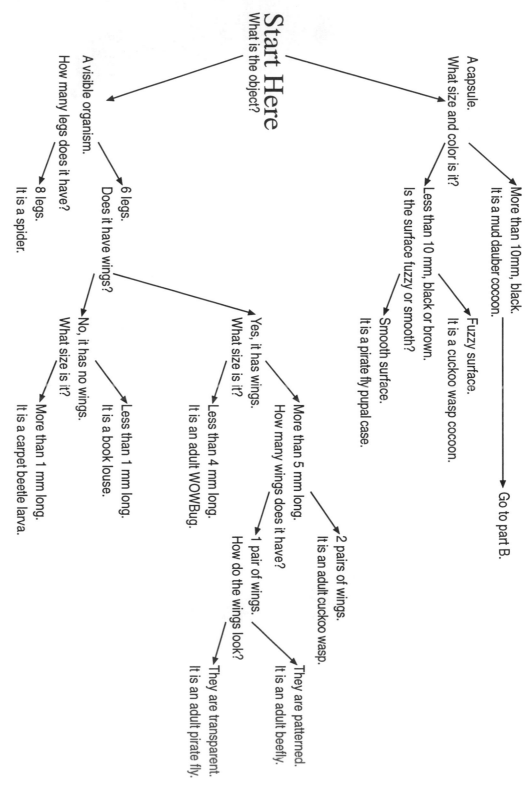

Start Here
What is the object?

A visible organism.
How many legs does it have?

6 legs.
Does it have wings?

8 legs.
It is a spider.

Yes, it has wings.
What size is it?

No, it has no wings.
What size is it?

Less than 4 mm long.
It is an adult WOWBug.

More than 5 mm long.
How many wings does it have?

Less than 1 mm long.
It is a book louse.

More than 1 mm long.
It is a carpet beetle larva.

1 pair of wings.
How do the wings look?

2 pairs of wings.
It is an adult cuckoo wasp.

They are transparent.
It is an adult pirate fly.

They are patterned.
It is an adult beefly.

A capsule.
What size and color is it?

More than 10mm, black.
It is a mud dauber cocoon.

Less than 10 mm, black or brown.
Is the surface fuzzy or smooth?

Fuzzy surface.
It is a cuckoo wasp cocoon.

Smooth surface.
It is a pirate fly pupal case.

Go to part B.

A key to the most common arthropod inhabitants of a current-year organ pipe mud dauber nest, Part B (cocoon contents).

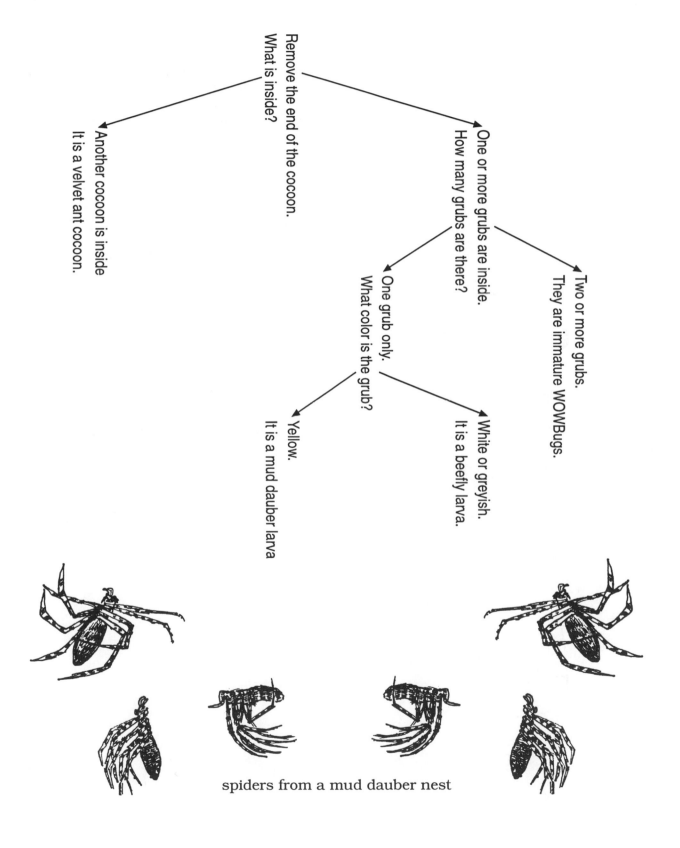

Remove the end of the cocoon.
What is inside?

Another cocoon is inside
It is a velvet ant cocoon.

One or more grubs are inside.
How many grubs are there?

One grub only.
What color is the grub?

Yellow.
It is a mud dauber larva

White or greyish.
It is a beefly larva.

Two or more grubs.
They are immature WOWBugs.

spiders from a mud dauber nest

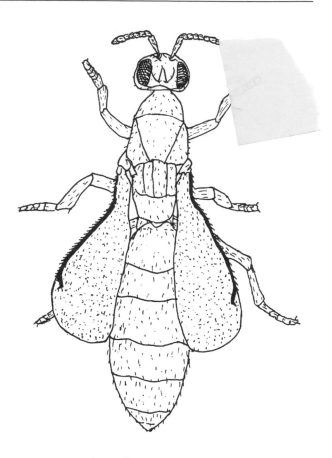

A male WOWBug

A female WOWBug

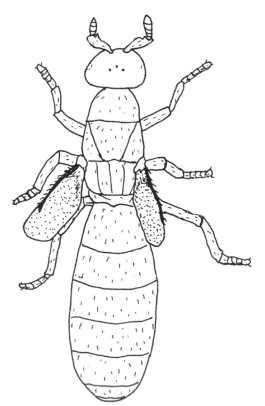

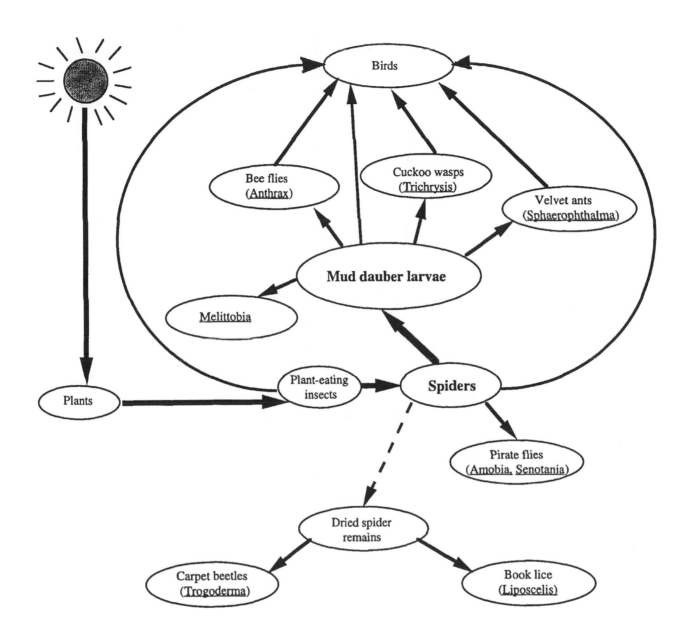

Ecological interactions in a mud dauber nest

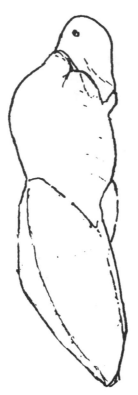

Male (above) and female (below) WOWBug pupae

**Adult female finds a
new host and lays eggs**

Eggs hatch into larvae

**Adults emerge from
pupae and leave cocoon**

The WOWBug life cycle

**Larvae feed on host
until fully mature**

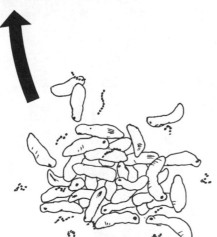

**Larvae pupate inside
host's cocoon**

Female WOWBug

Electronmicrographs of WOWBugs

1 millimeter

Male WOWBug

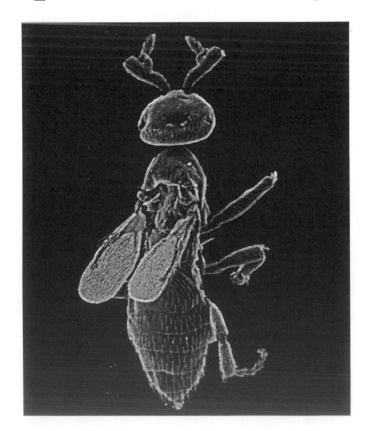

Female WOWBug

Male WOWBug

1 millimeter

Organ pipe mud dauber nest inhabitants

pirate fly pupal cases

pirate fly

cuckoo wasp cocoon

cuckoo wasp

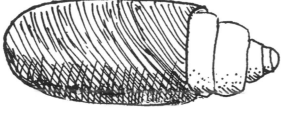
bee fly larva

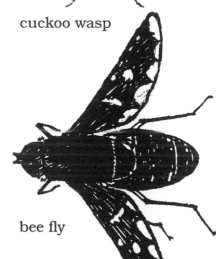
bee fly

book louse

velvet ant (male)

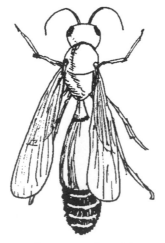
carpet beetle larva

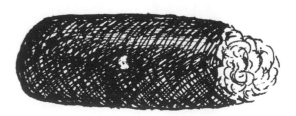
velvet ant cocoon

Sensory Response Choice Test Summary

Left   Right
Branch   Branch

Trial 1.

Left branch: One condition of the manipulated variable is _____. In ___ minutes, _____ entries were made into this branch. At the end of this time, there were _____ insects in this branch.

Right branch: The other condition of the manipulated variable was _____. In ___ minutes, _____ entries were made into this branch. At the end of this time, there were _____ insects in this branch.

There are _____ insects in the bottom or Y tube connector who did not choose either branch.

Trial 2.

Left branch: One condition of the manipulated variable is _____. In ___ minutes, _____ entries were made into this branch. At the end of this time, there were _____ insects in this branch.

Right branch: The other condition of the manipulated variable was _____. In ___ minutes, _____ entries were made into this branch. At the end of this time, there were _____ insects in this branch.

There are _____ insects in the bottom or Y tube connector who did not choose either branch.

Combined Results:

First condition : _____ . Number of insects entering this branch: _____. In ___ minutes, _____ entries were made into this branch. At the end of this time, there were _____ insects in this branch.

Alternate condition: _____. Number entering this branch: _____. In ___ minutes, _____ entries were made into this branch. At the end of this time, there were _____ insects in this branch.

Insects that did not choose either branch: _____

Assembling A Bioassay Chamber

Wrap small ribbon of hand-warmed poster putty around the end of clear plastic straw section. Insert into hole in film canister so straw is flush with inside wall. Mold putty to cover any leaks. Repeat with remaining straws.

Replace canister lid. Number straws with a permanent marker. Use section of cotton swab to close straw ends.

Sound Choice Tunnel Assembly

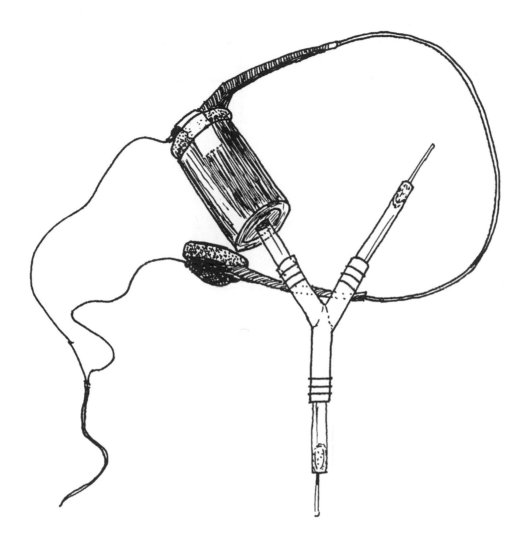

Put one end of the straw segment through the hole in the bottom of the film canister. Connect the other end to the choice tunnel.

Tape one earphone to the opening in the canister. Position the other earphone away from the choice tunnel.

Data Charts For "Speedy WOWBugs"

WOWBug Ground Speed

Jump
Number   Distance (mm)

1.

2.

3.

4.

5.

6.

7.

8.

9.

10.

Total distance:

Average jump length:

Range:

Crawling WOWBugs

Trial
Number   Seconds to Finish

1.

2.

3.

4.

5.

Total time in seconds:

Average time:

Range:

Making And Using A WOWBug Choice Tunnel

1. Using the ruler and scissors, cut a straw in two. Put one end of each on a branch of the "Y" connector. The length of the straw arms is not critical, but both should be the same length.

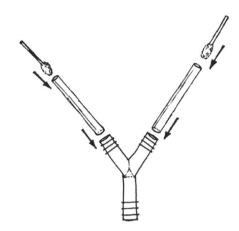

2. From another straw, cut a piece about 4 cm long. After you use it to collect the WOWBugs (step 4, below), it will be the stem of the "Y". It is a little shorter so you don't have to wait so long for the insects to choose between the branches. Vary its length if necessary.

3. Cut two double-ended cotton swabs in half with scissors. (The "handles" do not have to be the same length.) Put the plump end of one swab in the end of each branch to keep the insects from escaping. (Occasionally a WOWBug may get out if the connection to the Y is not tight or if a swab fits too loosely. If this happens, fix the "leak" and continue with the remaining insects.)

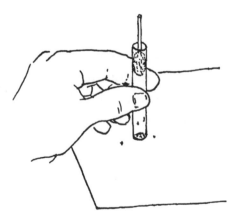

4. Use the 4-cm "stem" straw as a collecting tube. Plug its top with a swab. Gently shake 6-10 WOWBugs from the culture onto a piece of paper. Quickly turn the straw straight up. Place it over the insects, one at a time, so they will crawl or hop up inside it. (While doing this, have someone else use a paintbrush or pipe cleaner to gently keep the remaining insects on the paper.)

5. After about 6 insects have entered the straw, they begin to fall or crawl out about as fast as another new one can be added. Pick up the tube and quickly plug the open end with another swab.

6. When you are ready to begin your experiment, unplug one end and insert the straw into the "Y" connector stem.

Chapter Nine.
The Georgia
WOWBugs Project

Any creative endeavor is only as good as the people it involves. From its inception, this National Science Foundation sponsored project has been fortunate to have the involvement of a dedicated and creative group of Georgia middle school teachers.

This chapter reviews the history of the Georgia WOWBugs Project and lists the teacher participants. The hundreds of students who have worked with WOWBugs have also been essential to the Project's success. We thank them all.

The Georgia WOWBugs Project History

The Georgia WOWBugs Project was funded by a grant from The National Science Foundation and directed by Dr. Robert W. Matthews in the Department of Entomology. The project is dedicated to promoting public understanding and enjoyment of the biological sciences, with special emphasis on young people and those who teach them.

The Georgia WOWBugs Project was organized around the development and introduction of WOWBugs (*Melittobia digitata*) as a "new" organism for middle school (grades 5-9) life science curricula. One of the project's major goals was to involve teachers at all stages in developing the potential of WOWBugs to teach biological concepts and principles. Another has been to provide explicit guidance to teachers as they incorporate WOWBugs into their teaching practice.

The project began by soliciting the counsel of two master middle school life science teachers as advisors, Joseph Conti of Oglethorpe County Middle School, Lexington, Georgia and Jean "Chatty" Wight of the Athens Academy, Athens, Georgia.

Then a 13 member Development Team for the project was recruited from certified middle school teachers attending a *Melittobia* workshop held at the annual Georgia Science Teachers Association meeting in February 1994. The Development Team (see the list on the next page) worked with the project staff to conceive, develop, and field-test possible activities, meeting in full day sessions in March and May 1994. The ideas for most of the activities in this manual originated from these sessions.

The Development Team continued their active role by helping to present the first WOWBugs workshop held July 23-25, 1994. Experiences with the Development Team helped to shape the nature of the workshop, and team members provided considerable leadership during the workshop. Workshop activities mirrored many of the experiences of the Development Team and were greatly enhanced by commentary regarding their own classroom experiences with the WOWBugs.

Workshop participants, all middle school science teachers, were asked to pilot test as many of the prototype activities as possible during the subsequent year in their classrooms and return evaluation forms for project staff to use in refining and revising the activities. Revised prototype activities were provided to participants of the second WOWBugs workshop in July 1995, who were given the same charge. Final revisions and extensive editing of the activities to achieve coherence and a uniform format were accomplished during summer 1996, in time for the third WOWBugs workshop.

Development Team Members

Jan Baggett, Villa Rica Middle School, Villa Rica, GA

Era Hall, Bartlett Middle School, Savannah, GA

Deborah Heineman, Sharp Middle School, Covington, GA

Suzanne Jarrard, North Hall Middle School, Gainesville, GA

Brian Lucy, J. C. Booth Middle School, Peachtree City, GA

Cathy McGraw, Glenwood Elementary School, Rome, GA

Sarah Paul, Oak Vista Elementary School, Jesup, GA

Kathy Perry, Carver Middle School, Monroe, GA

Lynda Pollock, Lilburn Middle School, Lilburn, GA

Jennifer Ritter, J. C. Booth Middle School, Peachtree City, GA

Cathy Robinson, Windsor Forest Elementary School, Savannah, GA

Donna Whiting, Ralph Bunche Middle School, Atlanta, GA

Mark Yount, Carver Middle School, Monroe, GA

The original project goal was to develop a set of ten activities, but teachers requested more activities, additional content, and more teacher background information. Thus this manual now consists of twenty activities, each with detailed teaching notes. All together, 98 science teachers have attended one or more of the summer WOWBugs workshops. These teacher participants and their schools are listed on the following pages, with the years attended shown in parentheses.

Materials developed during the project include this manual of laboratory activities; a series of three "Working With Wowbugs" videotapes, describing the insects' behavior and demonstrating techniques for rearing and handling; a set of 2x2 color slides on mud dauber biology; and a quarterly newsletter, *WOWBugs Bulletin.* This newsletter provides suggestions for new activities and/or extensions, summaries of current research findings, and other recent developments of interest to teachers and students using WOWBugs.

These materials greatly support the use of WOWBugs in the curriculum. All are available from Riverview Press, P. O. Box 5955, Athens, GA 30604-5955. In addition, the WOWBugs Project has established an e-mail address (bugdoc@arches.uga.edu) to promote communication between project personnel, teachers, and their students.

Through the University of Georgia Research Foundation, Inc., the project staff has negotiated with Carolina Biological Supply of Burlington, North Carolina, to provide living WOWBugs and related support materials for national distribution.

WOWBugs Workshop Teacher Participants

Joyce Abbott, Matt Wilson Middle School, Tifton, GA ('95)

Vicki L. Albritton, Brittin Elementary School, Ft. Stewart, GA ('95)

Kay Anderson, Willow Hill Middle School, Portal, GA ('94)

Karen Barlow, M.L. King Middle School, Atlanta, GA ('94)

Mark Barton, North Hall Middle School, Gainesville, GA ('95)

Kim Berry, Lilburn Middle School, Lilburn, GA ('94)

Deborah Breedlove, South Hall Middle School Gainesville, GA ('96)

Letty Bridges, Oconee Middle School, Watkinsville, GA ('94)

Nancy Brinson, Ben Hill County Middle School, Fitzgerald GA ('94, '95, '96)

Nancy Brown, St. Marys Middle School, St. Marys, GA ('94)

Pam Burkhead, Jasper County Middle School, Monticello, GA ('95)

Linda Caldwell, Chattanooga Valley Middle School, Flintstone, GA ('95, '96)

Patricia Carr, DeRenne Middle School, Savannah GA ('94, '95)

Marybeth Chassagne, Thurgood Marshall Middle School, Atlanta, GA ('94, '96)

Angela Clark, South Paulding Middle School, Dallas, GA ('96)

Wanda Cole, South Paulding Middle School, Dallas, GA ('95, '96)

Belinda Coleman, Matt Wilson Middle School, Tifton, GA ('96)

Deborah Crawford, DeRenne Middle School, Savannah, GA ('96)

Vickie Joe Davidson, Lawrenceville Middle School, Buford, GA ('95)

Loretha Daymon, Lawrenceville Middle School, Buford GA ('94, '95)

Melissa Dennis, Arnold Middle School, Columbus GA ('94, '95)

Gwendolyn Edwards, Thurgood Marshall Middle School, Atlanta, GA ('96)

Lynn Faust, Barnett Shoals Elementary School, Athens, GA ('96)

Tracey Fletcher, Ralph Bunche Middle School, College Park GA ('94, '95)

Heather Fosgate, Madison County Middle School, Danielsville, GA ('96)

Ruth Foster, Shiloh Middle School, Stone Mountain GA ('94, '95)

Audrey Fowler, J. H. Arnold Elementary School, Jonesboro, GA ('94)

Fredericka Garlinghouse, Wesleyan Day School, Atlanta GA ('94, '95)

Mary Georgetti, Eagle's Landing Middle School, McDonough, GA ('95)

Sharon Green, Crawford Long Middle School, Tucker GA ('94, '95)

Adria Griffin, Clements Middle School, Covington, GA ('95, '96)

Dianne Hall, Lanier Middle School, Buford, GA ('94, '95)

Mary Hensien, Barnett Shoals Elem. School, Athens, GA ('95, '96)

Elizabeth Hezekiah, Marshall Middle School, Columbus, GA ('96)

Mona Howard, Morgan County Middle School, Madison, GA ('95, '96)

Richard Howell, Richard, Kemp Creek Middle School, College Park, GA ('95)

Linda Hughie, Chattanooga Valley Middle School, Flintstone, GA ('96)

Brenda Hunt, North Habersham Middle School, Clarkesville, GA ('94, '95, '96)

Gayla Jackson, Northside Middle School, Warner Robins, GA ('96)

Steve James, Sweetwater Middle School, Lawrenceville GA ('94, '95, '96)

Joan Jordan, Elbert County Middle School, Elberton, GA ('95)

Patricia Kent, Islands Elementary School, Savannah GA ('94, '95)

Charlotte Kimbrell, Baldwin Middle School, Baldwin, GA ('95)

Sandra Kimbrell, Banks County Elementary School, Oakwood, GA ('95)

Sallie Kirby, Pickneyville Middle School, Norcross, GA ('94)

Jill Kirkland, Whitewater Middle School, Fayetteville GA ('94, '95)

Judi Sue Krumnow, Banks County Elementary School, Homer, GA ('96)

Jeanette Lincoln, Islands Elementary School, Savannah GA ('94, '95)

Dianne Mapp, South Paulding Middle School, Dallas, GA ('95)

Sue Matthews, Elbert County Middle School, Elberton GA ('95)

Dawn McCaskill, Cousins Middle School, Covington, GA ('94, '95, '96)

Katie McCloud, Diamond Elementary School, Ft. Stewart, GA ('95)

Christine McKinney, W. C. Abney Elementary School, Dallas, GA ('96)

Cheryl Meadows, Franklin County Middle School, Carnesville, GA ('94, '95)

Nancy Meyers, Holcomb Bridge Middle School, Alpharetta, GA ('96)

Vannie Middleton, DeRenne Middle School, Savannah, GA ('95, '96)

Hallas Midgette, Fort Middle School, Columbus, GA ('94, '96)

Susan Mitchell, Banks County Elementary School, Homer, GA ('96)

Renee Mosley, DeRenne Middle School, Savannah, GA ('96)

Rebecca Oliver, Northside Middle Middle School, Warner Robins, GA ('96)

Brenda Oulsnam, Riverdale Middle School, Riverdale, GA ('94, '95, '96)

Mima Owens, Nevils Elementary School, Statesboro, GA ('94)

Joy Parham, South Hall Middle School, Gainesville GA ('94, '95, '96)

Parr, Rachael, Jackson County Middle School, Jefferson, GA ('94, '95, '96)

Alice Patton, Dickerson Middle School, Marietta, GA ('94, '95)

Diana Pearson, Barnett Shoals Elementary School, Athens, GA ('95, '96)

Evelyn Peebles, Clarke Middle School, Athens, GA ('96)

Minnie Peek, Morgan County Middle School, Madison, GA ('95, '96)

Margie L. Pendergraph, Islands Elementary School, Savannah GA ('94, '95)

Kelly Peppers, Banks County Elementary School, Homer, GA ('96)

Memorie Pierce, Venice Area Middle School, Venice, FL ('94)

Jenny Poole, Lanier Middle School, Buford GA ('94, '95)

Debbie Pope, Williams Heights Elementary School, Waycross, GA ('96)

Anna Belle Pyle, Duluth High School, Duluth, GA ('96)

Norma Quinn, Whit Davis Elementary School, Athens, GA ('96)

Marybel Rivera, Frank Long Elementary School, Hinesville, GA ('95)

Jane Rollins, Savannah Christian School, Savannah, GA ('95)

Jacquline Russell, Evans Middle School, Newnan GA ('94, '95)

Deanna Ryan, Pointe South Middle School, Jonesboro, GA ('94)

Tonya Saunders, Ralph Bunche Middle School, Atlanta, GA ('94)

Sheila Scoggins, Commerce Middle School, Commerce, GA ('95)

Frankie Shaw, Dobbins Middle School, Dallas, GA ('96)

Tammy Shiflett, W. C. Abney Elementary School, Dallas, GA ('96)

Catherine Sims, Jackson County Middle School, Jefferson, GA ('96)

Kay Smith, Pinckneyville Middle School, Norcross, GA ('95)

Tami Smith, Ralph Bunche Middle School, Atlanta, GA ('94)

Frances M. Steele, Arnold Middle School, Columbus GA ('94, '95)

Wanda Stevenson-Randolph, DeRenne Middle School, Savannah, GA ('95, '96)

Mary Nell Storey, Matt Wilson Middle School, Tifton GA ('94, '95, '96)

Milton Sutherlin, Warner Robins Middle School, Warner Robins, GA ('96)

Eric Taylor, C. T. Walker Trad. Magnet School, Augusta, GA ('96)

Kimberly Truslow, Northside Middle School, Warner Robins, GA ('96)

Reva Utz, Ashworth Middle School, Calhoun, GA ('94, '95)

Lisa Voigt, Barnett Shoals Elementary School, Athens, GA ('96)

Tom Wellnitz, The Paideia School, Atlanta GA ('94, '95)

Clara Williams, DeRenne Middle School, Savannah, GA ('95, '96)

Debbie Woods, Ben Hill Middle School, Fitzgerald, GA ('95)

David Zvonar, Adamson Middle School, Rex, GA ('94, '95, '96)

Biologically Speaking: A Glossary of Terms

Basic scientific literacy includes familiarity with at least some of the language of biology. However, memorizing terms should never be an end in itself in life science instruction. Students will understand and remember words best by associating them with their use in hands-on investigations.

New terms important to understanding a particular activity are listed at the end of the teacher's version of each activity. Each special biological word or term of importance is printed in boldface type the first time it appears in this book, and the text is worded so as to reveal the meaning of the word by context. The inclusion of this glossary is for the convenience of teachers and their students who may do these activities in different order than the one we've presented.

accuracy. Correctness or precision in measurement.

acoustic. Pertaining to hearing.

adaptation. Any genetically controlled characteristic that helps an organism survive and reproduce in the environment it inhabits. Modification to perform a specialized activity.

ambient temperature. The temperature of the air and surroundings.

anterior. Toward the front end.

asexual reproduction. Production of new individuals in plants and animals by a process that does not involve gametes. See also parthenogenesis, clone.

bioassay. An analysis that makes use of living organisms.

chevron. A v-shaped bar worn on the sleeves of a uniform. A similarly shaped mud strip that comprises part of the organ pipe mud dauber wasp nest.

clone. A group of individuals derived asexually from a single ancestor, hence genetically identical.

consumer. Any organism that ingests other (usually) living organisms in whole or in part to obtain organic nutrients. Herbivores, carnivores, omnivores, and parasites are consumers. Compare producer.

cuticle. A thin outermost layer of skin or other covering.

data (plural; the singular is **datum**). Facts or figures from which conclusions can be inferred.

diapause. A period of dormancy or arrested development much like hibernation.

diploid. Having two chromosomes of each type (that is, homologous chromosomes, one coming from each parent) in the body cells. Compare haploid.

dormancy. Cessation of growth under physical conditions that could be quite unsuitable for growth. See also diapause.

dorsal. Pertaining to the back.

dorsum. The back.

electron microscope. An instrument for focusing rays of electrons, rather than light rays, to form a greatly enlarged image of an object.

electronmicrograph. A picture of an image formed with an electron microscope.

evolution. In biology, successive changes in allele frequencies in a population, as brought about by events such as mutation, genetic drift, gene flow, and selection pressure.

external morphology. The form and structure of the outside of an organism.

eyepiece. In a microscope, the lens or combination of lenses nearest the viewer's eye.

fertilization. Fusion of sperm nucleus with egg nucleus.

field of view. In a microscope, the area which can be seen through the eyepiece.

food web. Network of many intermingled food chains, encompassing primary producers, consumers, decomposers, and detritivores.

gamete. A sexual reproductive cell that must usually fuse with another such cell before development can begin; an egg or sperm.

geotaxis. An animal's oriented response to gravity.

gestalt. The overall structure, form, and pattern of an experienced situation, which is more than merely the sum of various elements of it.

habitat. Place where an individual or population of a given species lives; its "mailing address."

haplo-diploidy. A type of sex determination mechanism in which fertilized (diploid) eggs always produce females and unfertilized (haploid) eggs always produce males. This mechanism is characteristic of bees, ants and wasps.

haploid. State in which a cell nucleus contains half the paren-tal number of chromosomes characteristic of the somatic (body) cells of a species. A haploid state is characteristic of sperm and egg cells. Compare diploid.

hermaphrodite. An organism which is sexually both male and female so that reproduction can take place without two individuals, as in certain worms, mollusks, and barnacles.

host specific. Said of a parasite that can live only on or in certain other organisms.

host. The living body from which a parasite gets its nourishment.

humidity. The atmosphere's moisture content.

larva (plural, **larvae**). A sexually immature, free-living and free-feeding animal that grows and develops into the sexually mature adult form.

life cycle. For any species, the genetically programmed sequence of events by which individuals are produced, grow, develop, and themselves reproduce.

locomotion. The spontaneous movement of an organism from one place to another.

malnutrition. Undernourishment resulting from insufficient food, improper diet, or inadequate nutrition.

mean. A quantity with a value intermediate between the values of two or more other quantities. The average (also called the arithmetic mean) obtained by dividing the sum of these quantities by the number of these quantities.

micrometer. One millionth of a meter. One thousandth of a millimeter. Abbreviated with the symbol μm. Also called a micron.

micron. One millionth of a meter, one thousandth of a millimeter. Abbreviated with the symbol μ. Also called a micrometer.

nest cell. A space partitioned off within a nest for occupancy by a single offspring.

nymph. A young insect that resembles the adult, but is wingless and sexually immature.

objective lens. On a compound microscope, the lens or combination of lenses mounted on the telescoping tube at the end furthest from the viewer's eye.

order. In scientific classification, a group of related organisms that is next larger than the family and smaller than the class.

orientation. The act of turning or moving in relation to some external feature such as a source of light.

ovipositor. In insects, a special organ for depositing eggs, usually situated at the end of the abdomen.

parasite. A type of consumer that lives on or in a living host organism during some part of its life cycle, obtains nutrients from the host's tissues, and may or may not end up killing the host as a consequence of the association. (It usually produces an intermediate level of negative effects.)

parasitism. A feeding relationship in which one party benefits at the expense of the other.

parasitoid. An insect whose larval stage kills a single host insect by completely consuming its soft tissues, but whose adult stage is free living.

parthenogenesis. Production of offspring without fertilization. See asexual reproduction.

pedigree. A recorded or known line of descent, record of ancestry, or family tree.

pheromone. Chemical secreted by an exocrine gland that serves as a communication signal between individuals of the same species.

phototaxis. The oriented response of an animal to light.

polyphagous. Capable of subsisting on many kinds of food.

population. In ecology, a group of individuals belonging to the same species living in a specific area.

posterior. Toward the hind end.

predation. The feeding of free-living organisms on other organisms.

prepupa (plural, **prepupae**). The development stage that occurs just after an insect larva stops feeding and before it transforms to a pupa.

primary host. The host which a parasite uses most often.

producer. An autotrophic organism, such as most plants. Able to build its own complex organic molecules from simple inorganic substances in the environment.

propagate. Reproduce or multiply.

range. In statistics, the difference between the greatest and smallest values in a series of measurements.

raw data. Facts or figures in the original form in which they were collected.

relative humidity. The ratio of the actual water vapor content of air to its total capacity at a given temperature.

scale bar. A series of marks along a line at regular or graduated distances, used in measuring the proportion that a drawing, model, etc. bears to the thing that it represents.

sex ratio. The proportion of males and females in an animal population.

sexual dimorphism. A reference to the different anatomy of males and females in parts of the body used in reproduction or courtship.

sexual reproduction. The process of reproduction that begins with meiosis, proceeds through gamete formation, and ends at fertilization.

stability. The capacity of an object to return to its original position after having been displaced or deformed.

sternum. The ventral part of an arthropod's thorax, from the Latin and Greek words for breastbone.

stimuli. Actions or agents that cause a response or change an activity in all or part of an organism.

taxis. A continuously oriented movement of an animal in response to some external stimulus. Movement away is called negative; toward is positive. The equivalent term for such movement by plants is "tropism."

thorax. In insects, the body region between the head and the abdomen, bearing the walking legs and wings.

transformed data. A complete and consistent conversion of a set of data from one form of presentation into another. For example, the conversion of fractions into decimal equivalents.

variable. Anything changeable. Variables are given many different names according to the role they play. An **independent variable** in science or mathematics is one chosen arbitrarily as the one upon whose value that of another (the **dependent variable**) shall depend. A **manipulated variable** is an independent variable that is chosen to be changed by the experimenter. A **responding variable** is the dependent variable that changes in response.

ventral. Toward the side of the body where the belly is located.

viewing power. The magnification that results from the use of a particular combination of lenses in a microscope or other optical device. Also called magnification.

Alphabetical Listing Of Activities

Index

Note: pages in bold are illustrations or figures

Add WOW to Your Life Science Classes!

☐ **WOWBugs™: New Life for Life Science.**   **$19.95**

By R. W. Matthews, T. R. Koballa, Jr., L. R. Flage, & E. J. Pyle. Meet WOWBugs™ — pint-sized insects with 17-day life cycles, fascinating behaviors and strange morphology! Over 20 classroom-tested activities, experiments, and extensive support materials in this teacher-friendly book. 320 pages. Grades 5-12. ©1996

☐ **WOWBug™ Biology Video**   **$29.95**

The life cycle of insects is one of nature's most amazing phenomena. Watch WOWBugs™ from egg to larva, pupa and adult. Introduce concepts such as adaptation, locomotion, competition, and reproduction. Includes Teacher's Guide. 17 minutes. ©1996

☐ **WOWBug™ Rearing And Maintenance Video**   **$29.95**

Make your WOWBugs™ culture last forever! Learn about diet, housing, hosts, and tips that spell success. Ideal for students using WOWBugs™ for science fair projects. Includes Teacher's Guide. 14 minutes. ©1996

☐ **Organ Pipe Mud Dauber Biology Video**   **$29.95**

Gain firsthand appreciation of ecological interactions in the microcommunity that centers around the WOWBug's preferred host. Introduce concepts such as food chains and webs, parasitism, and predation. Includes Teacher's Guide. 21 minutes. ©1996

☐ **Set of <u>all three</u> Working With WOWBugs™ Videotapes & Guides**   **$79.95**

Get comprehensive support and save 12% over the single-video prices.

☐ **What's Inside A Mud Dauber's Nest? A Teacher's Guide With Identification Keys**   **$4.95**

Well-illustrated, 32-page stand-alone booklet with directions for dissecting the nest of this solitary wasp, and keys to the inhabitants. Includes biological information about parasites, predators, and scavengers commonly found within the nest.

☐ **Organ Pipe Mud Dauber Slide Set**   **$39.95**

Students eagerly learn about predator/prey relationships through the analysis of mud dauber wasp nests, often called "poor man's owl pellets." Highly motivational for regular class or independent study. Includes 20 full-color 35-mm slides, numbered narrative, and a Teacher's Guide (What's Inside A Mud Dauber's Nest?) with keys to nest contents. ©1996

☐ **WOWBUGS™ Bulletin**   **per year $17.00**

Four times a year, this multi-page newsletter brings the newest ideas, from classroom activities to science fair ideas, board games to book reviews, newest research, and tips from teachers successfully using WOWBugs across the country! A valuable addition to the classroom and to the teacher's resource shelf. (Price includes mailing.)

Sales Tax: Please add 7% for materials (except *Bulletin*) shipped to Georgia addresses: _____

Mailing Costs: Add $3 per item (except $5 per 3-video set , $1 for *What's Inside?*): _____

Total Payment Enclosed or Charged: _____

Name: _____

Address: _____

_____   Daytime Phone: _____

If using a credit card: VISA   MasterCard   Expiration Date: _____   Card Number: _____

Name on Card: _____   Signature: _____

To order, fax this form to (706) 369-0931, call **1-800-847-6540**, or mail this form with payment to:

Riverview Press
P. O. Box 5955
Athens, GA 30604-5955